Praise for *Jack Ruby*

"As a conspiracy buff, I leapt into Danny Fingeroth's *Jack Ruby* with gusto, only to realize how little I actually knew about Jacob Rubenstein, a.k.a. Jack Ruby. . . . You have to read the book. Fingeroth takes you beat by beat through that fateful weekend and Ruby's array of costars: strippers, club owners, policemen. He paints a disturbing portrait of a manic Ruby desperate to be in the center of the action, who just wanted to be important."
—**David Mandel**, showrunner of *Veep* and
director of *White House Plumbers*

"Why did Jack Ruby do what he did? . . . Fingeroth brilliantly takes us through a dazzling array of twists, turns, and possible motivations in telling it, in all its labyrinthine complexity."
—**Jeremy Dauber**, author of *Mel Brooks: Disobedient Jew*

"It's likely that no book will ever answer whether Jack Ruby was a lone gunman or part of some vast conspiracy. But cultural sleuth Danny Fingeroth's fascinating biography offers something more revealing—showing us how this irony-laden icon offers a lens into America's low-level underworld, its multitiered Jewish community, and a baby boom generation robbed of its hero-worshiped president."
—**Larry Tye**, author of *Bobby Kennedy*

"Danny Fingeroth's book does what few books on the JFK assassinations have even attempted by painting a humanized depiction of the many complex layers of Jack Ruby, the killer of the one of the most notorious presidential suspected assassins."
—**Mark S. Zaid, Esq.**, JFK assassination historian

"Sixty years after the events that changed the world comes this important biography, a gripping, deeply researched investigation into a crucial thread of pivotal history."
—**Lisa Napoli**, author of *Up All Night*

JACK RUBY

THE MANY FACES OF OSWALD'S ASSASSIN

DANNY FINGEROTH

CHICAGO
REVIEW
PRESS

First hardcover edition published in 2023
First paperback edition published in 2024
Published by Chicago Review Press Incorporated
814 North Franklin Street
Chicago, Illinois 60610
ISBN 978-0-89733-332-0

The Library of Congress has cataloged the hardcover edition
under the following Control Number: 2023943198

Cover design: Jonathan Hahn
Cover photo: Bettmann/Getty Images
Typesetting: Nord Compo

Printed in the United States of America

For Varda, once again, always . . .

John F. Kennedy was Cary Grant in the White House. Lee Harvey Oswald shot and killed Cary Grant, and the next morning we all understood we were living in another country. And by the end of the week, when Jack Ruby shot Oswald, surrealism was in the saddle and rode mankind.

—Jules Feiffer, *Backing into Forward*

CONTENTS

PREFACE

"You Killed My President, You Rat!"

I WAS TEN YEARS OLD when President John F. Kennedy was assassinated and Jack Ruby murdered presumed assassin Lee Harvey Oswald on live television. I don't remember if I saw it live or on replay. Upset by the killings, I was also, like many boomer kids, annoyed that TV programming that weekend was all JFK all the time and I couldn't see my favorite TV shows.

As it has been for everyone else, the JFK murder was a touchstone for my life. "Where were you when it happened?" is a common question. (I was buying used comic books at a secondhand magazine store on First Avenue in Manhattan, in case you were wondering.)

I pretty much accepted the official story of who had killed JFK and why: Oswald, because he was crazy. Over the years, I would hear one conspiracy story or another about the assassination and at a certain point just didn't have room in my brain for even one more contradictory narrative. (Interestingly, as a Marvel Comics writer and editor, my job for much of my life was to come up with stories in which conspiracies and secret dealings were par for the course.)

Like everyone else, I was being asked to choose between a random world, where things happened for no good reason, and its polar opposite: a world where everything was managed and manipulated as if humanity were some sort of massive lab experiment where we were being put through paces to see how much we could tolerate—you know, like life today.

So it was certainly comforting to believe that both Kennedy and Oswald had been killed by "lone nuts." I was clearly not alone in feeling exhausted

On November 22, 1963, President John F. Kennedy—accompanied by his wife, Jacqueline, and Texas governor John Connally and wife Nellie—rides through the streets of Dallas. The motorcade would soon be violently interrupted by bullets and Kennedy would be pronounced dead half an hour later. *Photo by Victor Hugo King, courtesy of Wikimedia Commons*

by trying to figure out the two murders and other traumatic assassinations through the years. They were readily absorbed into popular culture, to the point where *Seinfeld* had an episode that spoofed the "magic bullet" theory of the JFK murder and *Saturday Night Live* presented a sketch about the imagined assassination of an adult Buckwheat from the Our Gang short films. These and other cultural references embodied the feeling that the idea of *Who did what and when, and why did they do it?* was simultaneously too big to think about and also too big to ignore.

In the mythos of the John F. Kennedy assassination, Jack Ruby is the wild card. With his lunge into history, on live television, and his assassination of the presumed assassin of JFK, Ruby shattered the entire narrative of the assassination into a thousand pieces.

It's not that no one thought someone might well try to kill the guy who killed the president—but not *that* guy, not *that* way.

A slick professional hit man, an enraged Dallas cop, a foaming-at-the-mouth political extremist—these would be the types you would expect to do it, the types you'd be on the lookout for. Not that Willy Loman of strip club operators, Jack Ruby. If anything, based on his life story, Jack Ruby is the guy you'd expect to be hit by a stray bullet fired by the professional assassin, the classic *shlimazel*—recipient of bad fortune—that Ruby often seemed to be.

But none of those people showed up to kill Oswald on live TV. Jack Ruby did (while, by at least his own account, exclaiming, "You killed my president, you rat!" as he pulled the trigger). In so doing, he changed history and how we view it.

On November 24, 1963, as Lee Harvey Oswald is being escorted through the basement of Dallas city hall, Jack Ruby rushes from the crowd of reporters and police to fire one fatal shot into Oswald's abdomen. *Photo by Robert H. Jackson, courtesy of Wikimedia Commons*

Like it or not, Jack Ruby is a key part of the story. What part exactly is kind of a Rorschach test. We all see in Jack Ruby what and who we need to see—which includes *not* seeing him much at all.

Needless to say, there is somewhere an objective truth behind what happened in Dallas that weekend and why it happened, beyond the televised action of Ruby shooting Oswald. We know, at least, who killed the young prisoner. And we know that someone (someones?) murdered JFK, probably for some logical reason, or at least one that seemed so at the moment of the murder. Similarly, there must be a definitive backstory as to why and how an armed Jack Ruby was present at the exact place and time to shoot Oswald. But we will likely never know it.

———————

Not knowing can be maddening for any number of reasons, but especially since so much of our world today seems to ripple out from those killings. In 2016 Donald Trump maligned rival Ted Cruz by implying the latter's father was somehow mixed up with Oswald. More recently, in 2021 thousands of people congregated in Dallas's Dealey Plaza—site of the shooting of Kennedy—awaiting the Christlike return of JFK Jr., who died in a 1999 plane crash and who, teamed up with Trump, would in some magical way save the country.

But discovering the objective truths of the history-shattering events of November 22–24, 1963, and the motives behind them is unlikely. Any discovery at this point will be impossible to prove beyond a shadow of a doubt. Any confession, no matter what evidence backs it up, will be derided as a forgery or deception. For all we know, perhaps the unalloyed truth *has* been revealed and we just didn't notice. Many have confessed to being part of or behind the events. Many claim—not without reasonable backup—to have discovered the truth.

Still, the events of that weekend are so dramatic and so long ago that the only satisfactory outcome will be if, like a novel or movie, everything is wrapped up and explained. That isn't likely to happen. (Not everyone believes the preceding of course. Perhaps some indisputable, undeniable proof-backed truth will emerge, as unlikely as that seems. Or perhaps you yourself were involved and are even now laughing at my gullibility and naïveté.)

But I'm not immune to being fascinated by the defining event of my generation. Why else would I be writing this? Besides being a boomer, I'm also an American-born Jew, the son of US-born children of Eastern European immigrants. I come from a similar background to that of one Jack Leon Ruby. And it is on Ruby that my obsessions have settled. I want to know more about this guy who could easily have been my weird cousin—or yours.

Perhaps unsurprisingly, the more I research Ruby's life, the less sure I am of precisely why and how he did what he did. The path of least resistance is to say that he was simply a lone nut who was able to get close to Oswald because he was known to the Dallas police—who, even if they didn't all like him, certainly didn't see him as any kind of threat. Lots of smart people with no apparent agendas think that both Ruby and Oswald were unhinged individuals whose madness led them to the point of exploding in violence. Both were trained as shooters in the military, so using firearms was not alien to them. Oswald even got in trouble with a gun during his brief residence as a teen in the Bronx, where he fired a BB gun at a neighbor's windows across the street.

Of course, many believe that the scenario described above is too simple and too easy to be true, that in this case the simplest explanation is *not* the correct one. Ruby must have been part of a larger plot, they believe. Maybe he was allowed in by the police, who wanted revenge on Oswald for killing Officer J. D. Tippit. Maybe he was hired by the mob, despite no known record as a hitman, to "clean up" Oswald, who had somehow (as decoy shooter? as patsy?) been involved in the larger plan to exact revenge for Bobby Kennedy's attacks on the mob, sending a message to RFK that no one is untouchable. Or, possibly, the Russians had contracted the killings out to the mob because of their anger over Kennedy's handling of the Cold War. Or perhaps the CIA was behind it, or a power-hungry Lyndon Johnson. And on and on. The mind, unsurprisingly, boggles.

But when all is said and done, in all those not-implausible theories and scenarios, we really know only two things: Someone killed John F. Kennedy as his motorcade was driving through Dallas. And, two days later, Jack Ruby shot Lee Harvey Oswald on live television. That's a lot of responsibility for Jack Ruby.

In the movie in his mind, Jack Ruby was a star. Hustling and bustling his way through the demimondes of 1950s and early 1960s Dallas, he was well aware that he didn't meet any traditional standards of male beauty, be they of the tall, blond Texan vintage or the dark, brooding ethnic type. He was a central casting thug, replete with thinning hair, beak-like nose, and beady eyes. He spoke with a flat Midwest accent.

Still, Ruby wanted to be noted and remembered. As mystery novelist, musician, and fellow Jewish Texan Richard "Kinky" Friedman said of him, "Jack Ruby, that bastard child of twin cultures, [was] death-bound and desperately determined to leave his mark on the world." Ruby would regularly ask people, "I'm colorful, ain't I? I'm a character, ain't I?" He ultimately got the recognition he desired. But did he get it the way he desired? That's hard to say. As Friedman noted, Ruby, until his death in January 1967, was "possibly the last living piece in a puzzle only God or Agatha Christie could have created"—or Kinky Friedman.

It's a puzzle that's been put together many times by many people, some of them in a convincing manner. When people ask me what I think was the real story behind the murders of Kennedy and Oswald, I reply that it's whatever theory I read last, whatever book I read last, whatever movie or documentary I saw last—although some of them retain a sense of credibility longer than others.

Still, whatever his true motivations, Jack Ruby's role in history is significant and fascinating. Not unlike Oswald, Jack Ruby's lifelong history of erratic, unpredictable behavior makes it difficult, if not impossible, to ascribe definitive motives to many of his actions, especially those connected to the Kennedy and Oswald murders. I hate to say it, but he was a nut. While his behavior certainly could fit any number of conspiracy theories, much of it could also be viewed as the inconsistent workings of a confused, erratic mind. Add to this Ruby's various testimonies and statements that contradict themselves and each other, and pinning this guy down becomes a maddening challenge—which doesn't make him any less important or compelling.

Who wouldn't like to link Ruby's actions to some sort of plan? But his life doesn't seem to have ever been planned out in any way, shape, or form. Ruby seemed to be constantly improvising and reacting, dealing with each situation as it emerged. Many of his actions and reactions were extreme, often sudden and violent. Jack doesn't seem to have been a guy who ever did much advance planning, nor did he appear to have thought much about the potential consequences of his actions—actions that were often spontaneously taken. (He did, however, seem to have endless *regret* over things he'd done and not done.)

———————

Of the three key players in the assassinations, Ruby's motivations are the most difficult to theorize about or understand.

Kennedy was a seeker and holder of power. He enjoyed wielding it, seemed to bask in the fame and attention it brought him, and seemed to genuinely feel he could use that power to do good in the world.

Lee Harvey Oswald, too, was obsessed with history and politics. He loved the spotlight and was actually something of a low-wattage public figure in Dallas and New Orleans, owing to his own seeking of attention and courting of controversy. He, too, didn't want simply to be famous. He wanted to affect history. The guy joined the US Marines and then, once in, proclaimed that he was a Communist. His situation was so weird that a fellow marine—Kerry Thornley, who would go on to play a role in the assassination investigations of Jim Garrison and others—wrote a novel in 1962, *The Idle Warriors*, based on the very strange Lee Oswald. That Oswald would take, or be part of, actions intended to affect history seems very much in character. He had grandiose visions of himself his entire life. Most (but, of course, not all) historians believe that it was Oswald who took a shot at right-wing extremist General Edwin Walker in Dallas several months before the JFK assassination, only through a fluke not killing him.

Jack Ruby, too, wanted to be famous, but in the way a lot of people want to be famous—so people would admire and love him and make him feel important. He enjoyed being the center of attention. It's not difficult to imagine him coveting a career as a Vegas-style singer or comedian. You could even say that he at times had a desire to make the world a better place. In his youth, he was known for beating up Nazis in his native Chicago, a visceral response to the rise of these antisemitic thugs who threatened him and his fellow Jews. His pursuit, in the same period, of power in that city's Scrap Iron Handlers Union could be seen as political, but in a local and personal way. Jack Ruby wasn't someone who wanted to be taught about in history classes. The world he wanted to change had very narrow boundaries.

That Ruby would end up standing at a crossroads of history, and would pull the trigger that changed history, wasn't something anyone would or could have predicted. But he *was* there and he *did* pull that trigger. And whether he was paid to be there, ordered to be there, or brought there by the compulsions of his own mind, at some point the entire thing seems to have become personal for Jack Ruby.

No matter who or what may have been manipulating, ordering, arranging, this was a man on a mission. No matter what narrative one may choose to overlay atop Jack Ruby's actions, at a certain point he became convinced that he was somehow fulfilling a grand destiny that fate had ordained for him. Indeed, of all the contradictory and confusing things he said in the more than three years following his history-changing action, he never expressed any remorse over murdering a shackled man who was innocent in the eyes of the law.

———————

Given what he did and its repercussions, it's unlikely that Jack Ruby will ever be forgotten. Six decades later, people know his name and the famous image of him shooting Oswald. You can watch the video on YouTube. Besides that, he shows up frequently in fiction and documentary. It would be so satisfying to fit him into one of many possible theories. But there are two days' worth of behavior that just don't comport with *any* theory. Ruby's forty-eight hours of manic behavior, acted out all over Dallas, in the period between the two killings fit no logical pattern at all. Jack traversed the metropolitan Dallas area, acting part of the time as if he, himself, was somehow going to solve some kind of mystery but also as if he was hosting a big party for his friends in Dallas and his guests from all over the world. Certainly, this is not how we think of a hired gun, biding his time in the shadows, waiting for the right moment to strike.

This is what's frustrating and fascinating about Ruby's story. Every narrative beyond "lone nut" becomes impossibly unlikely and complicated. Maybe that's why Ruby's story has been relatively neglected. It's too difficult to explain this guy.

———————

For many baby boomers, the Kennedy and Oswald assassinations were the first indication we had that conflicts, outside of war, were not always resolved peacefully and reasonably, according to rules and regulations and defined modes of behavior. Suddenly the orderly world of the 1950s was shattered; the ugly realities of human behavior that our Greatest Generation parents had tried to shield us from had instantly become visible. We saw Kennedy and Oswald get shot in a way that was as real—and unreal—as any TV violence we had seen on *Gunsmoke* or *77 Sunset Strip*. Except, in this case, real bullets had killed real people.

Every boomer kid—every boy, anyway—had a collection of toy guns, often cowboy-style guns, used, we were told, in places with weird names, like Dallas. We grew up playing with guns and seeing countless killings by gun—always bloodless—in the movies and TV shows that we consumed with avid regularity.

Suddenly, here was real violence with real repercussions. And, sure, a bad guy shot the president. But what about the guy who shot the guy who shot the president? Was he a good guy—or some other kind of bad guy? And what's that some people are saying on those boring talk shows our parents were watching—there might have been a whole bunch of people planning all this? But then, who were those people? Let's find out who they are and have the good guys find those bad guys and put them in jail. Wait—what? Now you're telling me the good guys *are* the bad guys? So—everybody's a bad guy? Except President Johnson, right? He's doing all that great stuff for civil rights, and he put together the Warren Commission to get to the bottom of the assassinations—what—*they're* not trustable? And neither is *he?* Vietnam? Where's that? I think I saw something about it in *My Weekly Reader*.

So the boomers had multiple—inevitable—shocks to the system. And Jack Ruby was a big part of that. Here was a guy who could have been a thug in an episode of *The Untouchables*, striding gracefully into a real-life scene and changing not just history but our perception of what reality was and wasn't.

———————

Even if Oswald did kill Kennedy, we have no photo of him firing his rifle, no visual image or eyewitness report equivalent to John Wilkes Booth leaping flamboyantly onto the Ford's Theatre stage after shooting Abraham Lincoln.

What we do have is the gruesome frames of the Zapruder film, fraught with ambiguity regarding where the killing shots that hit the young president originated and who fired them.

And, what we also have is film and still photos of Jack Ruby, the chubby everyman, the surprisingly graceful "regular guy," stepping up and firing point-blank into Lee Harvey Oswald's abdomen. Like all regular guys, Jack Ruby was more complicated than he seemed, with an entire lifetime of experiences and emotions and relationships and successes and failures leading to his most famous moment.

Who was this guy? Does it matter?

How can it not?

1 | KILLING THE KILLER

THE ASSASSIN MOVED STEALTHILY through the shadows. It was essential no one see him.

The president's full head of wavy hair was in his sights. The trigger was pulled, and the leader's head erupted in a splash of blood and bone and flesh.

Before anyone could stop him, the shooter leaped from the balcony and landed hard on the stage, breaking his ankle in the process. "Sic semper tyrannis!" the dapper man shouted, and fled from the spot, hurrying to meet his coconspirators.

President Abraham Lincoln was mortally wounded. John Wilkes Booth—and those who aided him in his violent, history-shattering act—would soon be brought to justice.

———————

Close to a century later—a period that witnessed two other presidential assassinations—President John F. Kennedy was shot to death as his motorcade snaked its way through the streets of Dallas on November 22, 1963.

But though a suspicious-acting young man named Lee Harvey Oswald was arrested for this killing and much evidence would point toward his guilt, there was no similar room full of eyewitnesses as there was to Lincoln's assassination, no triumphant Latin phrase intoned by a famous Shakespearean actor to put the exclamation point on his deed.

Nonetheless, Oswald was soon arrested for Kennedy's murder, as well as for that of Officer J. D. Tippit of the Dallas Police Department. Found hiding in the Texas Theatre during a daytime screening of *War Is Hell* (which starred Baynes Barron, born the same day—May 29, 1917—as John F. Kennedy), Oswald would, reportedly, try to shoot the police officers coming for him, but had the misfortune of having his gun jam as he tried to fire it.

On Sunday morning the twenty-fourth, having been in custody and questioned for close to forty-eight hours, Oswald should have been the most closely guarded person in the world. What he did and how he did it and why he did it and who—if anyone—he was in cahoots with were urgent concerns, especially if it was with America's Cold War enemy, Russia. It had only been a little more than a year since the Cuban Missile Crisis, which had brought the world to the brink of nuclear war.

For those two days, from 12:30 PM on Friday, November 22, 1963, to this morning, about 11:20 AM Sunday, while Oswald was hidden behind closed doors in Dallas police headquarters, the world outside was making the city the spot on the planet to which the most attention was being paid. Reporters from every major city were converging on downtown Dallas. The events of the weekend were being scrutinized via live television in a way that no event in history had ever been before. Pretty much all a viewer anywhere in the United States could see on network television was coverage of the aftermath of the assassination of the president. At a certain point, especially for children looking for their favorite kiddie shows, it was, despite the shock of the killing, actually growing tedious.

Now, on Sunday morning, there would be some break in the tedium. Oswald was to be transferred from the custody of the Dallas police into the hands of Dallas County, the assassination considered neither a local nor a federal crime but rather an offense against the state of Texas. In other situations, this would be the enactment of a simple bureaucratic formality. But of course, this was anything but an ordinary case. Lee Harvey Oswald was the target of widespread hate. And for all its sophistication and wealth, Dallas was in many ways still part of the Old West—a "shootout town," as some described it.

Therefore, this potentially vulnerable moment is when you'd think the Dallas police, having kept Oswald alive for two days, would be most aware that they had to keep this guy safe. If he was killed, any secrets or clues he possessed would die with him. Two days before, as he was paraded past reporters, he had denied any connection to the murders. "I'm a patsy," he insisted. Could that possibly have been true? Were there secrets he might yet reveal?

Oswald was escorted through a corridor that had been checked and double-checked for security. As reporters, cameramen, and police looked on, the suspect, flanked by two police officers and handcuffed to one—James Leavelle—walked to an awaiting car. They were escorting him to a different vehicle than the armored van that people thought he'd be taking, so any attackers en route would hopefully be fooled. Also, intentionally or not, Oswald was moved at a different time than the one that had been announced the day before. And really, who would be crazy enough to attack the guy here and now? It would be the literal definition of a suicide mission. Fire a gun, and a dozen cops would fire at *you!*

With police standing guard and reporters shouting questions and taking photos and shooting movie and video footage—indeed, with the event being broadcast over live TV—it seemed that the Dallas police would soon have this headache off their hands. It would be the state's problem now.

And then, in a sudden burst of activity, a short, stocky—but quite graceful—man in a fedora and dark suit pushed—almost danced—his way into the scene. He shoved a .38 caliber Colt Cobra revolver into Oswald's abdomen and fired once.

"You killed my president, you rat!" the shooter was reported to have declaimed (what he actually said would become a matter of debate), eschewing any Latin catchphrases.

It happened so fast, so casually. Where did that guy come from?!

Oswald collapsed, pulling Leavelle down with him. Before the gunman could get off another shot, he was grabbed, tackled by police and reporters, the Cobra wrested from his hand. The fedora was gone now, lost in the scuffle, betraying a man who seemed somehow puzzled at the extreme situation he found himself in. As if in explanation, seeming confused as to why these people were suddenly swarming all over him, trying in vain to break their hold, he could only repeat, like a mantra:

"You all know me. I'm Jack Ruby. You all know me . . ."

2 | DEATH OF A DREAM

JOHN F. KENNEDY HAD BEEN DECLARED DEAD twice in his forty-three years. He'd had last rites read over him. Clearly, those reports of his death were premature.

On the morning of Friday, November 22, 1963, he'd seemed as full of life as ever, touring through Texas to shore up support for his run for reelection the following year. If there was a walking dead man, it was Vice President Lyndon Baines Johnson, brought on to the Kennedy campaign in 1960 to help unite the Democrats in the South in general and Texas in particular in their support of Kennedy. And in that year, he had succeeded. But in the interim, discord between the liberal and conservative elements of the Texas Democratic Party had grown toxic, while Johnson's political capital had lost much of its value. His relationships with local politicians had weakened, and his finances were under scrutiny in relation to DC political operative Bobby Baker.

As the presidential plane descended on Dallas Love Field that morning—a bit of political showmanship, since the trip from Fort Worth would have been quite short by car—Kennedy had cracked to his wife, Jackie, that they were "heading into nut country." Less humorously, he had once reportedly opined to her that "if somebody wants to shoot me from a window with a rifle, nobody can stop it, so why worry about it?"

After touching down, Kennedy took some time to press the flesh with admirers at Love Field. Then he and his motorcade made their way to Dallas, huge crowds lining the streets of downtown. "You can't say Dallas doesn't love you, Mr. President," Nellie Connally, wife of Governor John Connally, cooed as the procession wove through town. The cars were headed for Dallas's recently built Trade Mart, a glass-fronted model of modern architecture, where the president was scheduled to speak at a luncheon of civic and religious leaders, including Rabbi Hillel Silverman, spiritual leader of Congregation Shearith Israel, whose members included one Jack Leon Ruby.

But as the motorcade left downtown and headed for the Trade Mart, shots rang out (three? four?), and—as filmed by local businessman Abraham Zapruder—Kennedy was mortally wounded, though still alive. Someone had shot the president—but it didn't look like anyone had paid the price of his or her own life in doing so.

Speeding up, the presidential limousine made its way at breakneck speed over highways and streets, soon arriving at Parkland Hospital. And while the president's entourage, including Secret Service agents, went into action to get their charges to the hospital safely—the extent of the president's wounds was as yet unknown—the Dallas Police Department also mobilized, fanning out to search for the shooter or shooters, who had also seriously wounded Governor Connally. A bullet—one that some would later sarcastically call "magic"—had pierced Connally's body and leg, blood oozing all over his off-white western-tailored suit.

Elsewhere in Dallas, at the office of the *Dallas Morning News*, reporters mobilized into action, several heading for Parkland to get the story. They left a customer in their classified ad department stranded in the middle of writing and submitting ad copy for his nightclubs. But rather than stand there waiting to hear what was happening, the customer, Jack Ruby, also mobilized for action.

What he did next and why he did it have become, over the decades, subjects of debate and controversy.

———————

Ruby was an attention-seeking, glad-handing nightclub owner, a perennial small-timer looking for validation from everyone with whom he came into contact. His bottom line was attracting customers to his nightclubs—not only the Carousel Club, which was primarily a strip club, but also, at various points, other venues, including a couple of country-western music halls where performers as diverse as Hank Williams Sr. and the Hawks (later renamed the

Band, of Bob Dylan fame) would perform, coming away with stories about the strange impresario who hired them to play. (Ruby did, however, pass up the opportunity to engage a pre-fame Willie Nelson, telling the person who brought Nelson in that he'd "better leave this Willie fella alone.")

One thing that was generally observed about Jack Ruby: he wanted to be where the action was. Most likely, this was because he felt that any popular event could affect the status of the businesses in which he was engaged and could also be a good excuse for him to promote those businesses. Ruby never went anywhere without a pocketful of risqué Carousel Club promotional cards. He took a proprietary interest in whatever was happening in Dallas. How would it affect the city? How would it affect his business? And how would it affect the city's—the country's, the world's—Jewish population?

Ruby lived simultaneously in multiple worlds. To some, he was a self-important buffoon, a struggling entrepreneur, perennially hanging on to solvency by his fingernails. The name Jack Ruby was synonymous with loser and busybody. Who could ever take this guy seriously? Certainly not those in the upwardly striving echelons of Dallas society, whether the members of his synagogue or the professionals he made it his business to be on a first-name basis with.

But there were many worlds within Dallas. And in some of those worlds, Jack Ruby was indeed taken seriously, if not universally liked. For instance, the world of Dallas nightclub operators had mixed feelings about Ruby, to say the least. It was a closed fraternity that may have found Ruby strange, annoying, and eccentric but still counted him as one of their own. Some, notably the Weinstein brothers, Barney and Abe, who ran enterprises similar to—and, as considered by most, classier than—Ruby's, had good reason to dislike and distrust Jack. Nonetheless, they had no choice but to accept him as someone they would sometimes have to deal with.

Ruby had all sorts of connections, including among Dallas's police. That was a matter of survival, important to his being able to function in the world of Dallas nightlife's arcane rules and regulations, especially those that defined what was obscene and what was not, as well as those that determined what manner of and delivery system for alcoholic beverages were allowed within the walls of the city's nightclubs. So Jack Ruby made it his business to be on friendly terms with the city's police, many of whom, despite his many connections to criminals, he seemed to genuinely like and admire.

As his brother Earl told Gus Russo, there was an "incident" where "two Dallas policemen were . . . trying to arrest some hoodlums. About half a dozen. But they couldn't do it. They weren't strong enough. But Jack joined the policemen to help them arrest the hoods. And from then on, he got a real close relationship with the cops." Ruby would often bring sandwiches to on-duty police officers. (Some believed this was more than simply currying favor with the powers-that-be, that Ruby was involved with, even key to, the drug trade in Dallas and that what he brought the police was more potent than pastrami.)

Besides the worlds of Dallas's nightclubs and police, there was the world of the entertainers and performers—strippers, of course, but also musicians and comedians and providers of quirky "revues"—whose circuits took in the clubs of Dallas, including Jack Ruby's. Some of these people genuinely liked and admired Jack, some feared him—he had a notoriously violent temper—some simply tolerated him. While many saw his violent side, many often saw his generous side, sometimes one right after the other.

Ruby was a fixture of the world of downtown Dallas, that neighborhood where nightclubs and hotels—notably the upscale Adolphus and Baker Hotels—and restaurants and government and police and courthouses and prisons and bail bondsmen and pawn shops—most famously, the optimistically named Honest Joe's—overlapped. Whether Ruby was seen as "mayor" or mascot, bully or buffoon, one thing was certain: there was no getting rid of the guy.

And there was the world of Jewish Dallas, a world that encompassed the North Dallas congregation to which Ruby belonged—an institution that had fought hard to be allowed to even have a home there—and its rabbi, Hillel Silverman, who had spearheaded that fight. The synagogue was now situated in this affluent community, its neighbors counting among their ranks New York Yankees superstar Mickey Mantle, who spent the off-season there (and who was an investor in a rival nightclub run by mobster Benny Bickers). Other members of the community included dermatologist Coleman Jacobson, who treated Ruby regularly for venereal disease and with whom Ruby traded gossip and news. Ladies' sportswear manufacturer—and home movie buff—Abraham Zapruder may have belonged to the congregation (more likely he belonged to the more religiously liberal Temple Emanu-El), but he was certainly a part of the city's Jewish community.

Ruby's week had been full of stress and anxiety. His business and his finances nearing rock bottom, he was in the middle of the usual feuds with his staff and his entertainers. A popular stripper named Jada was giving him considerable agita, but so were Abe and Barney Weinstein. The brothers were holding "amateur nights," featuring dancers Ruby believed were not actually amateurs, unfairly competing with his attractions. Ruby's attempts to persuade the performers' union—the American Guild of Variety Artists (AGVA)—to intervene had been unsuccessful in getting the Weinsteins to stop.

But worse than all that was the brouhaha surrounding the pending visit to the city of President Kennedy. Texas was then a Democratic state, but its most prominent government officials were feuding, despite Texan Lyndon Johnson's status as Kennedy's vice president. And so the president and his second took what they hoped would be a fence-mending trip to Dallas. The city was aflutter with excitement over this rare presidential visit. But not all of the excitement was positive. Many in the city virulently hated Kennedy and everything associated with him.

Among the criticism aimed at the president was a large ad printed in that morning's *Dallas Morning News*—the very paper at whose offices Ruby was present, readying his Carousel Club's ads for the weekend. (He was there in person—instead of phoning his ads in—because the newspaper would no longer honor his credit.) The ad that infuriated Ruby was headlined WELCOME MR. KENNEDY TO DALLAS. It asked a series of loaded questions, the overall effect being to accuse Kennedy of being incompetent and a Soviet dupe. The ad was signed by a "Bernard Weissman," which, to Ruby, seemed an obviously Jewish name. Ruby felt the hostile ad would reflect badly on the city's Jews. He even wondered if Jew haters had signed the Jewish-seeming name to the ad specifically to inflame hatred.

"Are you so money hungry?" he demanded of John Newman at the newspaper's advertising department, even as he was composing the ad for his clubs. (Ruby also ran the Vegas Club, a nightclub in the Oak Lawn neighborhood that was a place for people to drink and dance, but not a show venue like the Carousel.) Ruby feared that if anything untoward happened during the president's visit, it would be blamed on Dallas—bad for business—and blamed on the Jews—bad for the Jews.

WANTED

FOR

TREASON

THIS MAN is wanted for treasonous activities against the United States:

1. Betraying the Constitution (which he swore to uphold): He is turning the sovereignty of the U. S. over to the communist controlled United Nations. He is betraying our friends (Cuba, Katanga, Portugal) and befriending our enemies (Russia, Yugoslavia, Poland).
2. He has been WRONG on innumerable issues affecting the security of the U.S. (United Nations-Berlin wall-Missile removal-Cuba-Wheat deals-Test Ban Treaty, etc.)

3. He has been lax in enforcing Communist Registration laws.
4. He has given support and encouragement to the Communist inspired racial riots.
5. He has illegally invaded a sovereign State with federal troops.
6. He has consistently appointed Anti-Christians to Federal office: Upholds the Supreme Court in its Anti-Christian rulings. Aliens and known Communists abound in Federal offices.
7. He has been caught in fantastic LIES to the American people (including personal ones like his previous marriage and divorce).

Anti-Kennedy flyer distributed in Dallas in the days leading up to his visit. It gives an indication of extremist hostility toward the president in the city at that time. *Courtesy of Wikimedia Commons*

And so, when the shocking news of the president's shooting in Dealey Plaza reached the newspaper offices, many of the paper's staff unsurprisingly raced out to get the story. It also couldn't be considered surprising that Jack Ruby ran out too. He always wanted to be where the action was.

But where did he go?

Ruby would claim that he made his way directly back to the Carousel at 1312½ Commerce Street. That makes sense. He needed to decide what a frivolous—even shady—entertainment locale like his should do when a president was shot virtually next door, whether or not the man died. And he certainly did end up at the club, where he would make and receive numerous frenzied phone calls.

But some say that, like the reporters, Jack Ruby—before arriving at the Carousel—went to Parkland Hospital, where the gravely wounded president had been taken. Notably, reporter Seth Kantor claimed that he saw Ruby there and that Ruby even asked him if he thought he should close his clubs for the weekend out of respect for the president. Kantor wasn't surprised to see Ruby. This was just the kind of event Jack Ruby would be attracted to. And yet, Ruby would deny he was ever there.

Overall, this wouldn't seem to be that important, except when the idea started circulating that Ruby had somehow tampered with evidence at the hospital.

Kantor came to believe that, whether he tampered with evidence or not (Kantor thought this unlikely, actually), Ruby had somehow been involved in a larger scheme, in part because of Ruby's denial of his presence. *If Ruby would lie about that,* Kantor wondered, *what else would he lie about?*

This is the type of uncertainty that colors so much about Jack Ruby's story. We know, of course, that he shot Lee Harvey Oswald at point-blank range on national TV at 11:21 AM central time on November 24, 1963. But so much else of Ruby's story is ambiguous. And yet, as much as the president's killer or killers, Jack Ruby changed history.

But who *was* this guy?

Why, despite the blunt, shocking nature of his murder of Oswald, are Ruby's reasons for his deed so shrouded in uncertainty? Why has Jack Ruby's assault on history left us, sixty years later, still reeling?

To find out, we need to take a trip to his—and America's—past.

3 | WORLDS APART

IN 1871, JACK RUBY'S FATHER, Joseph Rubenstein, was born in Poland—then controlled by czarist Russia—in a little town called Sokolov. Joseph was charming and affable, loved to tell a good joke, often one with a double entendre punchline. His fifth child, born Jacob Rubenstein, would share those characteristics. Another trait they shared was a violent temper, which would lead them into ceaseless conflict, both within and outside their family.

Joseph's charm wasn't enough to keep him from being drafted into the Russian army, where he was assigned to the artillery, serving in China, Korea, and Siberia. In the army, he was trained as a carpenter. It was also in the army that he developed a serious drinking habit. While serving, Joseph entered into an arranged marriage with Fannie Turek Rutkowski. The marriage would prove to be tempestuous, marked by frequent, often violent, conflict between the spouses.

Knowing the fate of Jewish inductees in the Russian army was either death in combat or lifetime servitude, one day in 1898 Joseph decided that he'd had enough and deserted. After first stopping off in England and Canada, he made his way to America, as did so many of his generation, winding up in Chicago in 1903. In Chicago he settled in the Maxwell Street area, one of several now-legendary Jewish neighborhoods—or ghettos, if you will—in that city. (Years later, as a Black ghetto, it was the setting for John Lee Hooker's performance of "Boom Boom" in the 1980 *The Blues Brothers* movie. Following that, it was razed for the edifices that stand there today, buildings owned by the University of Illinois Chicago.)

The neighborhood produced prominent Jewish Americans, including jazz legend Benny Goodman, Supreme Court Justice Arthur Goldberg, and CBS founder

William S. Paley. Maxwell Street's alumni also included gangsters such as Jake "Greasy Thumb" Guzik, who handled Al Capone's financial affairs.

In Chicago, Joseph joined the carpenters union and found regular work in that occupation, sending for his wife Fannie and two children a couple years later. Over the next years, she would give birth to six more children, for a total of eight surviving offspring—four boys and four girls. (A daughter had died as an infant as a result of a horrific scalding accident.) Fannie would never become fluent in English, preferring to speak in Yiddish whenever possible. Possessed of a mercurial personality, she never released her hold on her children, though often swearing that she hated them—and they her.

Unsurprisingly, given Fannie's extremes of mood and the rage that would be unleashed in Joseph by his alcoholism, the couple spent much of their time in America living separately, their children spending much of their time in foster homes. Joseph seemed to have no lack of female attention, though whether that was a cause or an effect of his marriage's troubles is hard to say. When husband and wife were together, there were frequent, often violent, arguments. Jacob was the fifth child and the second-oldest male (Hyman was nine years older than Jack), born sometime in March or April 1911. Like so much about Jack Ruby's life, even this basic fact is hard to pin down. Throughout his life, he would give different birthdates, though always the same year, always March or April. His headstone gives it as April 25.

Author Ira Berkow's Uncle Jerry, whose family was neighbors with the Rubensteins, recalls that Joseph was thrown out by his wife for some combination of real violence and real or imagined infidelities. Joseph then lived in a nearby apartment, where he constructed a homemade still.

"His sons Jack and Earl would come and we'd all put in cherries to give the gin some color," Uncle Jerry recalled. He told Berkow that Joseph "was a great storyteller. . . . Sometimes he'd say things that would have shocked our mothers. His favorite saying was 'Six-and-seven-eighths measurement.'" When asked by Berkow what he meant by that, Jerry responded, "He was a carpenter. You figure it out. He would laugh and say, 'It's six and seven-eighths.'" Apparently, Jacob came by his preoccupation with sex naturally.

In 1913, when Jacob was two, his mother became convinced that she had a fish bone lodged in her throat. She would complain of this for years. She even had surgery performed to dislodge the nonexistent obstruction, but there was no curing her of this delusion. By the time he was eleven, Jacob was the oldest male living at home with Fannie, his brother Hyman having left the nest. Missing many days at school, Jacob was brought before Chicago's Children's Court as a truant. The court sent him to be evaluated at the Institute for Juvenile Research. The reason given for his examination in the institute's report is

> boy's truancy, incorrigibility at home and mother's extremely erotic [sic] temperament. Mrs. R . . . admits she loses her temper with the children and beats them . . . she cannot control them and is always getting into quarrels because of their delinquencies, i.e., principally their destructive tendencies and disregard for other people's property.

The report also notes that Jacob, at age two, fell from a table and injured his head. One could imagine this might have been a blow to the head from his mother or father, as opposed to the reported fall. In later years, doctors would claim this and other blows to the head affected Ruby's judgment as an adult. Psychologists' findings during Ruby's 1964 murder trial, including an electroencephalogram reading, indicated that Ruby's brain showed an injury that could have resulted in his often-extreme behavior.

In those later examinations, psychologist Roy Schafer detected indications that Ruby felt "disruption and confusion" in his "experience of his own body. He feels generally damaged, impaired and repulsive." Psychiatrist Renatus Hartogs and Lucy Freeman, in their 1965 book *The Two Assassins*, speculate that this was because of Ruby's boyhood "undescended testicles," which would have made him feel like a freak. They noted that the institute reported Jacob as having engaged in "frequent masturbation," perhaps "as a way of gaining some pleasure from a life that for him is too harsh." The two pointed out how Ruby slept in the same bed as his younger brothers, which they felt could have led to "sexual arousal."

Correspondence dated July 1922 from the institute to the Jewish Social Service Bureau indicated about Jack that

> he has some sex knowledge and is greatly interested in sex matters. He stated that the boys in the street tell him about these things. This

patient is egocentric, states that he can lick everyone and is as good as
anybody at anything he wants to do . . . and expects much attention
[at home] and is unable to get it as there are many children at home.
His behavior is rather colored by his early sex experiences, his great
interest [in sex] and the gang situation in the street.

A follow-up document from March 1923 noted, "In our last conversation
with the boy it was noticed that he felt that the mother was inferior, therefore,
he did not have to abide by her rules." It was recommended he be placed in a
foster home. Asked by the institute if she felt that Jacob ever planned to injure
anyone, Fannie replied, "Yes." As a result of these findings, in July 1923, Jacob
was placed in a foster home, as were his younger siblings.

Fannie appealed for help to local Jewish welfare agencies. The four younger
children, including Jacob, lived in foster homes for somewhere between four
and five years. At one point Jacob was sent to live on a farm, though he was
later reunited with Earl (the youngest brother) and Sam (the second youngest)
in another foster home.

Jacob was on the farm long enough, though, for someone there to make
the comparison between him and the bumbling, lovable racehorse Spark
Plug—nicknamed "Sparky"—from the popular *Take Barney Google F'rinstance*
newspaper comic strip. Sparky became Jacob's nickname too. Jacob hated the
name—the horse was kind of an equine buffoon—but the name stuck. Some
said it also fit him because of his "sparky" temper, always ready to erupt in
anger and violence.

At age nine, Jacob had enough of an entrepreneurial streak that he would
travel fifteen miles to Maywood, Illinois, and bring back firecrackers that he
would sell on the streets of Chicago at a profit.

When Jacob was fourteen, his oldest brother, Hyman, brought the children
back together with their mother, though Joseph was still not living with them.
Hyman later recalled he "felt an obligation to . . . help take care of the family,"
since his father had left home. Nonetheless, with Jacob's family life continually and regularly disrupted, not least of all by his mother's madness and his
father's instability, the atmosphere was not conducive to a serious approach to
education. Jacob would not formally drop out of school until he was sixteen,
but it's unlikely that he progressed beyond the eighth grade. From 1927 on,
Jack Rubenstein focused full-time on making a living.

His brother Hyman described him as "a hustler." He elaborated, "Anything that he could go out and sell and make a dollar [he would do] . . . he wouldn't have a steady job, but he was always on the go." Hyman recalled Jack scalping tickets for sporting events. He recounted that in 1928 "Ruby had a fight with two plainclothes policemen, when he was selling tickets outside Soldiers Field."

In his book *Gangsters vs. Nazis*, Michael Benson notes that "Jacob learned to fight when the Italian kids visited from Taylor Street in Little Sicily to beat up Jews. Jacob made sure he dished out more than he got. . . . At sixteen [in 1927], he was scalping tickets for Bears football games outside Soldier Field and at William Harley's Mills Stadium" and other sports venues. Benson also notes that "Jacob worked legitimate jobs, too, but always in a venue where one was apt to see gangsters. . . . At least three times a week, he'd get into a fight."

One consistent element in young Jack Rubenstein's life was his friendship with another Maxwell Street kid, Beryl Rossofsky, born a year earlier than Jack. Rossofsky, whose father was a neighborhood grocer and rabbi, was headed for a career as a Judaic scholar when violence changed his plans. In 1922 Rossofsky's father was murdered during a holdup at the family store, shattering Beryl's family and his faith. Beryl abandoned his studies and turned his attention and his rage to boxing, although he also claimed (and then denied) that he and Jacob Rubenstein earned money from time to time by delivering packages for gang boss Al Capone. Rossofsky—who would become famous as boxer Barney Ross—asserts in his autobiography, *No Man Stands Alone*, that they contained nothing illicit or illegal.

Both Jacob and Beryl were enamored of the world of boxing, in an era when, as today, it was a route out of poverty for sons of immigrants. In the 1920s and '30s, that group included young Jewish men from the ghettoes of New York and Chicago. Rubenstein and Rossofsky spent their time at local gyms, including Kid Howard's and Davey Miller's. Miller himself had mob ties, not uncommon for those in the boxing field. Cartoonist Irwin Hasen, best known for cocreating the syndicated *Dondi* newspaper strip, recalled that the boxing magazine office where he worked drawing portraits of fighters was frequented by gangsters, including a "Mr. Gray," the codename for mobster Frankie Carbo.

Infamous Chicago mob boss Al Capone, for whom young Beryl Rossofsky (Barney Ross) and Jacob Rubenstein (Jack Ruby) were said to have performed errands.
Courtesy of Wikimedia Commons

Ross was the more skilled boxer and would go on to have an illustrious career in the ring, amassing a variety of championship titles. His fame would continue through the decades, well beyond his achievements in the squared circle. Eventually, his and Ruby's lives would reconnect, even ending within two weeks of each other. Author Douglas Century refers to Ruby as "the Jungian shadow of Ross."

Even before his father's murder, Ross was already a tough kid. According to Jeffrey Sussman, in *Max Baer and Barney Ross: Jewish Heroes of Boxing*, "Sparky and Beryl were an intimidating team; if you were not a resident of Maxwell Street, you would have wanted to cross the street when you saw these two coming at you." Sussman adds that "they were said to have rolled drunks, offered protection to peddlers . . . and run errands for Big Al [Capone]."

When Ross finally made the leap to professional boxing, he was rumored to be backed by "the Outfit" and have again attracted the attention of Capone himself, who supposedly steered the young man from a life of hands-on criminality to one where he wouldn't be in direct contact with underworld forces.

Ruby's lifelong friend Barney Ross during his 1930s reign as welterweight boxing champion. *Courtesy of Wikimedia Commons*

Regarding Ruby, Ross's brother, George Rasof, recalled that on a trip to a Chicago Bears game, a fan made the mistake of blocking Jack's car in the parking lot. Ruby, Rasof recounted, "flew into an uncontrollable rage that ended in a physical assault." There are numerous stories like this about Ruby, from childhood to the end of his life, stories of erratic behavior, often erupting, with minimal provocation, into violence.

Century observes, "Throughout his life, Jack Ruby idolized Barney Ross—carried his water bottle at the gym and lived for the days when he could get into the ring with him to spar. And Ross . . . never abandoned his childhood friend, even when Ruby was on trial for first-degree murder."

One may ask what, if any, level of involvement Jacob Rubenstein had with the criminal side of Chicago, loosely called "the mob." Rumors of mob involvement would dog the entire Ruby family, and, of course, are crucial to various theories as to why Jack acted as he did in November 1963. His siblings testified before the Warren Commission that the Rubensteins knew criminals and gangsters just by dint of where they grew up and who they grew up among. Ruby himself just said that, in the course of daily life on the streets of Chicago, especially when engaged in ticket scalping and selling horse race tip sheets, he inevitably came across mobsters but was never engaged in business with them.

Of course, few people would come forth under oath and brag of their membership in organized crime—certainly not unless they'd already secured some kind of a deal with prosecutors or were resigned to serving a long stretch for crimes of which they'd been convicted. Too many of Ruby's associates and business partners have been accused and convicted of crimes of various levels for it to be credible that Ruby would have had no knowledge of their subterranean activities. Still, as Joe Kraus, in *The Kosher Capones*, notes, "Gangsters make excellent protagonists because we know so little about them and they seem such a potential outlet for aggression. Organized crime shrouds itself in uncertainty. . . . In that space, in the middle ground between the reputation they need for intimidation and the deniability they need for protection, they create mystery. And mystery, like a vacuum, draws scraps of story into it."

Indeed, that he associated with criminals—perhaps even committed his share of criminal activity—isn't the same as designating Jack as some kind of "made man" or regular mob bagman or envoy. And it certainly isn't the same as saying that he was picked out of all the shady characters in Dallas to be the long arm of the mob, tasked with slipping in and executing Lee Harvey Oswald.

But it doesn't mean he wasn't, either.

While his friend Barney Ross was making a name for himself as a fighter, Jack Rubenstein was struggling to figure out where in the world he might fit in. Having abandoned formal education at age sixteen in 1927, what Jack Ruby did with his life between that dubious milestone and his departure for the West Coast in 1933 is unclear. For large swaths of Ruby's life we know where he most likely was—Chicago—but very little sense of what he was doing.

We can be pretty sure that Jack worked various hustles, perhaps with Ross or other local toughs. We can figure he had to mediate conflicts between his siblings and his parents. It's likely he engaged in various business enterprises with his brothers, as he would in later years. (The phrase "it's likely" is the bane of researching anything related to the Kennedy assassination.) With a large, intermeshed family, many of whom were at the very least neurotic, and with an insane mother and a complicated, violent, irascible, and often unemployed father (Joseph was frequently out of work from 1928 on), anyone's hands would be full.

During these years, there's no record of Jack dating anyone or of any friends as close as Barney Ross that he palled around with. Some of the Maxwell Street no-goodniks were interviewed by the FBI and the Warren Commission after Ruby killed Oswald, but most of these people indicated—truthfully or not—that they never really knew Ruby well and, anyway, they hadn't seen him for decades. There's no record of specific books or magazines or radio programs or movies that he loved or that motivated or comforted him.

Nevertheless, here was a young man who, as Hartogs and Freeman note of his personality traits, "appears to have suffered from a great hunger for recognition and affection, something he apparently never received from his mother or father."

That search for recognition and affection would lead Jack Ruby to find and lose both in wrenching ways that would inform his most famous act.

But long before that act, there would be an economic disaster and a westward move.

4 | A WORLD GONE MAD

THE ROAR OF THE TWENTIES came to an abrupt halt on October 24, 1929, when the stock market crashed, sending America into the Great Depression. Groucho Marx famously received a call from a friend who ominously warned, "Marx, the jig is up!" And, indeed, it was—except perhaps for businesses such as those run by Joseph P. Kennedy, the future president's father, which thrived throughout this period, multiplying his wealth and amplifying his political influence and ambition.

Unrest that had been festering in Europe, especially in Germany, metastasized into the racism and territorial expansionism that brought the Nazi Party to power. Adolf Hitler rose violently and inexorably through Germany's shattered political world, gathering power, while Joseph Stalin carved a path of bodies as he consolidated his own power in the USSR.

On January 30, 1933, Hitler assumed the office of chancellor of Germany. In the United States, Jews—already dealing with ongoing antisemitism, especially as embodied by the publication in Henry Ford's *Dearborn Independent* of the bogus *Protocols of the Elders of Zion* and by the rantings of radio preacher Father Charles Coughlin—listened to the dire reports coming from the lands from which many of them, or their parents, had recently emigrated.

The market crash and ensuing economic disasters propelled President Herbert Hoover to an election loss to Franklin D. Roosevelt in November 1932. Roosevelt was slated to take the oath of office on March 4, 1933. In his inaugural address, he informed the nation that "the only thing we have to fear is fear itself."

Roosevelt had good reason to know fear. His life had nearly come to a violent end a few weeks before. On February 13, 1933, in Miami, Giuseppe Zangara fired a shot that mortally wounded Chicago mayor Anton Cermak, who was standing next to Roosevelt. Cermak died on March 6, two days after his ally's inauguration. While it's generally thought that Roosevelt was Zangara's target, a school of thought holds that Cermak was the intended victim, part of a complicated scheme that was essentially revenge from Capone lieutenant Frank Nitti for a Cermak-backed attempt on *his* life. Either way, the bullet came far too close for comfort to FDR.

And on March 23, Barney Ross became lightweight boxing champion in a classic matchup with his ongoing adversary, Tony Canzoneri, at Chicago Stadium. It's likely Jack Rubenstein was there, as he was at almost all of his friend Beryl's Chicago fights. It's also likely he was scalping tickets before the fight. (Perhaps for this reason—as well as a desire to be in the spotlight—Ruby would often arrive at his own seat just as a boxing match was beginning, calling attention to himself as he greeted the VIPs in attendance.) Still, whatever money that or his other activities might have been bringing in, it didn't seem to be enough.

Right around this time, Jack and "several Chicago friends," despairing of earning much of a living through whatever means, made their way to the West Coast. One can imagine them hitchhiking or even riding the rails to get to the Promised Land of California.

One of Jack's first forays into making a living on the West Coast was working as a singing waiter in a Los Angeles Italian restaurant. If the unnamed restaurant prided itself on the vocal prowess of its waitstaff, this could only have ended badly. Though Jack Ruby would be accused of many things in his lifetime, having a beautiful voice was not one of them.

After finding no success in Los Angeles, Ruby made his way to San Francisco, where he engaged in ticket scalping at sporting events and ran crews of men who peddled newspaper subscriptions door-to-door. Jack's sister Eva, who would soon join him in San Francisco, explained to the Warren Commission that she believed Jack was aggressive and successful in his subscription sales, indicating perhaps a certain amount of intimidation used to persuade people that they absolutely needed to have a newspaper delivered to their door daily during the depths of the Depression.

According to the Warren Commission investigation,

One friend, who stated that he resided with Ruby and Eva [in San Francisco] for about a year, described him as a "well-mannered, likable individual who was soft spoken and meticulous in his dress and appearance." Another friend described him as a "clean-cut, honest kid," and the manager of a crew with which Ruby worked stated that he had a good reputation and appeared to be an "honest, forthright person." The crew manager reported that Ruby associated with a sports crowd, some of whose members were involved with professional boxing, but not with criminals.

During Ruby's years of self-imposed exile from Chicago, his childhood friend, Ross, continued punching a path through a championship boxing career, with but a single loss among the dozens of bouts that he fought. He was making himself a legend—and rather wealthy—while Jack was shlepping newspapers up and down the hills of San Francisco.

Eva had been married in Chicago in 1930 to a man named Hyman Magid, who was a partner in a butcher business. With him, she had a son, Ronald. Eva and Magid divorced in early 1934.

Later that year, she moved to San Francisco, where she and Ronald shared an apartment with Jack. In 1936 she married Frank Grant, and she, her husband, and her child shared an apartment with Jack, although who was paying the bulk of the expenses is unclear. Eva reported that she relied on Jack for "advice and support." She divorced Grant in 1940. Ronald Magid remembered Jack also working in the linoleum-laying business.

Eva recalled that Jack "was always guiding me." She explained that there was good money in the newspaper subscription work "considering the times, because they were paying 90 cents an order and we would go out and get eight or ten or fifteen orders a day, which you couldn't get in any other job, and our obligations were great. My son's expenses were $65 a month, and my brother helped support half of the fellows that didn't work—who wouldn't do this." (Who those "fellows" were is unclear.) In other words, Jack Rubenstein wasn't afraid of or incapable of hard work. Jack returned to Chicago in 1937, apparently not finding whatever he was looking for on the West Coast.

Perhaps the most notable thing about Ruby's time on the West Coast was his relationship, in San Francisco, with Virginia Belasco, granddaughter of the legendary Jewish playwright and actor David Belasco and herself an actress.

Ruby met her at a dance at the city's Jewish Community Center in 1936 while she was still a teenager and saw her regularly in San Francisco and then other cities, including New York, until 1941, when she saw him numerous times in that city, the last being right after the December 7 attack on Pearl Harbor by Japan. She described the Jack Ruby of that year to the FBI as "a young man who dressed very well and was a personable date." The FBI report described Virginia as "a very wealthy woman, who has never been married." Years later, Ruby would refer to a "Virginia Fitzgerald" as the only woman he ever truly loved. It's reasonable to speculate that he was really referring to Belasco, changing her name for some reason known only to himself.

Returning to Chicago in 1937, Ruby hustled scalped tickets and bought and resold watches and other small items. But soon, his relationship with Local 20467 of the Scrap Iron and Junk Handlers Union began. His job title was "organizer," although there's no evidence that he had any experience or interest in, or history with, organized labor. It wouldn't be shocking to imagine that Jack's idea of negotiating with potential union members and union rivals would somehow involve brass knuckles and baseball bats, or at least the threat of such items being put to persuasive use. Kraus, in *The Kosher Capones*, states that Ruby "acted as hired muscle" for the union.

This becomes especially tempting to assume because, not long after signing on with the union, Jack and some of his Jewish pals—fellow ne'er-do-wells hanging out at the mob-connected Davey Miller's legendary pool hall and boxing gym—would reportedly spend considerable time and force breaking up Nazi Bund meetings in Chicago. These confrontations reached their peak in November 1938—the days leading up to Kristallnacht—when, with Aryan-looking Jewish Chicago reporter Herb Brin acting as their inside man, Jacob Rubenstein and others broke up rallies held by the Bund and another Nazi group, the Silver Shirts.

Interestingly, his boxing career pretty much over, Barney Ross himself took part in these incursions. As Benson writes, Ross told Ruby he couldn't go on one particular foray: "You guys get caught, it's assault. I get caught, attempted murder. My hands are lethal weapons." Ruby had a solution. He provided Ross with a leather blackjack he could use instead of his fists. Ruby's brother Hyman Rubenstein recalled that people would tell him, "Your brother is terrific. He just goes in there and breaks up the joint."

Though Local 20467 would within a few years become infamously mob-controlled under the thumb of gangster Paul "Red" Dorfman, it's generally believed that the union was fairly clean when Ruby first became involved with it. His point of first contact with the union is unknown for sure, but it seems to have been through its founder, attorney Leon Cooke.

For a union getting started and striving to survive in that era, a tough guy—a *shtarker*—like Jack Rubenstein would be seen as a necessity. In the course of his relationship with the union, Ruby came to admire Cooke, who was intent on keeping the organization focused on aiding its severely underpaid members. Whatever other motives he would have for his actions over the years, Jack Ruby seemed to be genuinely inspired by people he considered idealistic. Cooke was one of them.

During this period, Fannie Rubenstein was committed to psychiatric hospitals for lengthy stays in 1937 and 1938, following years of erratic behavior. Dr. Hyman I. Rubenstein, the son of Joseph Rubenstein's brother (i.e., Fannie's nephew), remembered that she ran "an irregular household" and seemed to be "a rather disturbed person of poor personal appearance with no incentive for cleaning or cooking." As the Warren Commission report noted, "According to the Michael Reese Hospital, whose clinic she had visited since 1927, Mrs. Rubenstein was suffering from psychoneurosis with marked anxiety state."

The commission report goes on with this litany of Fannie's suffering:

> By order of the county court of Cook County, Mrs. Rubenstein was committed to Elgin State Hospital on July 16, 1937. She was paroled on October 17, 1937, 3 months after her commitment. On January 3, 1938, the Chicago State Hospital informed Elgin State that the family desired that she be readmitted to the mental hospital. The family reported that she was uncooperative, caused constant discord, was very noisy, and used obscene language. A State social worker observed that Mrs. Rubenstein refused ever to leave the house, explaining that her children would have thrown her things out had she left. Mrs. Rubenstein rebuffed a suggestion by the social worker that she help with the dishes by stating that she would do nothing as

long as her "worthless" husband was in the house. She was readmitted on January 14, 1938.

Mrs. Rubenstein was again paroled on May 27, 1938, and was discharged as "improved" on August 25, 1938. She stayed in an apartment with [her daughter] Marion, and her separation from the rest of the family apparently ended most of the difficulties.

On September 1, 1939, German troops invaded Poland, signaling the beginning of World War II. Less dramatically—but also of historical import—the following month, on October 18, to be specific, Lee Harvey Oswald was born in New Orleans to the recently widowed Marguerite Oswald.

And in Chicago, Scrap Iron and Junk Handler's union executive Leon Cooke's idealism was not finding appreciation. Gangster Johnny Martin—believed to be employed by mob boss Dorfman, who would eventually take over the union himself—had muscled in, naming himself head of the union. In December 1939, Cooke confronted him about it and ended up with three bullets fired into his back by Martin, who claimed *self-defense*—and was acquitted!

Questioned about this killing was Jack Rubenstein, who might have been in the room when the shooting happened, though he was never charged with having any part in it. In fact, according to his recollection, Ruby took on the middle name Leon in honor of his fallen friend. Ruby would recall—although no one else mentioned it—that he actually tried to take over the union, assuming that Martin would be convicted, the jury seeing through his absurd alibi. Such was not to be the case. Martin was released and returned to the union, leading Ruby, as he himself recalled, to beat a hasty retreat from Chicago.

It's also possible that Ruby never left town and just liked telling the story with himself at the center of a major event. It would not be the first or last time Jack Rubenstein would attempt to aggrandize himself in the eyes of the world.

5 | WAR AT HOME, WAR ABROAD

ONE WAY OR ANOTHER, Jack Ruby's tenure with the union was done by late 1939. He still had to find a way to make a living. Was he actually run out of town, or was his recollection that he was just an excuse for his inability to continue rising in the union or to develop any kind of serious career accomplishments?

We do know that, by 1941, Ruby was back in Chicago and in business with partners, including Martin Gimpel, Martin Shargol, and brother Earl Ruby, as the Spartan Novelty Company. The firm sold small, candy-filled cedar chests and "punchboards," which were sort of low-tech, low-paying versions of instant lotteries. For this venture, Ruby would travel all over the Northeast, which would explain why he was able to spend considerable time in New York with Virginia Belasco. Virginia seemed to have been genuinely fond of Ruby, although not, apparently, in a serious romantic way.

In the wake of the December 7, 1941, attack on Pearl Harbor, Ruby and several friends (whether still as the Spartan company is unclear) decided to go into business manufacturing souvenir plaques commemorating that fateful day. Unfortunately, Ruby's fixation on the items meeting some high level of quality that only he could determine delayed their release into the market. By the time they met his standards, the market for such souvenirs was saturated. Ruby also tried selling busts of President Roosevelt in another attempt to market patriotic memorabilia that doesn't seem to have been very successful. In the year or so after Pearl Harbor, Ruby also worked for Globe Auto Glass and Universal Sales Company. One can only guess what these businesses did.

Early in 1941 Ruby had, after being classified 1-A by his Chicago draft board, been reclassified as exempt from the draft because of his age (he had turned thirty in 1941) and because he was the main support for his mother.

Ruby was remembered in this period, as over his entire life, for erupting in anger, often taking the form of violence, at any perceived or—all too often— real instance of antisemitism he'd encounter. Earl recalled that Jack had many battles because of "being called . . . names, referring to his Jewish parents. . . . He was always quick tempered and just couldn't take it." Once Jack came home with blood all over his clothes. "Somebody called me a dirty Jew," he told Earl by way of explanation. And his sister Eva recalled that if anyone "said words like *Sheeny* or *kike* or *Jew*—he belted it out of them."

Ruby's anger could also be triggered by injustices besides antisemitism. His brother Hyman recalled Jack picking up a chair in a bar to hit someone who had made a disparaging comment about President Roosevelt. Two men kept him from hitting the guy with it. Someone else remembered that Jack brawled with a couple of college boys who'd insulted an African American musician.

In 1943 Jack, though already thirty-two years old, lost his deferment and was again classified 1-A. After unsuccessful appeals to the draft board, on May 21, 1943, he was inducted into the US Army Air Forces. His brothers were already in the armed services. Earl was serving with the navy's construction arm, the Seabees; Sam, like Jack, was in the Army Air Forces, but in their intelligence division in Langley, Virginia; and Hyman was trained in army field artillery in Washington State.

Stationed mostly at air bases in the South, Jack Rubenstein didn't see combat. He did earn marksmanship and sharpshooter ratings, and, somewhat surprisingly, his character and efficiency ratings were excellent. This was despite, as the Warren Commission report noted, Jack being, while in the service, "extremely sensitive to insulting remarks about Jews. When . . . a sergeant called Ruby a 'Jew bastard,' Ruby reportedly attacked him and beat him with his fists."

Betraying perhaps some of its own prejudice, an FBI report to the Warren Commission on Ruby's activities during his military service described Jack as a "conniver with much nerve." The report related that, one night in a Savannah hotel, Ruby was talking to a woman on the telephone "when Bob Hope [who Ruby didn't know] walked through the lobby. Ruby reached out, took . . . [Hope's] arm . . . and persuaded him to speak to the girl." Though this was an arguably endearing act on Ruby's part, it does indicate his brashness as well as his affinity for celebrities and for inflating his own importance.

Though he didn't see combat (at least, not on a battlefield), Ruby seems to have to some degree thrived in the air force, spending much of his time gambling and engaged in a variety of side businesses. He regularly returned to Chicago on leave, and photos exist of him seeming to be enjoying himself at nightclubs, often in the company of attractive women.

In April 1944 Fannie Rubenstein died of heart disease and pneumonia. She had been reunited with her family, living with her daughter Marion, as well as her husband, with whom she seems to have reconciled. It doesn't seem as if this loss spurred any sort of religious interest in Ruby, though when his father died in 1958, something sparked in him by *that* death would lead him to participate in mourning rituals at his synagogue.

Unlike Jack Ruby, his friend Barney Ross saw more than his share of combat. Well over draft age and possessed of connections that could have provided him with a deferral or a cushy stateside assignment, Ross instead used his clout to get a special age waiver and to enlist in the marines. He then maneuvered himself into the heart of deadly combat. He told columnist Irv Kupcinet, "I'm frank enough to admit I don't like being a soldier, but our country needs me and that's where I belong." Ross's brother George, though, years later recalled things as being more complicated. Having been badly injured in his last professional fight in 1938, Ross had tried his hand at the restaurant business and as an entertainer and actor, but none of it succeeded or satisfied him. His marriage had crumbled, and he was seized by depression.

His brother related, "He'd gone through money like shit through a tin horn. He was down and he was disgusted . . . when he came down, he came way down . . . he felt that there was no place left to go. He figured, what the hell, I'll go out fighting."

In the marines, Ross became a hero in the Pacific theater, rescuing his platoon in the Philippines by catching and throwing back Japanese grenades, dragging his comrades to safety, and reciting the biblical Shema Yisrael prayer in Hebrew. Badly injured, Ross became addicted to the morphine used to treat his pain. He would fight to overcome the addiction, but it would leave him vulnerable to the influence of criminals and lowlifes.

Barney Ross's fame was so great and his life story—of escape from the Maxwell Street ghetto, a triumphant boxing career, and World War II heroism—was so dramatic, it was made into a comic book story in 1943, in *Real Life Comics* #13. The story was written by novelist Patricia Highsmith, with art by Maurice Gutwirth. Jack Ruby does not appear in the story. *Courtesy of Wikimedia Commons*

(Ross's life was thought so compelling that a thinly veiled version of it was used as the basis for the John Garfield–starring movie *Body and Soul*. The borrowing was so apparent that the boxer sued the movie studio and, as he so often did in the ring, triumphed.)

Though they saw each other infrequently in their later years, Ross would play a significant part in the drama that the life of Jack Ruby would become.

In April 1945 President Roosevelt died, and—like so many others—Jack Ruby wept. Harry Truman became president. On May 8, 1945, Germany surrendered, ending the war in Europe. With atomic bomb detonations at Hiroshima and Nagasaki that August, the world entered the atomic age. Japan surrendered on September 2, 1945.

His military record free of any serious misbehavior, despite anecdotes relating to violence and gambling, Ruby was discharged from the US Army Air Forces in February 1946, having received the Good Conduct Medal and the rank of private first class.

Upon his discharge, he returned to Chicago, where he joined his three brothers, who had received earlier discharges, in the Earl Products Company (bankrolled by Earl), once again manufacturing and selling novelty items. Jack was in charge of sales. But the business wasn't successful, which led to quarrels between the brothers.

Hyman left to go into business for himself. And in 1947 Earl and Sam bought out Jack's share for $14,000. Splitting off from them, Jack attempted to set himself up as a bookmaker, taking bets on sporting events. This business, too, did not succeed. Jack claimed that he was run out of town by rivals, not unlike the way he claimed he was forced to leave town when his union job imploded. In any case, he did indeed leave Chicago again.

Here, as in so many aspects of Jack Ruby's life, accounts diverge as to the origins and reasons behind his actions as well as those of his relatives and associates. Eva Grant, Jack's sister, had moved to Dallas, where, she reported, she had at first represented her brothers' manufacturing business. Once there, because of experience she'd had managing a nightclub on the West Coast, she was bankrolled by them in managing a new nightspot called the Singapore Supper Club. But, she testified, Jack was "mad that I got involved in that with [losing] so much money and then all this work," and he came to take it over from her. So one version of Jack's move to Dallas is that it was a combination of arguing with his brothers and being sent by them to rescue their sister, who was in over her head in this club that was in Dallas's "tenderloin district," an unsavory part of town.

However, former Dallas sheriff Steve Guthrie reported to the FBI during its investigation of the assassination that "shortly after his [Guthrie's] election as sheriff in July 1946, Paul Roland Jones, representing other Chicago criminals, offered him a substantial amount of money to permit them to move in and manage illegal activities in Dallas. Although he never met Ruby, Guthrie asserted that these criminals frequently mentioned that Jack Ruby would operate a 'fabulous' restaurant as a front for gambling activities." So, in this version of the story, Ruby was part of the Chicago mob's incursion into Dallas, a city seen as lawless but one where criminal activities were not yet centralized.

According to the Warren Commission report, "before she opened the Singapore in 1947, Eva Grant engaged in the sale of metal products" (possibly manufactured by Hyman). The report continues, "In that year she met Paul Roland Jones, who allegedly was seeking customers for iron pipe and whom she referred to Hyman Rubenstein. Jones had, at about that time, been convicted of attempting to bribe" Guthrie, and "on October 24, 1947, [Jones] was arrested for violating Federal narcotics statutes."

According to Seth Kantor, Jones appealed the bribery conviction. During that period, he had dealings with Eva, who was "hooked up with a con-artist named Dr. Waldon Duncan." Eva and Duncan, a chiropractor, were romantically involved and were preparing to open the Singapore Supper Club together.

Jones, according to Kantor, had become involved in narcotics smuggling in 1945. That year, he met with Jack and Hyman in Chicago. Hyman and Eva were involved with the shipping of pipe samples in the mail. This led to Jack and Hyman being questioned regarding narcotics smuggling. "For all I know they were shipping narcotics in iron pipe but I didn't know anything about it," Ruby told the Secret Service.

Also, Kantor reports, "In the week before he was arrested on the narcotics deal, Jones made arrangements with Hyman Rubenstein to ship seven hundred gallons of four-year-old whiskey to a bootlegger in Oklahoma, which still was a dry state. The shipment was to be made in cases indicating there were salt and pepper shakers inside."

"Meanwhile," Kantor continues, "Waldon Duncan and Eva Grant were arrested in Dallas on a . . . swindle charge. Jack Ruby bailed her out and got the charge against her dropped." (How he got the charges dropped is unclear.) That ended her affair with Duncan, and "Ruby remained to help his sister run the Singapore. But they couldn't get along." Ruby gave Eva $300, and she returned to California. He changed the name of the club to the Silver Spur, giving the place a country-western music theme. As for Jones, he and "his sinister associates hung out at the Silver Spur until Jones went away on the narcotics rap to Leavenworth and on the bribery conviction to the state penitentiary . . . in a pair of back-to-back sentences."

Of course, these multiple narratives are not necessarily mutually exclusive. Some combination of Eva's and Jack's personal and professional situations could have made them likely and willing candidates to be part of a move by organized crime into new territory. That they were pawns in that game, willing or not, is the theory of more than one historian, including Michael Benson, author of numerous books on the history of organized crime, and Kantor, who believes that Ruby was heavily mobbed up. Broadcast journalist Steve North, who knew Eva and other Ruby family members, also believes that there was family involvement with organized crime. In a 1976 Geraldo Rivera interview with Eva, produced by North, she vigorously denied any involvement by her family in criminal activities. Nonetheless, a viewing of the video of the interview, which provides her voice tone and body language, does leave a viewer feeling that perhaps Eva did protest too much.

On the other hand, nephew Fred Ruby—Sam's son—for one, isn't convinced his uncle was in the mob. When asked if Jack was mob-connected, Fred sarcastically responded with what he himself referred to as "the smartass answer":

> My uncle was *very* involved with the Mafia. He had to *pay* them to get musicians. He had to *pay* them to get girls. He had to *pay* them to get his drinks, his alcohol and his nonalcoholic drinks. He had

to *pay* them to get the snacks for the club. He had to *pay* them to get all the provisions and meat to cook in the kitchen. So, yeah, he was "involved" with the mob. They were taking a lot of his profit margin away.

In 1947, Earl, Sam, and Jack Rubenstein agreed to change their last name to Ruby, although Hyman kept his original surname. (The sisters already had different last names through marriage.) It would be reasonable to assume that was done to make their last name seem less obviously Jewish. From then on, Jack would be known by his new, chosen name.

Jacob Rubenstein of Chicago was now Jack Ruby of Dallas.

6 | THE OLD FRONTIER

TAKING OVER THE SINGAPORE Supper Club from Eva, Jack had changed the name the to the Silver Spur and transformed the Asian-themed venue into a country music and after-hours club, not a strip club. Besides his sister and other siblings, a mobster named Joe Bonds (born Joseph Lecurto in the Bronx) was involved as a partner with Rubenstein and with Ralph Paul, a former fruit merchant, also from the Bronx, who described himself as Ruby's best friend. Paul was an investor in many of Ruby's ventures.

Seeking advice on the local Dallas entertainment world, Ruby went to see Abe and Barney Weinstein, brothers who were owners of two downtown Dallas strip clubs. They refused to help him. The Weinsteins were part of a subculture of Jewish-owned entertainment venues in and around Dallas. Many were likely mob-connected to some degree or other. The brothers saw Ruby as not worthy of trust and just plain didn't like him. They believed he was an informant for the police and the FBI—which, it turned out, he was. And though Ruby swore he'd never open a strip club to compete with them, they didn't believe him.

In a 1994 interview for Dallas's Sixth Floor Museum—a research facility focused on the Kennedy and Oswald assassinations, which is run by the Dallas County Historical Foundation and housed in the former Book Depository—Abe Weinstein (former owner of the Colony Club; he and Barney owned separate clubs near each other) said that he "wasn't surprised" that Ruby killed Oswald. "He'd do anything." Weinstein recalled Ruby as "a kind of Jekyll and Hyde." Clearly not an admirer, Weinstein noted that Ruby was "a real jerk." Indeed, in coming to Dallas, Jack Ruby had entered a world that he seemed to not yet

Abe Weinstein, seen here in his office at the Colony Club in Dallas, was one of Jack Ruby's main competitors in the city's strip club world. *Abe Weinstein in his office, 1940s, courtesy of the Dallas Jewish Historical Society*

really understand. He tried to appeal to the Weinsteins as a fellow Jew, but that didn't carry any weight with them.

"My club [the Colony Club] was a nightclub," Weinstein, who died in 2000, recalled in another interview. "His was just a joint. I had big names; he had nobody. When he came from Chicago to Dallas in '47, he came up to my club right away. He was told there's a Jew runs a club, that's how I met him."

According to Weinstein's son, Larry, Ruby threatened his father with a gun the day JFK was assassinated because Abe had kept the Colony Club open that night, and Ruby, who had closed the Carousel out of respect—and not wanting to be seen as doing anything inappropriate—was offended that he did so. As Rachel Stone wrote in the *Oak Cliff Advocate* in 2021 after speaking with Larry, "A 7-foot bouncer named Big Tex then threw Ruby out, and Weinstein says his dad later regretted opening that night, but he'd thought acting normal was the right thing to do at the time."

Abe's brother Barney, who owned the nearby Theater Lounge, also a strip club, seemed to feel at least somewhat more positive about Ruby. "He had a wonderful heart," Barney told Gary Wills and Ovid Demaris. "When he hardly knew me, he read about my mother's funeral in the newspaper and came to it." But the brothers agreed that Jack, with seeming good intentions, was as capable of escalating a situation as defusing it. Barney recalled that "once, he dropped by when my houseman had not come in. He said, 'Don't worry, I'll stay and take care of any trouble.' I told him, 'I don't *want* you to, Jack.' You know, he doesn't stop trouble, he starts it. But he stayed anyway."

As Ted Schwarz and Mardi Rustam explain in their book *Candy Barr: The Small-Town Texas Runaway Who Became a Darling of the Mob and the Queen of Las Vegas Burlesque*, Barney's Theater Lounge "was not a burlesque house. There were no comics, no singers, no athletic dancers popular on the vaudeville circuit, and no satirical plays. A girl got on stage, and . . . if she could parade around without falling as she dropped her clothes, she would be called a dancer." Abe owned "the upscale Colony Club . . . catering to the city's elite. The brothers had two different personalities. . . . Abe was the natural leader and promoter. Barney was the follower."

One of Barney's headliners was Juanita Dale Slusher, who worked under the name of Candy Barr, a name supposedly bestowed on her by Barney because of her love of, well, candy bars. Barr had already achieved notoriety as the star—unwilling, to the point of being drugged at fifteen years old—of what has come to be thought of as the first porn movie, 1951's *Smart Alec*. She was considered one of the top attractions on the strip club circuit. Her trademark look was a sort of sleazy cowgirl image, complete with cowboy hat (which she would hang on one breast) and six-shooters. After some unpleasant conflict with other dancers at Barney's, Barr "graduated" to Abe's Colony Club, where she was much happier and treated more like a star than a commodity. "I loved it at Abe's," she said.

Still, as Schwarz and Rustam were told by Abe, he always "made girls available [to dance] for private work, taking the attitude that what the girls did away from the club was their own business. 'Being in the business I was in, and being who I was, I never did anything crooked,' said Weinstein. . . . 'I was propositioned by everything—[by the] Mafia, by the prostitution, by the gambling. No, I treated my business like it was a shoe business. Consequently,

I made good friends in the district attorney's office, and the sheriff, and the police.'"

Though Barr escaped conviction when she shot—but did not kill—her abusive second husband, Troy B. Phillips, she would not be so lucky when she was arrested for possession of marijuana in October 1957. Barr claimed that she had actually taken the fall for prominent Dallas figure George Owen, best known as a star athlete for Southern Methodist University, later as an executive for the Dallas Cowboys, and for involvement in a scandal involving fees paid to student athletes. Her case went through numerous appeals, during which her fame and success in the stripping world only grew, and she became involved in a high-profile affair with mobster Mickey Cohen, who did what he could to help her beat the rap. Cohen helped her disguise her identity and move (with her four-year-old daughter) to Mexico. Growing bored there, Barr returned to the United States, where she was imprisoned. Her lawyers, including San Francisco–based legal star Melvin Belli, appealed her conviction to the US Supreme Court. The court denied her appeal.

Mobster Mickey Cohen (seen here in a 1961 mug shot) and Jack Ruby had at least two friends in common: Candy Barr (who was romantically involved with Cohen) and Melvin Belli (who represented Cohen in a murder case). *US Department of Justice, courtesy of Wikimedia Commons*

Barr began a fifteen-year sentence on December 4, 1959, at the Goree State Farm for Women near Huntsville, Texas. While there, she testified against Cohen (who seemed to not hold a grudge about it) in a tax evasion case and was paroled in April 1963. Her parole stipulations prohibited her from returning to Dallas, and she went to live in her hometown of Edna, Texas.

Well before that, in 1952, Barr/Slusher was headlining at Abe's Colony Club. After the club closed for the night, as often as not, she would unwind at the Silver Spur, as she had even before it was the Silver Spur. According to Schwarz and Rustam, "Eva Ruby's nightspot [the Singapore Supper Club] was an oasis of safety for a girl like Juanita. The older woman had strict policies about behavior that customers followed. . . . Juanita . . . found an end to loneliness through . . . going dancing at Eva's place, where Jack Ruby had come to work. . . . Jack Ruby was so taken with Juanita . . . that he began acting like her big brother. Let one of the men get out of line and Jack would have a quiet word with him or if need be . . . take him to an isolated place and beat him senseless."

Despite—or perhaps because of—their friendship, she was never a professional dancer at any of Ruby's clubs. Nonetheless, the relationship was less innocent than it might have seemed. According to Schwarz and Rustam, "always eager to help the local power figures, [Ruby] had provided her services for some of the [Dallas] stag parties." Ruby would "call the people for whom she did work, helping make the arrangements without Juanita's knowledge or approval." Still, the relationship with Jack Ruby would continue to be important to Barr.

Ruby would be arrested numerous times over the years in Dallas, mostly for relatively minor infractions involving violations of regulations relating to when and how alcohol could be served at his clubs and once for hosting a stripper's performance that was considered lewd. But there were a couple of weapons violations. And at least one arrest involved violence on Jack's part. According to the Warren Commission, Ruby's significant arrests were:

- "July 26, 1953, Ruby was suspected of carrying a concealed weapon; however, no charges were filed and Ruby was released on the same day."
- "May 1, 1954, Ruby was arrested for allegedly carrying a concealed weapon and violating a peace bond; again no charges were filed and Ruby was released on the same day."
- "February 12, 1963, Ruby was arrested on a charge of simple assault; he was found not guilty February 27, 1963."

Ruby also piled up, between 1950 and 1963, some twenty driving-related tickets and was twice put on six months' probation for his reckless road habits. In addition, he was regularly suspended by the Texas Liquor Control Board. For instance:

- "In 1953 Ruby received a 5-day suspension because of an obscene show, and, in 1954, a 10-day suspension for allowing a drunkard on his premises." Although it may seem strange that a club serving alcohol could get such a punishment, in Texas in that era, drinking was fine, but being obviously drunk was not.
- "On February 18, 1954, he was suspended for 5 days because of an obscene striptease act at the Silver Spur and for the consumption of alcoholic beverages during prohibited hours."

Despite the numerous arrests and suspensions, the only time Ruby had actually served prison time was in the 1930s, when he was sentenced to a month in prison for copyright violations on counterfeit sheet music he was selling.

The question raised by all these arrests and nonconvictions is, was he truly innocent in all the dropped cases—or were his mob connections so strong that the police could be bought off? Or was his relatively clean record a reward for Jack's habit of cozying up to police in general, comping them to his clubs, bringing them sandwiches at the police station, raising funds for the families of injured or killed police officers? If so, why would he have been arrested so many times—or at all—in the first place? This is yet another mystery of Jack Ruby's life. It does seem, according to historians including Schwarz and Rustam, that Dallas's police at the time were involved in what could be called performative policing, such as arresting Jack Ruby or, early in her career, arresting Candy

Barr while allowing some serious crimes—especially if committed by the city's elites—to go unnoticed.

In 1949, with Eva returned to the West Coast, Jack now ran the Silver Spur on his own. In addition to the club, right next door to it, was the Ervay Theater, a movie house that Jack also ran for a time, both venues in Dallas's tenderloin district. Unsurprisingly, the Silver Spur was known as much for its fights as for its music. At least one customer recalls Jack literally grabbing a gun out of the hands of a patron on the verge of explosive violence, then personally roughing the guy up.

Also in 1949, Ruby met divorced executive secretary Alice Nichols at, according to her, a Dallas bus stop. They proceeded to date, seeing each other once or twice a week for the next ten years. It's unclear what "dating" consisted of and whether their relationship was sexual. Nichols told investigators that she had dated other men during that period and that Jack had dated other women. She told the Warren Commission's Burt Griffin that he always treated her politely.

Nichols recalled that Jack claimed he could not marry her because he had promised his mother he would never marry a gentile woman. He once brought Nichols to meet with Dallas reform rabbi Gerald Klein of the city's Temple Emanu-El, a synagogue less religiously stringent than Shearith Israel, where Ruby was a member, and whose Conservative Movement rabbi, Hillel Silverman, would become significant in Jack's life. They were there to discuss the possibility of Nichols converting to Judaism so they could marry, but nothing ever came of it.

Klein recalled, in an interview recorded on March 10, 2005, for the Sixth Floor Museum, that when Nichols and Ruby came to discuss her converting he met with them briefly, gave them a book about the conversion process, and advised them to read it and get back to him, which they never did. Nichols later related that she had no interest in converting to Judaism. Besides that, she reported that she was troubled by what seemed to her to be Jack's habitual gambling.

Nichols told Griffin that Jack was devoted to his mother and explained how much her death had hurt him. She met Joseph Rubenstein and remarked that

Jack was "devoted" to him, as well. Beyond that, she recalled that Ruby had told her the only woman he had ever really been in love with was someone he knew in San Francisco, a woman he referred to as "Virginia Fitzgerald." Some speculate that this was how he chose to refer to Virginia Belasco, but this has never been confirmed.

Nichols said their 1959 breakup was "a gradual thing. We had no quarrel. . . . He quit calling me. We just quit going together." They would not speak again until the day of the Kennedy assassination, when, despite their estrangement, he chose to turn to her. He called her twice, and they discussed how upset he was about the killing of the president. Eva Grant testified that Nichols was "a very fine person, but I could never get to talk to her. . . . I never sort of pushed conversation." Eva recalled that Jack had given Nichols an engagement ring.

How this comports with reports from Jack's doctor of his regular treatment for a variety of sexually transmitted diseases and with reports from employees that he would engage in sex with women he'd pick up at bus stations and wannabe strippers (who he'd automatically send packing for giving in to him), in addition to reports of his being gay, is hard, if not impossible, to determine. As with so much else of his life, reports and rumors and gossip make his sexuality difficult to untangle. One former employee recalls Ruby calling her to engage in what's now called phone sex. Numerous people recall Jack bragging of his many female sexual partners.

A woman friend of a Carousel employee told the Warren Commission that Ruby had asked her out on dates regularly, although she never went out with him. She related that he called her "several times each week" and would recite obscene poetry over the telephone, describing "in minute detail how he would have sexual intercourse with her." She felt that he gained sexual gratification from just talking. Paradoxically, she felt that his "almost continuous occupation with sex and his continuous attempts to impress all of the girls with how great a man he was" indicated he was using this as an act to disguise the fact that he was a homosexual.

Her friend the Carousel employee, who worked for Ruby as a waitress and a stripper, said that he also called her on the telephone and recited obscene poetry. She thought that, in general, his aggressive behavior was employed "merely to cover up his homosexual tendencies."

A Carousel bartender claimed that, at a party, Ruby, who rarely drank, "seemed to have been drinking before he arrived with some of his strippers, and himself stripped down to his underwear and declared, 'Come on, man or woman. I'll take anyone on.'" And a stripper who had known Ruby for fifteen years until leaving his employ over a salary dispute claimed that she had been on the scene when a drunk Ruby "took off all his clothes and rolled naked on the floor." Another former employee referred to him as bisexual, a term which would certainly reconcile the various reports of his sexuality.

(It should be remembered that these Warren Commission and FBI testimonies, some in-depth, some very brief, were fueled by the personal agendas of those being questioned and of those doing the questioning. How much credibility any of the interviews holds is left to the reader to determine. Some seem designed to cast Ruby—and the interview subjects themselves—in as positive a light as possible, while others seem slanted toward the negative.)

It was at Ruby's Silver Spur that country music legend Hank Williams Sr. would perform—or, on occasion, become too inebriated to play—and hide out from Jack, despite the fact that Ruby was one of the few promoters who would still hire the singer, who grew less and less dependable as his drinking and his various medical conditions worsened. Kinky Friedman noted that Ruby was "one of Hank Williams' last friends on Earth." Of course, when Ruby was able to drag Williams into the club (after Williams would do his best to avoid the guy) and Hank would black out backstage, Jack reportedly charged irritated patrons to take photos of their unconscious hero.

Whether Ruby really had any interest in country music is unknown, but he also purchased, with Martin Gimpel, the Bob Wills Ranch House— formerly owned by that country music star—borrowing $3,700 from Ralph Paul. It was at the Silver Spur and the Ranch House that Ruby would dress up in an all-white cowboy outfit and act as MC, calling himself "the Chicago Cowboy."

One of the most striking of the tales of Ruby's short temper and propensity for violence comes from Willis "Dub" Dickerson, a guitarist who

Legendary country music singer-songwriter Hank Williams Sr., seen here in the late 1940s, played in Ruby's country-western clubs in the early '50s. *MGM Records, courtesy of Wikimedia Commons*

played in one of his clubs, probably the Silver Spur. Dickerson recalled for the FBI that, sometime in 1951, he dropped into the club after hours to hang out with Ruby's musicians. As he sat at a table with his friends, Dickerson's chair was in the aisle. Annoyed, Ruby kicked the musician's chair and told him to move. Dickerson told Ruby to "go to hell." And left—only to be followed by a now-enraged Ruby. Dickerson repeated that Ruby could "go to hell." This angered Ruby even more, and he punched Dickerson in the face, knocking him down.

Ruby then slammed Dickerson against a wall, kneeing him in the groin. During this beating, Ruby's left index finger got into Dickerson's mouth and the guitarist bit down on it hard, severing part of it.

Ruby would later need to have the top half of the finger amputated. No charges were filed by either party, and Dickerson would testify that the few times he saw Ruby after that, everything was fine between them.

Both the Silver Spur and the Bob Wills Ranch House failed. Ruby transferred the Silver Spur to his business partners Martin Gimpel and Willie Epstein, both probably mob-related figures, in 1952. In this period, Ruby suffered what he described to the Warren Commission as a "mental breakdown." He recalled that he "hibernated" in Dallas's Cotton Bowl Hotel for several months. Earl Ruby recalls Jack being severely depressed during this period, ominously reflecting to Earl, "Well, it looks like it is the end for me."

7 | THE PERSONAL AND THE POLITICAL

DEPRESSED AND DEFEATED, Ruby finally left Dallas and returned to Chicago.

His family, especially his youngest brother, Earl, tried to help Jack out of his situation. As Earl told Burt Griffin of the Warren Commission, "I would have said he was disgusted, not knowing that actually he was depressed until I really learned what the word 'depressed' means."

Earl would learn the meaning of the word when, after some business reverses in the mid-1950s, he himself became "depressed . . . and was thinking of doing away with myself." He spent several weeks in what he called the "psychopathic ward" of a veterans hospital, and soon recovered.

Earl recalled of Jack's state of mind when the latter returned to Chicago that it wasn't "hostility or belligerence" toward his financial situation that Jack exhibited, but more an attitude of "submission. He wouldn't go any places. . . . He didn't want to wash or clean himself up and I had to more or less force him to get in the shower and things of that sort. . . . He didn't even have much to say. He tried to keep to himself. . . . In other words, he would go in another room or sit in a chair and just sit there . . . just thinking to himself about whatever was going through his mind. He was listless."

Earl continued: "[Jack] was so depressed that I took him to try to cheer him up. I had to go to New York for a business trip, a show that was taking place there, and I took him for a ride, we were driving . . . and I thought it would pep him up a little bit, you know, to go on a trip. But it didn't help much. . . . I just thought he was disgusted with things, little realizing that he was in a state of depression. . . . That is why I took him on the trip. I tried to encourage him. I told him, 'Maybe we can find something for you to get into . . . some business we can get you started in or something.'"

Somehow, though, being back in Chicago seems to have eventually lifted Jack from his depression. It's yet another of the mysteries of Jack Ruby's life. Perhaps just being free of the crushing responsibilities of running his clubs had been enough to change his mental state.

Or perhaps his funk was lifted when, after six weeks in Chicago, Ruby was called back to Dallas. Gimpel and Epstein wanted to "sell" the Silver Spur back to him. This presents another tangle of mysteries in the Jack Ruby saga. Why was the club taken from him? Why was it returned? (The Bob Wills Ranch House would end up sold by Ruby during this period and seemingly never returned to his control. It eventually become known as the Longhorn Ballroom, where acts from Merle Haggard to the Sex Pistols would perform.)

Bankrolled by somebody—his family? Gimpel and Epstein?—Ruby returned to Dallas and the Silver Spur. He also somehow acquired some percentage of the Vegas Club—purchased from Abe Weinstein, of all people—and he ran it in partnership with Joe Bonds. Weinstein's disdain for Jack Ruby apparently didn't extend to his money.

The Vegas was not primarily a strip club, although strippers would occasionally perform there. Possession of the Vegas ping-ponged around until, in September 1953, Ruby, according to the ownership choreography established by the Warren Commission,

> informed Irving Alkana, who had retained a prior ownership interest, that he was unable to meet his obligations with respect to the club. Alkana then assumed management of the Vegas until June 19, 1954, when, following numerous disagreements with him, he sold Ruby his interest.
>
> Ruby still owned the Vegas Club at the time of his arrest on November 24, 1963. However, when Eva Grant returned from San Francisco in 1959, she assumed management of the club, receiving a salary but no ownership interest. The Vegas, which occasionally featured striptease acts, employed a dance band and served beer, wine, soft drinks, and some prepared foods.

According to country-western music legend Willie Nelson (who Ruby once declined to hire), the Vegas had a back room where "bosomy women were working two different roulette wheels. Green felt tables were set up for poker and blackjack."

The commission's chronology continued:

> In 1954, Ruby's Vegas associate, Joe Bonds, was convicted of sodomy and sent to a Texas penitentiary to serve an 8-year sentence. [What "sodomy" consisted of in practical terms in 1950s Texas is hard to know.] In 1955, Ruby sold the Silver Spur to Roscoe "Rocky" Robinson; however, Robinson could not obtain a license to operate the club and it was subsequently closed. For a few months during this period, Ruby also operated Hernando's Hideaway, but this venture proved unsuccessful.
>
> Sam Ruby testified that shortly after he sold his interest in Earl Products in mid-1955 and moved to Dallas, he loaned Jack $5,500 to enable him to pay Federal excise taxes on the Vegas. As security for the loan, Sam required Jack to execute a bill of sale of the Vegas. Upon Jack's default in payment, Sam instituted suit, claiming that he owned the Vegas and that Jack had breached his promise to repurchase it. The case was ultimately settled, with Jack retaining his ownership interest in the club.

You really do need a scorecard to keep track of the various clubs and the group of people among whom the Ruby-associated venues' ownerships seemed to bounce back and forth. A cynic might think all these different sales and resales were part of some kind of less-than-legal business scheme.

In any case, as Sam Ruby told Leon Hubert of the Warren Commission:

> SAM RUBY: We sued that I was the legal owner of the business and that he [Jack] told me he would . . . purchase the club from me. He wasn't satisfied with me as a partner and he said he was going to buy me out, but he failed to meet his financial promises and so . . . I hired an attorney. . . .
>
> HUBERT: And then he filed suit on your behalf?
>
> SAM RUBY: Yes.

HUBERT: And he obtained a judgment?

SAM RUBY: Right.

HUBERT: Was that a contested suit or did it go by default?

SAM RUBY: It was contested—he had his attorney there. . . .

HUBERT: He actually went to trial?

SAM RUBY: Yes.

HUBERT: And you won the case?

SAM RUBY: Yes, sir.

HUBERT: And the result of the judgment was that you were declared to be the owner of the Vegas; is that it?

SAM RUBY: Well, [Jack] agreed to pay me the amount of money he owed me, which at that time amounted to about $4,500. . . .

HUBERT: Has the $4,500 been paid off?

SAM RUBY: No, sir.

MR. HUBERT: How much is yet due upon it?

SAM RUBY: Oh, about $1,300 or so.

The conflicts between the Rubenstein/Ruby brothers, apparently, resulted in at least one lawsuit, one more expression of the volatility of the family's relationships.

The Silver Spur seems to have attracted at least some top talent in the country and western music world. Besides Hank Williams, Tennessee Ernie Ford (a radio and TV singing star, best known for his hit song "Sixteen Tons") also played the club. Ruby's relationships with talents like Williams and Ford—among other prominent performers he interacted with over the years—makes one ponder, what if Ruby's clubs had been more than marginally successful?

In 1952, another pivotal what-if in Ruby's life occurred when he became the manager of a twelve-year-old African American child named Ben Estes Nelson. Nelson, according to a contract Ruby signed with his guardian, Columbus L. Nelson, "has become well known in the Dallas Area under the name of 'Little Daddy,' as a singer and performer, and probably can earn large sums of money if properly managed and promoted."

Country music star Tennessee Ernie Ford (seen here in 1957), best known for his 1955 hit "Sixteen Tons," performed at one of Ruby's country-western venues, possibly the Silver Spur. *NBC, courtesy of Wikimedia Commons*

Little Daddy performed at the Silver Spur, the Vegas Club, and the Bob Wills Ranch House. In 1953 or 1954, Ruby took Nelson and his parents to New York and Chicago in hopes of finding TV work for the kid. On one of those trips, however, a woman showed up who claimed that *she* was Ben Estes's real mother, not the woman who Ruby had brought on the trip with them. At that point, Ruby gave up on representing Ben Estes Nelson.

A photo of Ruby with Little Daddy, taken when things were still hopeful, before the appearance of mother #2, certainly gives a viewer the feeling that he had genuine affection for the kid. (Over the years, Ruby seems to have also been involved with other up-and-coming, non-stripper entertainers, none of whose careers panned out as he'd hoped.) The photo, of Ruby and Nelson enthusiastically dancing their hearts out (or at least posing as if they were), is especially memorable. So is another photo of Ruby holding Ben Estes in an adorable, avuncular manner, the child planting a kiss on Jack's ear. How would history have been affected had Ruby been able to really make something out of managing Little Daddy Nelson?

Ruby and twelve-year-old singer and dancer Ben
Estes "Little Daddy" Nelson in around 1952. *Everett
Collection Inc. / Alamy Stock Photo*

Ruby's activities were, of course, not always so endearing.

For instance, on June 11, 1964, a woman named Eileen Curry told the FBI
that, in late 1955 or early 1956, she had moved to Dallas with a man named
James Breen and that "Curry planned to have two girls employed as prostitutes
at the Statler Hilton Hotel." In other words, to extrapolate on the "Just the
facts, ma'am" formal language favored by investigators, Curry would run a
small-scale brothel. She claimed her boyfriend, Breen, told her of attending a
meeting where Ruby was present. There, Jack discussed drug trafficking with
him, and Breen "was enthused over what he considered an extremely efficient
operation in connection with narcotics traffic."

Curry went on to say that she threatened to break up with Breen because
she didn't wish to engage in drug dealing, especially not heroin and cocaine.
While Breen was away on a possible drug deal, Ruby, she claimed, took her

to one of his clubs, and she "did not become intimate with Ruby despite his statement that he could send her influential clients if she were 'friendly.'" Curry added that Ruby knew she was employing two prostitutes . . . and, in fact, sent her customers. Curry also reported that Ruby had tried to "interest her in selling pornographic photographs to her customers, indicating that he had [access to] a large quantity of such material." While the rest of Curry's sordid story did not involve Ruby, she was not exactly serving as a character reference.

Nor, for that matter, was Jack Hardee Jr., who was interviewed by the FBI on December 26, 1963, while serving time on federal charges in Mobile, Alabama. Hardee testified that he came to Dallas in 1962 to "set up a numbers game, and he was advised . . . it was necessary to have the clearance of Jack Ruby . . . [who] had 'the fix' with the county authorities." Hardee added that he didn't like Ruby, and so that and other factors led him to give up the numbers idea.

Hardee also didn't like Ruby because he was told Ruby was "running around" with Hardee's girlfriend. Hardee, accompanied by two "friends," warned Ruby to "keep his hands off the girl." Ruby, according to Hardee, then showed him a .357 Magnum revolver he had stuffed into his pants. That ended the confrontation. Hardee also claimed to know that Ruby "hustled the strippers and other girls who worked in his club. Ruby made dates for them, accepting the money for the dates in advance, and kept half, giving the other half to the girls." Hardee opined that Ruby "impressed him as being the type of individual who would kill without much provocation."

Apparently, career criminals, for whatever reasons, were eager to make sure the FBI knew exactly the type of lowlife they thought Jack Ruby was. One can imagine their motives, and certainly it's possible that some of the many such stories were exaggerations or outright lies. Still, given a pattern of testimony in the many interviews, it's hard to not ascribe some degree of truth to the various tales of Jack Ruby as an outright brutal criminal.

For another example of witnesses eager to dish on Jack Ruby, FBI special agent Ralph J. Miles reported that, on August 1, 1953, he "chanced to be" in the office of Vincent Lee, the branch manager of the AGVA in Dallas, when Ruby barged into Lee's office and demanded some "girls" to entertain at the Silver Spur. Miles recalled that "Lee told Ruby that Ruby would have to put up a cash bond to guarantee the girls' salary, whereupon Ruby began to curse Lee, claiming that he was short on money and that Lee did not make his, Ruby's, competitors put up such a cash bond." After more arguing, "Ruby arose and in a threatening tone of voice asked Lee: 'Do you want to know whether or not I'm packing a gun?' and 'What are you trying to do, be a tough guy in Dallas? Well, I'm just as tough as they come,' or words to that effect." Ruby then "stormed out . . . cursing all the while." Lee told Special Agent Miles that "Ruby and [Joe] Bonds always carried concealed pistols" and associated with "hoodlums and safe-crackers."

In 1954, another significant figure in Jack Ruby's life would appear on the scene.

Hillel Silverman, an accomplished young rabbi from a distinguished rabbinical family, came to Dallas to become spiritual leader of Congregation Shearith Israel, the synagogue that Ruby would eventually join. Silverman became active in the congregation's move from South Dallas to prosperous North Dallas, where newly affluent Dallas residents, gentile and Jewish, were moving. (Within a few years, New York Yankees superstar Mickey Mantle would move into an off-season home next door to the synagogue.)

The prejudice in their new neighborhood was such that Silverman had to attend a hearing to assure the community that, should they approve the building of a new synagogue there, the congregation would not conduct animal sacrifices as part of its services. Silverman recalled, "For years, the neighbors had protested the erection of a public building (never using the word 'synagogue') because it would create traffic congestion."

He remembered that the synagogue went to court to be allowed to construct its new home. (The congregation had been in existence for sixty years but was based in South Dallas.) "The lawyer for our neighbors questioned me with derision: 'Do you intend to slaughter chickens and animals in your new kitchen? The blueprints call for a meat and milk kitchen.' I carefully explained . . . the Jewish dietary laws, separating milk and meat."

Silverman and Shearith Israel's lawyer were able to convince the community that the synagogue should be built. As Silverman recounts it, it seems like his sincere testimony and the essential good-heartedness of his neighbors led to the congregation's acceptance. The synagogue still stands on the property that was the subject of the hearing.

Rabbi Hillel Silverman (seen here in a 1975 photo) led Dallas's Congregation Shearith Israel, where Jack Ruby was a member. Silverman would become heavily involved with Ruby's defense when Jack went on trial for Oswald's murder. *Photo by Ralph Samuels Valley Photo, courtesy of American Jewish University (formerly University of Judaism and Brandeis-Bardin Institute)*

Nonetheless, a 2015 visit to the synagogue grounds by this author revealed a reality that, even that recently, is perhaps not as rosy as Silverman had recalled. After a mildly antisemitic comment made by my cab driver as we approached the place, it was clear to me that the synagogue's architecture—both the original from the '50s and subsequent renovations—is designed to hold off anything short of an army attacking it. Windows are tall and narrow, walls are solidly laid red brick. North Dallas may be welcoming and open, but this house of worship doesn't seem to be taking any chances.

Eventually, Jack Leon Ruby would become a member of the synagogue, as would siblings Eva and Sam. Silverman recalled that Ruby "was a member of my congregation. He attended services occasionally, on holidays or to recite Kaddish on a dear one's Yahrzeit [death anniversary]. I really did not [at that point] know him."

And as Silverman told me in 2013, "He [Ruby] was looked upon in Dallas as neither a tough guy nor a Jewish tough guy. He was a guy making a living

from burlesque. He loved dogs. He really loved dogs. He once visited me . . .
with a bunch of puppies on my lawn. He said, 'Take one.' It was his idea. And
they were very nice dogs.

"Actually, when he came with his dogs to my yard, he said, 'These are my
children. And Sheba, the main dog, the mother, is my wife.' Kind of peculiar.
He loved the dogs."

When Silverman and his family took a trip to Israel a year or two later, the
rabbi recalled, "I didn't know what to do with the dog, so I brought the dog
to Jack and said, 'Jack, will you take care of the dog until we come back?' He
said, 'Yes.' But when I picked the dog up, the dog was acting very peculiarly.
It had been with all these burlesque queens, and the dog was shaking."

Silverman also recalled Jack's sister Eva: "She was a sicko. . . . She talked
and talked and talked. She was a little unstable."

It would be a few years from his debut as the temple's spiritual leader until
Silverman would get to know Ruby better. The relationship would prove to be
intense and pivotal for both men.

Ruby's famous words upon being tackled after shooting Oswald—"You all
know me! I'm Jack Ruby!"—were quite true, at least for some portion of the
city's population. Though certainly not the classic Texan, or even the classic
Dallasite, Ruby was a classic "type." Whatever his motivation, he spent much
of his time schmoozing and networking, much of that activity focused on
downtown Dallas and its numerous businesses and restaurants, many Jewish
owned and operated, which catered to a mix then found in older American
downtowns: entertainers, lawyers, politicians, businessmen, students, restauran-
teurs, barkeepers, bail bondsmen, reporters, disc jockeys—as well as strippers,
con artists, hustlers, criminals, and people generally tagged as "degenerates"
or "characters." It was almost a city within a city.

As Schwarz and Rustam observe,

> The top people in Dallas were the ones who worked together in creat-
> ing, benefitting from, and using the special district where they tried to
> keep the clubs. There were officials in the sheriff's office, the police,
> the courts, and politics, all carefully coordinating what took place.

They also protected everyone from the media, for this was an era when scandals could still be covered up.

Schwarz and Rustam quote Joe Ashmore, a former judge and Dallas insider:

> There was a special district set aside for the clubs no one admitted patronizing. Everything was all downtown. . . . The downtown locations were all controlled by the "boys." If you wanted to play, you went down there to play. There was very strict zoning.

By the "boys," Ashmore meant not just mobsters but also "a group of politicians, high officials in the police and sheriff's office, businessmen, and the like. They had to approve what was taking place or nothing would happen."

Schwarz and Rustam explain further that "the downtown club district . . . was a region with its own rules. . . . The 'good' people of Dallas never went there. Or such was the myth perpetuated by the regulars, the Baptist ministers, and the long-suffering spouses of secret philanderers."

Within this downtown nucleus, Jack Ruby made it his business to be known. Whether this would make him viewed as almost the mayor of downtown or—as lawyer Melvin Belli later characterized him—the "village idiot" is hard to pin down. He spent much of his time gathering information; promoting his clubs; taking the local pulse; dispensing, if not wisdom, opinions; and carving out a reputation for himself that could be best described as mixed. He would bring deli sandwiches to the police and to radio and newspaper staffs. Jack was on a one-man charm offensive that never ended. (Not everyone was charmed, however, and not everyone thought his activities were so benevolent. Some thought that his endless comings and goings were in actuality cover for drug dealing and payoff-distributing activities.)

Of course, as insular as Dallas could be, it was also part of the larger world. Political and business interests from all sides of the spectrum were vocally and visibly part of Dallas's reality. Its influential Dallas Citizens Council, while not free from the prejudices of the American South of the 1950s and early 1960s, also realized that demonstrations and riots would not serve the city's larger goals of economic expansion. The city instituted its own program of desegregation, although tales still abounded of demeaning treatment of Black people at the hands of police. But the city had avoided the violent, fiery disruptions that had occurred in other American cities.

In 1958 Joseph Rubenstein passed away at age eighty-seven. Jack Ruby increased his attendance at Silverman's Shearith Israel synagogue, regularly going to services to say mourner's prayers. And around this period, Mantle of the Yankees did indeed move in next door to the house of worship. Mantle would himself come to own an interest in a Dallas nightclub and would be among the pallbearers at gangster and club owner Benny Bickers's 1967 funeral.

And at the end of 1958, Ruby became entangled in the brewing revolution in Cuba led by Fidel Castro and Che Guevara. But was it as player or pawn—or both?

8 | CONVERGING FORCES

ON JANUARY 1, 1959, Fidel Castro's forces overthrew Fulgencio Batista in Cuba. As part of his revolution, Castro disrupted the mob's gambling interests at Cuba's hotels, marking him as their enemy.

Still, in the early days of the revolution, it wasn't clear where Castro's sympathies lay. Batista was indeed a corrupt dictator, and Castro presented himself as a nonpartisan liberator, not yet as a full-blown Communist and ally of the Soviet Union. And while Castro had overthrown the government, there was an ongoing civil war as Batista's forces continued in their efforts to retake control. It was a bull market for anyone who could supply either side with weapons. And, depending on what source you listen to, Jack Ruby was likely involved with channeling weapons and vehicles to either or both.

In August of that year, Ruby traveled to Cuba to, according to him, go on vacation and visit his friend Lewis McWillie, an executive at the Tropicana Hotel there. (McWillie was described by Seth Kantor as someone who "had run crime syndicate gambling operations in Texas and was identified in Dallas police criminal intelligence section records as a murderer.") Ruby reported being bored there, perhaps expecting that the hotel and casino scene would have been unchanged from before the revolution.

But some, including Kantor, see a sinister motive behind Ruby's Caribbean excursion. At the very least, he seemingly was there to convey information between imprisoned mob boss Santo Trafficante and his connections in the United States. Castro wanted to deport Trafficante but, facing indictments in the United States, Trafficante found it in his interest to remain in the "relative luxury" of his Cuban prison. In yet more head-spinning, contradictory but reasonable suppositions, it's possible Trafficante was acting as a double agent, working for both Castro *and* for his enemies, betraying each to the other, with an unclear endgame, except, perhaps, just a desire to make money off both sides.

What Trafficante's strategy was—and what Ruby's role in his plots and schemes might have been—are, once again, ambiguous. It does seem safe to say that Ruby's trip to Cuba (and other possible "ghost trips" there) was not for a vacation. (Ruby later admitted to his legal team and others that he'd purchased four guns and mailed them to McWillie, which even at its most benign seems rather sinister. Even Ruby realized that would look bad if brought out at his murder trial, and he worriedly confided it to his legal team, as well as to visitors in jail, as a possible problem, one he endlessly obsessed over.)

Mobster Santo Trafficante in a Havana nightclub around 1955. Ruby may have brought money and/or information to Trafficante when the latter was imprisoned in Cuba after the 1959 revolution. *Courtesy of Wikimedia Commons*

Jack Ruby had survived more than a decade in the nightclub business in Dallas. The word that comes to mind to describe him is *competent*. He wasn't brilliant. He wasn't terrible. But he seemed steady enough to be entrusted to run multiple venues simultaneously. The question was, on whose behalf was he competent? Was he working for himself, his brothers, and various investors—or was he somehow running mob fronts? If the latter, why was he living such a hand-to-mouth existence?

In any case, in late 1959 Ruby went into business with Joe Slatin to create the Sovereign Club at 1312½ Commerce Street in downtown Dallas, very close to the Weinsteins' clubs, especially Abe's Colony Club, which was literally next door. (Barney's Theater Lounge was around the corner.) The Sovereign was on a second floor, over a takeout barbecue restaurant. Significantly, it was very close to the fashionable Adolphus and Baker Hotels, from which it hoped to draw clientele. The club, which didn't yet feature strippers, was private, permitted to sell hard liquor to "members," which public nightclubs weren't allowed to do. (The latter could only sell beer, wine, and setups for harder drinks.) Ruby invested $6,000 in the club, money he borrowed from his brother Earl, and now he had the Sovereign as well as the Vegas and the Silver Spur. Yet none of them seemed to do well enough to provide him an adequate income.

In the summer of 1960 John F. Kennedy won the Democratic presidential nomination, making his famous New Frontier speech at the party convention. He named Texas senator Lyndon Johnson as his running mate, figuring Johnson would appeal to a demographic—old school southern Democrats—that he could not.

In Dallas, Ruby and Slatin's Sovereign Club was not successful, although the Vegas club—managed by Eva, who had returned to Dallas in 1958—seems to have consistently been in business, though not doing well enough to balance out the siblings' losses. The Vegas didn't run without conflict between brother and sister. Jack's roommate, George Senator, testified to Leon Hubert Jr. of the Warren Commission that Jack and Eva fought "like cats and dogs. . . . As well as Jack could holler, let me assure you, she can holler, too." Senator added that Sam Ruby once worked at the Vegas with Eva, and they, too, quarreled. Hyman Rubenstein told Burt Griffin of the Warren Commission that one time Jack "popped Eva on the nose. . . . Something broke in him and he hit her . . . which isn't like our family." And Eva, herself, said that she and Jack had a relationship "like a disagreeable man and wife." Nonetheless, the Vegas, under Eva's management, did manage to survive.

The Sovereign Club was not so lucky, and before long, Slatin left the partnership. Ruby took Ralph Paul in as a partner again. Ruby still owed Paul money from the Bob Wills Ranch House partnership, but Paul loaned him more, Ruby now owing him $3,400. By September, when that proved to be insufficient, Paul agreed to loan Ruby more money on the condition that the Sovereign become a public nightclub and start featuring strippers. Ruby agreed, and they changed the Sovereign's name to the Carousel.

Jack Ruby was now doing exactly what he had promised Abe and Barney Weinstein he would not do: competing directly with their burlesque businesses. ("Strippers" and "burlesque queens" were terms that were used interchangeably in Ruby's era. Those performers, though daring for the time, were relatively tame by modern standards. Still, some could definitely generate heat.)

Once in the strip club business, Ruby seemed to fall easily into the role of volatile father figure to the equally volatile dancers, performers, and staffers who worked for him. He would travel great distances to entice the most popular dancers on the circuit to work at the Carousel, his obsession with a mercurial star-stripper called Jada being perhaps the most extreme. He did indeed convince her to perform at the club, but his fascination with her ended when she would regularly perform an especially graphic strip routine that could have gotten the place closed down. Jack got more than he had bargained for, although he put up with it for quite a while, hoping the scandalous Jada would bring in customers.

Ruby maintained relationships with a steady core of regular employees. He would regularly fire and rehire certain employees—or they would quit and then return—who formed the core of his staff of dancers, musicians, and comedians. Of course, there were regular lunatic, violent outbursts (on Ruby's and often on the employees' parts), but somehow they would make up and continue working together.

And it seems that Ruby's interpersonal style with customers, too, was consistent throughout his career. He often acted as his own bouncer, and as the Warren Commission report put it,

> On about 15 occasions since 1950, [Ruby] beat with his fists, pistol whipped or blackjacked patrons who became unruly. At other times, he ejected troublesome customers without a beating, in many instances, justifiably. However, many people stated that he employed more force than necessary, particularly since he often ended a fracas by throwing his victims down the stairs of the Carousel. . . . In about 1958, Ruby disarmed a man who had drawn a gun on him at the Vegas, beat him almost to death, put the gun back in the man's pocket, and threw him down the stairs. . . . In [another] fight at the Vegas . . . Ruby severely beat a heavyweight boxer who had threatened him.

The commission also noted,

> Buddy Turman, a prizefighter and Ruby's friend, stated that Ruby "picked his shots." According to Turman, a bouncer at the Vegas for about a year, Ruby's victim was frequently drunk, female, or otherwise incapable of successfully resisting Ruby's attack. The evidence indicates that . . . Ruby was often malicious.

It went on to say that he

> frequently felt contrite, however, when his anger had passed or when his victim was an old acquaintance, and he would seek to make amends for his violent temper.

In fact, after such an outburst, he would only vaguely—if at all—recall his behavior. (These blackouts would be important at his trial.) He would often offer money and food to his victims to make up for what he'd done and to keep them from complaining to the police.

As an outgrowth of his tempestuous relationships with Carousel employees, Ruby also seemed to run a crash pad of sorts at the club and at whatever apartment he lived in. Strippers, staffers, and random entertainers always had a place to stay, at least for a while. Ruby's car seemed to double as his own prime office and second home. It was filthy and worn, his dogs having wrecked its interior, even seeming to crap at will in it.

Ruby ordered his dancers and other female employees to entice patrons to drink overpriced champagne with them. Any hooking was done off premises. Jack would proposition new dancers. If they agreed to have sex with him, he fired them. Nonetheless, Ruby regularly set certain customers up with dancers who moonlighted. (What they did with those customers was up to them, but it seems that Ruby would be in for a percentage of their take.)

Ruby would often take the microphone and kibitz with the audience at the Carousel. He would become especially touchy if someone, audience member or performer, said anything remotely antisemitic, and would not allow his comedians to tell ethnic jokes of any kind. Wary of strict obscenity laws, Ruby would police the language performers used at his venues.

Comedian Gabe Kaplan, famous for his 1970s sitcom *Welcome Back, Kotter,* recalled, on an episode of the late Gilbert Gottfried's podcast (cohosted by Frank Santopadre), an encounter with Ruby early in Kaplan's career.

Having heard that the Carousel might be open to trying out a new comedian, Kaplan went over to meet with Ruby. Ruby told the young man that he didn't have any openings but might be able to find him a tryout spot between strippers that night. And that was exactly what happened—Ruby gave Kaplan a ten-minute audition slot.

Recycling a number of mildly off-color jokes that he'd heard other comics on the strip club circuit tell, Kaplan told a joke that involved Dracula admiring a woman's "tits," but, as a vampire, being more interested in her neck. It was no more or less obscene than other jokes heard on similar stages all over the country. Nonetheless, the previously friendly Ruby angrily called Kaplan into his office.

"Do you think this is a toilet? Do you think I'm running a toilet here?" demanded the agitated club owner. "What makes you think you can say 'tits' in my club?!"

Kaplan explained that it was the type of material he'd heard comics do in other clubs and didn't know there were any rules about it at the Carousel. Ruby calmed down and told Kaplan to make sure to leave his phone number in case he wanted to have Kaplan fill in for his regular comedian for a couple of weeks sometime.

Later that week, Kaplan was informed that Ruby wanted to see him. They met up at a poker game being held by a mutual acquaintance. Ruby was holding a paper bag, out of which he took . . . a Dracula mask. Ruby felt that he'd been too rough on Kaplan and had brought the mask as a peace offering.

"You can wear the mask next time you do the Dracula routine," he informed Kaplan. "Try it now."

Kaplan put it on, but it was hard to breathe while wearing it, so he did a short Dracula impression and then took it off. Ruby seemed pleased and Kaplan figured that perhaps Ruby really would call him about that possible gig.

The call never came. And months later, when Ruby had killed Lee Harvey Oswald on nationwide television, Kaplan told people, "I know that guy." No one believed him.

Another memory of Ruby's odd behavior comes from musician Jaime "Robbie" Robertson of the Band fame, who recalled an early gig at Fort Worth's Skyline Lounge (also, it seems, called the Skyliner Lounge or sometimes the Sky Lounge), on Jacksboro Highway, also known as "Thunder Road," a famous—and famously dangerous—nightlife area, a "three and one half mile strip that sported eighteen restaurants, six liquor stores, seven nightclubs and ten motels." The Skyline was "one of the wildest and most colorful clubs on the strip." At that point, the band was still called the Hawks, backing the colorful Ronnie Hawkins. Ruby was, according to Robertson, the owner of the club, though it seems more likely he was managing it on someone else's behalf. Ruby's behavior was strange, and the club itself bizarre. Robertson recalled, in his 2016 memoir, *Testimony*, that

> the club was burned out, blown up. It was hard to imagine it was habitable, never mind the kind of place that would actually attract paying customers. . . . But inside we learned why the place was called the Skyline Lounge: there was no roof. A fire had burned it up, and the owner [who at this point they only knew as "Jack"] either had decided to go with it or couldn't afford to fix it.

At their first show of the engagement, there were fewer than ten customers in attendance:

About halfway through our first song, a girl started dancing her way toward the stage from the back of the joint. As she came closer, I gradually realized that the club employed a one-armed go-go dancer to entice people to get up and dance.

The dancer succeeded in getting two couples out onto the floor, but they were only a fraction of what the space was designed to accommodate. Robertson feared they might not get paid. He continued:

> Suddenly, a tussle broke out in the middle of the dance floor. . . . The next thing I knew, one of the guys . . . shot tear gas at the other guy from very close range. The man clutched his face and crumpled immediately. Everyone shrieked and ran from the dance floor.

As the band was finishing up, the guy Robertson remembered as the club's owner told them, "Boys, this building ain't exactly secure enough for you to leave your musical equipment unattended. . . . If I were you, I'd stay here and guard 'em"—which they did. And throughout the week, the owner

> would pop in on us in the middle of the night. . . . "Does that guy ever sleep?" [band member] Rick [Danko] groaned. . . . You could tell by Jack's grinding jaw that he was into uppers. . . .
>
> We got paid—not as much as we'd hoped—and hit the highway, thinking that the strangeness was over. . . .
>
> Only it wasn't. A few months later . . . [as Oswald's] assailant's face was splashed repeatedly across television and newspapers for days on end, a bizarre realization settled in for all of us Hawks: Jack . . . of the Skyline Lounge . . . was none other than Jack Rubenstein— otherwise known as Jack Ruby.

One more entertainer who remembered Ruby's combination of harmful and helpful behavior was Jewel Brown. Brown, a well-known African American jazz vocalist, had, as a teen, worked as a singer at the Carousel when it was still the Sovereign. She was still relatively unknown at the time, but her marvelous voice helped her develop a following among people who frequented the nearby Adolphus Hotel and, hearing there about her vocal skills, would come to see her at Ruby's. She worked for him for a year and a half, quitting in a dispute over her tips, which he felt entitled to share in. After angrily leaving him, she went on to sing for seven years with Louis Armstrong's All-Stars, thanks to Armstrong's manager, Joe Glaser, who had heard this amazing talent.

Brown saw Oswald's murder on a motel TV while on tour in Terre Haute, Indiana, and recognized Ruby immediately. Seeing that momentous event triggered a memory of something *nice* Jack had done for her when she had unjustly gotten a $125 traffic ticket while working for him.

Upset, she had told Ruby what happened. He took the ticket and tore it up. Brown was worried this would get her in trouble with the police, but Ruby just said, "Forget about it." She did, and she never heard anything about the ticket again. To Brown, this meant that Ruby had some kind of influence with the police. "He definitely knew his way around downtown, if you know what I mean."

Ruby would later try to get Glaser to have Brown come back to work for him, but Glaser refused, feeling Ruby was a "mental case" and a "phony" and that Ruby tried to make people think he and Glaser were close friends when, as Glaser saw it, they barely knew one another.

Ruby had established himself as a familiar figure on the Dallas nightclub and entertainment scenes. Many stories told about him—like those told by Kaplan, Robertson, and Brown, in addition to those recalled by other performers and by Dallas businesspeople and newspeople—portray him as a volatile and violent character, but one ultimately good of heart and intention. Even many of those who disliked him seemed to feel that Ruby was someone who tried hard, whose failings and foibles were those of someone who did the best he could despite whatever limitations he might have had.

This is the benign version of Jack Ruby, the version that shows up in many popular culture interpretations, such as the Ruby of the streaming superhero series *The Umbrella Academy*. This Jack Ruby is relatable, an everyman character who could be us, who, even if he was involved with organized crime, was actually more of a bumbling, sometimes adorable, often pitiable figure, a comic version of a ruthless criminal.

That's an appealing fantasy: Ruby as an eccentric or pathetic figure, acting out some heroic fantasy only he could understand or see. But if he was in some ways a sort of Ralph Kramden everyman figure, there were, of course, disturbingly sinister aspects to him, as well.

Perhaps Ruby could have carried on a life as a person of such contradictions indefinitely, someone of interest only to other members of the various Dallas subcultures he inhabited. But fate had something else in store for him.

9 | THE NEW FRONTIER

TEXAS HAD BECOME CRUCIAL in national politics, a battleground state in the 1960 presidential election. Lyndon Johnson had been included on John F. Kennedy's ticket as candidate for vice president specifically to win Texas. Few had sharper political instincts than Johnson, as he would demonstrate time and again.

Though Dallas had many hallmarks of a conservative southern city, including segregated schools, restaurants, and movie theaters, its civic leaders were nevertheless hoping to avoid the upheaval that was roiling other southern cities. A prominent cadre of liberal citizens—notably Stanley Marcus, head of the prestigious Neiman-Marcus department stores—were hoping that the city could progress beyond the headline-grabbing activities of ultraconservative groups like the John Birch Society and the followers of divisive General Edwin Walker.

On November 4, 1960, just days before the presidential election, the campaigning Lyndon Johnson and his wife Lady Bird were attacked in Dallas—not far from the Carousel Club—by right-wing protestors (the so-called Mink Coat Mob), led by conservative congressman Bruce Alger. Days later, Kennedy would be elected president, defeating Richard Nixon. Rumors abounded that Kennedy was put over the top when organized crime made sure that he won Chicago's Cook County. Similar rumors—especially promulgated by archconservative billionaire Haroldson "H. L." Hunt and others—were bandied about regarding Kennedy's victory in Texas. Indeed, though JFK lost Dallas itself, he and Johnson won the state overall.

Jack Ruby, who probably didn't even vote in the election, claimed to have felt a connection to the Kennedy family, admiring them for prospering despite prejudice against Catholics, which he saw as not unlike the prejudice Jews faced. And despite JFK's father Joseph Kennedy's well-known disdain for Jews, Ruby believed that the son did not harbor such biases. Ruby seemed to closely equate Catholicism with Judaism as minority religions. As he told the Warren Commission on June 7, 1964,

> I want to show that we [Jewish people] love our president, even though we are not of the same faith. And I have a friend . . . a fellow whom I sort of idolized [Lewis McWillie, who] is of the Catholic faith, and a gambler. Naturally, in my business you meet people of various backgrounds. And the thought came, we were very close, and I always thought a lot of him, and I knew that Kennedy, being Catholic, I knew how heartbroken he was, and even his picture—this Mr. McWillie— flashed across me, because I have a great fondness for him.

Ruby was aware that JFK had Jewish friends and advisors and admired him for that. For Ruby, struggling to stay afloat, Kennedy's election was a moment of optimism and hope for the future. But it didn't change the fact that Ruby's life was heading nowhere good. His family, especially his brother Earl, were constantly "loaning" him money, which they never really expected to get back. As Earl Ruby told historian Gus Russo in an unpublished 2003 interview,

> He would feed people that were hungry and didn't have anything to eat. Some of them even slept [at the Carousel]. He had rooms there. . . . That's the kind of fellow he was. And he didn't have any money. He used to get the money from me . . . and he'd act like . . . a big shot. He wasn't. That's the way he was, though. He loved to help people.

Trying without success to sell the Carousel Club, Ruby essayed countless strategies to make a go of it. In debt to his brothers and, more seriously, to the IRS (and, one can imagine, less savory parties), Ruby was desperate and in despair, his future once again bleak. According to the Warren Commission report,

Ruby's financial records were chaotic. One accountant abandoned efforts to prepare income tax returns and other financial statements because of the hopeless disarray of Ruby's data. . . . Ruby was frequently weeks, if not months, late in filing Federal tax forms and . . . held numerous conferences with Internal Revenue agents who attempted to obtain the delinquent statements.

It continued that Ruby had obtained inaccurate advice from an attorney and

became liable to the Federal Government for more than 6 years of [business] taxes, amounting, with interest, to almost exactly $40,000.

Ruby also fell behind on his personal income tax payments. At the time of his arrest, he owed more than $4,400 for 1959 and 1960.

———

On Friday, January 20, 1961, at his inauguration, President John F. Kennedy made his famous "Ask Not What Your Country Can Do for You" speech, during which he exhorted Americans to boldly explore what he called the "New Frontier," an era in which the country would take on fresh challenges in a variety of areas. The oration brimmed with enthusiasm and optimism.

In contrast to Kennedy's stated hopes, tensions were rising in the country over recent Supreme Court decisions, especially those concerning civil rights. The personification of these tensions was Chief Justice Earl Warren, who had been considered a middle-of-the-road Dwight Eisenhower appointee, but who was now seen as the avatar of all things liberal—and therefore a target for the hatred of the right wing in Texas and elsewhere. The most extreme, and also most aggressively vocal, embodiment of this hostility was the relatively new John Birch Society, which was spearheading a movement to impeach Warren. General Walker would become a key figure in the movement and organization—and in the saga that would lead to Jack Ruby's explosive moment in the spotlight.

Meanwhile, whichever side—or perhaps both—in the Cuban Revolution that Jack Ruby might have been helping supply with weapons, that revolution was far from a done deal. Cuban exiles, trained by CIA operatives, had mounted an attack on Cuba on April 17, 1961, expecting they would be the vanguard of an assault on the Castro regime that would be supported by US air attacks. The Kennedy administration, though, had, at the last minute, decided against active participation, and the exiles were routed, with at least hundreds of casualties. Many in the exile community felt betrayed by JFK.

In Dallas, Jack Ruby was fighting his own sort of battle for survival. The Vegas Club was struggling but—largely under Eva's guidance—still in business. But the Carousel was losing money. Despite his insistence that it was a "class" joint, it actually bordered on being skeevy. It was the Weinsteins' venues—especially Abe's Colony Club—that seemed to provide more of a feeling to customers of being somewhere special, someplace sophisticated. While they may have been selling pretty much the same product as the Carousel, they seemed somehow be more respectable.

And, as always, there was time for Ruby to get into conflicts—verbal and physical—with anyone and everyone. For instance, actor Breck Wall, who would become the union representative of the performers union, AGVA, recalled for Bob Porter, in an interview for the Sixth Floor Museum, a violent encounter with Ruby and its aftermath. In the interview, Wall noted that Ruby didn't have many friends, that people didn't really like Jack, and that "I would say that I was one of [Ruby's] best friends if not his best friend." (Ralph Paul, too, claimed to be Ruby's best friend. The was something about the guy that attracted some people, despite Ruby's erratic behavior toward them.)

Wall recalled that he and his performing troupe were doing a comedy revue—tastefully called "Bottoms Up!"—for the Carousel (or its predecessor, the Sovereign Club) for Ruby in 1960, one they had previously been doing a version of across the street, at the Adolphus Hotel. Wall recalled,

> We got a bid to go back across the street at the Adolphus. . . . When we told him [Ruby] that we were going to go back . . . he got very angry. . . . He hit my partner, Joe Peterson, and knocked him down the stairs and knocked out a tooth. . . . We had no idea it was even coming. . . . He was just talking to us. And then he said, "Oh yeah?" And he belted Joe down the stairs.

Several months after this violent encounter, Ruby came across Wall on a downtown street. Wall recalled the chance meeting:

> I was really angry with him. And we needed like $900 to open the show [at the Adolphus] to get some costumes and stuff, and he met Joe on the street and he said, "What's happening?" And [Joe] told him and [Ruby] said, "Well, look, I was wrong. I shouldn't have done that, and what can I do?" And Joe ... teasingly—you know, just jokingly—said, "We need $900 to open the show." And [Ruby] said, "Well, come with me." And he went to the bank and made [the troupe] a loan. And that's the kind of person he was.

Whatever his temperament at a given moment, Ruby's businesses were indeed in big trouble. He was in continual panic mode. He owed all that money to the IRS. And he felt that the Weinsteins were engaging in unfair business practices and hurting him but was unable to get AGVA to do anything to help him. In reality, both Ruby and the Weinsteins were using the "amateur" gimmick to get around paying full union rates to dancers. They also were possibly engaged in kickback schemes, in which dancers would be paid full rates but would then be expected to return some of their fees to the club owners, in effect being paid below union rates. The Warren Commission's summary biography of Ruby explained:

> Ruby apparently believed his two competitors, the Weinstein brothers, were scheduling amateur shows in a manner calculated to destroy his business. Ruby's discontent with AGVA grew particularly acute during the late summer and early fall of 1963 when, in addition to meeting with AGVA officials, he called upon several acquaintances, including known criminals, who, he thought, could influence AGVA on his behalf.

As Abe Weinstein's son Steven recalled, his father and uncle "came up with this thing called amateur night ... [which] basically was a way to have dancers come in and work and not have to pay dues to the AGVA." Steven wasn't sure, since he was a kid at the time, but his recollection regarding the dancers was "Well, maybe they weren't [amateurs]. Or they may have been starting out the business—maybe they weren't doing it full time as a full-time living."

———————————

During this period, George Senator, an often-unemployed fifty-something salesman from upstate New York, was working part-time at the Carousel, doing a variety of odd jobs. At the same time, he was also, as he had in the past, sharing an apartment with Ruby. Senator has said that he was unable to stay more than five months with Ruby because, as he told Burt Griffin of the Warren Commission,

> Jack likes to live alone in the overall picture. First of all, it is an interference of the time that I wake up and the time that he goes to bed which don't coincide. . . . And then Jack don't live too clean . . . in other words, he comes home, he is reading a newspaper, on the floor, if he is in the bathroom the newspaper goes on the floor and things of that nature. Though he was very clean about himself, he wasn't clean around the apartment.

Nonetheless, at some point, Senator and Ruby seemed unable to afford, even together, the rent, and they actually moved into the Carousel for a time. In early 1963, though, Senator moved, with a different roommate, into a nicer building, at 221 South Ewing in Dallas and informed Ruby of a vacant apartment next to it that Ruby proceeded to rent. When Senator's roommate got married and moved out, Senator could no longer afford the apartment on his own, and he, in early November 1963, moved into Ruby's second bedroom.

It's partly this living arrangement, and the fact that Senator would refer to Ruby as his "boyfriend," that led some to assume that Ruby and Senator were lovers. Nonetheless, Senator insisted to Griffin of the Warren Commission that

> It is a word I have used all my life, when I was even a kid. There was no particular reason. My boyfriends. Some people may say, "This is my acquaintance." It happens to be I have always used this word, no

particular reason. Maybe I would probably say it was a habit more than anything else.

Senator attributed rumors of his—and Ruby's—homosexuality to hostile, insinuating questioning by prosecutor Bill Alexander at Ruby's first bond hearing:

> When I read this "boyfriend" and how many times that has been quoted . . . it has never been quoted [to] me direct, but I have heard it [as] hearsay, you know, things like that. At the . . . first bond hearing, Mr. Alexander said to me:
> "You and Jack Ruby lived together?" And I said, "Yes." He says, "How many bedrooms in the apartment you live in?" I said, "Two." He says, "What are the other rooms?" I says, "There is a bathroom, kitchen, and a living room." Then he come out with this live one, which I grasped right away. . . .
> "Where do you keep the TV?" . . .
> I said, "In the living room," [which is] where it is. But I caught the drift right away. . . . In other words, what this means is Jack Ruby and I are in bed together, probably holding hands, or whatever it might be, watching TV.

In August or September of 1962, according to Nancy Perrin, who claimed to have been a Carousel bartender (although no one at the club recalled her working there, according to Wills and Demaris), Ruby attended meetings in Dallas about smuggling weapons into Cuba on behalf of Castro. Conspiracy theorist Mark Lane—author of *Rush to Judgment*, one of the first books challenging the Warren Commission's conclusions—made much of her commission testimony, though its content was among many unsubstantiated claims she made about many things over the years. Wills and Demaris were told by her husband, "She is very nervous and imaginative. Things build up pretty easy like."

Whatever the accuracy of Perrin's testimony, some historians' research links Ruby to criminal activity. It's claimed that if a VIP was in town—including police—and wanted to be hooked up with drugs or prostitutes, Jack Ruby was the man who could provide them. It seems in character for Ruby. Would it be inconsistent with those who say that he fired anyone at the Carousel who he suspected of hooking?

Both could be true. Concern for his clubs' various licenses, the need to keep the doors open, could indeed have led him to make sure none of the illegal services he was alleged to have provided would be directly connected to his venues. Dallas of the era seemed to have been governed by very specific and esoteric rules of conduct and behavior, many unwritten, regarding what could be done, where it could be done, and by whom.

Nonetheless, for every story about Ruby's corruption, there's a story like the one told by a champagne girl who worked at the Carousel: "He fired me at least three hundred times—seven times in one night," she recalled for Wills and Demaris. But, she went on, with a history of miscarriages as well as several children she was supporting, she had once given birth at home, alone, to a son who died on arrival. "I lost four pints [of blood] by the time they got me to the hospital. I'm Rh-negative, and they needed two more pints than they had; so they called the place where I worked and Jack came right over. It was such an emergency they took both pints from him. He gave blood to lots of people. . . . When I tried to thank him, he just swore at me. . . . He had a soggy heart, but he covered it up with bluster."

And then there's the probably-not-unusual case of Connie Trammell Penny. As Jim Williamson reported in the *Texarkana Gazette* on November 22, 2013,

> Connie was a student at the University of Texas in Austin in 1962 and attending a junket [in Dallas] . . . "We had friends who met us in Dallas, . . . and we all said, 'Let's go across the street to the Carousel Club,'" Connie said. . . . "We were all sitting around a big table and we all had dates." . . . She got up from the table and was walking toward a restroom and a man started following her. . . . The man was Jack Ruby. . . .
>
> Ruby continued to pursue Connie asking her, "Would you like to work for me as a stripper? I own this club." Connie declined the offer.
>
> "I came back out of the rest room and he was still there," Connie said. . . . "He asked me if I liked little Dachshunds. I said, 'I love little Dachshunds.' . . . I followed him to the kitchen and he had about four or five Dachshunds. I thought he couldn't be all bad," she said. . . .

"He did dorky little things and I found him so harmless. . . . He was probably a lot safer than a lot of the guys who went to the University of Texas," Connie said. . . . "He [Ruby] was always a gentleman." . . . Ruby got Connie's telephone number at the dorm in Austin and called her weekly.

The next year, she would realize that Jack Ruby was not quite as harmless as she had thought.

In the universe outside Jack Ruby's personal sphere, events were happening rapidly in the worlds of national and international politics.

General Walker had been forced out of the army because of his aggressive promotion of extreme right-wing positions to his troops. President Kennedy targeted him specifically in a speech he gave on November 18, 1961, in Los Angeles. Walker was charismatic and handsome, with his own presidential aspirations. In 1962 he ran for governor of Texas, making Kennedy and liberals in general the targets of his campaign. He badly lost the Democratic primary—won by John Connally—but had established himself as a polarizing national figure.

On August 18, 1962, Walker led violent protests against Black student James Meredith, who was attempting to enroll in the University of Mississippi. Armed protestors rioted against the outnumbered defenders of the campus. Two people, including a reporter, were killed during the battle, which was finally quelled only by troops sent in by Walker's nemesis, John F. Kennedy. Meredith was able to successfully enroll. Despite the fact that he had, in 1957, commanded the soldiers who famously helped integrate the Little Rock, Arkansas, public schools, Walker's views had radicalized in the intervening years. After the riots, he was forcibly subjected to psychiatric hospitalization by Attorney General Robert F. Kennedy.

In light of this building notoriety, it was perhaps not surprising that, on April 10, 1963, an assassination attempt was made against this polarizing figure at Walker's Dallas home. Though never definitively proven, Marina Oswald would claim that the shooter was her husband, Lee. Walker—at least by his telling of the attack—avoided death only because the fired bullet was thrown off course by a piece of a window frame.

James Meredith, in 1962, walking to class at the University of Mississippi, protected by US marshals. The enrollment of this first Black student at the school sparked riots led by General Edwin Walker, a Dallas-based archconservative leader and outspoken foe of President Kennedy. *Library of Congress Prints and Photographs Division, U.S. News & World Report Magazine Collection, courtesy of Wikimedia Commons*

The Cuban Missile Crisis, in October 1962, brought the world to the brink of nuclear war. To avert disaster, compromises were made on both sides, including the removal of US missiles in Turkey in return for the removal of Soviet missiles in Cuba, though the former was not admitted at the time. There were those who looked at the avoidance of nuclear war with the Soviets as not a victory for rationalism but as a capitulation to Communism. Many of them placed the blame squarely on their perceived weakness of President Kennedy.

And adding to the tension of the year, on June 12, 1963, civil rights leader Medgar Evers was assassinated in Jackson, Mississippi.

What was Jack Ruby doing during this period of tumult? Well, he seems to have been simply running his clubs. But of course, for Ruby, there was rarely such a thing as "simply."

For instance, in February 1963 he was arrested by the Dallas police for getting into a fistfight at the Burgundy Room at the Adolphus Hotel. He was found not guilty the same day. Less violently, although probably more traumatically, he was told in March 1963 that he owed the Internal Revenue Service the $40,000.

Also in March, one of Ruby's dogs gave birth to a litter, one of which, as noted, he gave to Rabbi Silverman's family. Soon thereafter, in May, Ruby gifted another couple of dogs. Renting a car in Houston, he drove a hundred miles to Edna, Texas, to visit Candy Barr—Juanita Dale Slusher—who had recently been paroled.

"Dear Jack," recalled Barr. "He brought me several presents that day. Two of them were AKC dachshunds, a male and a female. He said that I should breed them and get wonderful puppies I could then sell."

She continued, "He also brought me an air conditioner because he knew how much the humid Texas heat bothered me. And then he gave me $50. . . . We talked for hours. Mostly he and I agreed how much we adored President Kennedy—that he truly was a savior for our country. It was very touching, the way Jack felt about that man." He predicted to Barr that there could be a Holocaust in America and that only Kennedy could prevent it.

Barr recalled that "he'd referred to himself as 'a black Jew.' I think he meant that he and his people never really had been accepted by so many Americans. . . . With Jack Kennedy, he could sense the change in religious attitude in the country. He said that President Kennedy would see to it that no one was discriminated against. After all, Jack [Ruby] said, Kennedy had to fight all odds because he was Catholic."

In any case, "Juanita took [Ruby's] advice and kept encouraging her dachshunds to have sex," but "her efforts were unsuccessful. 'They just didn't like each other that way, I guess.'"

Less humorously, months later, when Ruby murdered Oswald, Barr was intensively questioned in Edna by the FBI and later before the Warren Commission. Such was the "extra benefit" of having Jack Ruby as a friend. As Barr recalled, the FBI "yanked me up the night he killed Oswald. They bothered my family and me, way up into the seventies. . . . He'd been through Edna and they figured he was the bag man, and he'd come through here and I knew everything."

Soon after returning from Edna, Ruby ordered a .38 Smith & Wesson pistol from a gun dealer, requesting that it be delivered to Lewis McWillie in Las Vegas. Why and how Ruby decided to have the gun shipped to his friend is a subject of much controversy, and, in fact, McWillie declined to pick up the package containing the firearm when he was informed it had been delivered. And, although Ruby thought highly of McWillie, when asked after his arrest for shooting Oswald if anyone might wish him harm, he named McWillie. Clearly, something in their relationship had soured along the way. Perhaps the gun delivery was part of that.

In June, Ruby put great effort into engaging the dancer famous on the strip club circuit as "Jada" (real name Janet Conforto) to dance at the Carousel. He traveled to New Orleans, where Harold Tannenbaum, who ran a club called the French Opera House, introduced him to the star. She began her engagement at the Carousel later that month, at a salary nearly three times what Ruby's other dancers were being paid. The relationship between performer and club owner would soon become tempestuous.

You can get a sense of the style of burlesque entertainment—with strippers prominently featured—that was showcased at Ruby's Carousel Club in the poster for the 1950 movie *International Burlesque*. More than a decade later, this combination of eroticism and humor—including stand-up comedians—was still in vogue in some of downtown Dallas's nightclubs. *Courtesy of Wikimedia Commons*

Meanwhile, in his never-ending feud with the Weinsteins over their alleged misuse of "amateur" strippers, in early August Ruby contacted Mike Shore, an executive at Reprise Records, who had gone to high school with Jack's brother Earl. Ruby believed that Shore—reputed to be mob-connected—had some kind of influence with the performers union, but Shore would tell the late-1970s House Select Committee on Assassinations that he had been unable to offer Ruby any help. (He would later help Earl Ruby raise defense funds for his brother and with finding an attorney to represent him.)

Trying another tack, Ruby called AGVA headquarters in New York to once again plead for the union's help against the Weinsteins. Ruby spoke to an AGVA officer, borscht belt comedian Joey Adams—husband of gossip columnist Cindy Adams—hoping to enlist his aid, but to no avail.

Unable to make any headway via phone, Ruby *flew* to New York on August 4 to call on the union's offices in person and also to visit his old friend Barney Ross. The AGVA portion of the trip was no more successful than the phone call had been. The union paid lip service in agreeing with Ruby that the Weinsteins were probably engaged in unfair labor practices and ordered the brothers to stop, but it never made any serious attempt to enforce its own rulings.

And at the end of August, Jack and Eva got into a heated argument while they were driving with their sister, Eileen Kaminsky, who was visiting from Chicago. Reportedly, Jack was angry because Eva had accepted a person-to-person call that was meant for him, an expensive act in 1963 that would have been wasted money since Jack wasn't there to speak to whomever was calling. In what can only be seen as an overreaction—albeit in character for Ruby—he pushed Eva out of his car and continued on without her.

In the larger world, on August 28, the famous March on Washington for Jobs and Freedom took place, the event where Martin Luther King made his "I Have a Dream" speech. And then, on September 15, the 16th Street Baptist Church in Birmingham, Alabama, was bombed, killing four young Black girls. The nation was confronted with a churning mix of political tension interwoven with increasingly vocal demands for equal treatment by large numbers of Black Americans, all of which set off angry reactions in some quarters, with the most extreme responses coming from the likes of General Walker and the John Birch Society.

At about the same time, back in Dallas, Ruby placed an ad in the *Dallas Morning News* for a nightclub for sale. Starting in this period, Ruby's phone records are filled with calls to people with connections to organized crime. Much has been made of these calls in terms of possible conspiracy and pre-planning for the Kennedy murder. By the same token, a man desperately trying to keep his businesses afloat, especially someone who was as much of a networker and social animal as Jack Ruby, could well be expected to call, and be called by, people with less than impeccable backgrounds and connections. Ruby was fighting for survival, contacting anyone and everyone he could think of to help him.

On August 28, 1963, folk music idols Joan Baez and Bob Dylan sang at Martin Luther King's March on Washington for Jobs and Freedom. Later that year, a month after the Kennedy and Oswald murders, Dylan would excite controversy by saying that "I saw some of myself" in Lee Harvey Oswald. *Photo by Rowland Scherman, US National Archives and Records Administration, courtesy of Wikimedia Commons*

On the Ruby violence front during this period, Huey Reeves, a parking attendant at the garage next to the Carousel warned Jack that a stocky, "Jewish-
looking" man had come by the garage, stating that he was going to kill
Ruby. Instead of panicking or fleeing, Ruby got his gun from the trunk of
his car, found the man described by the attendant at a nearby liquor store,
and pistol-whipped him. Ruby's victim was hospitalized, and yet, for reasons
unexplained, later came to work for Ruby. In other words, it was business as
usual for Jack Ruby.

Meanwhile, also during this period, the maybe-gay-maybe-not Jack Ruby
argued with Eva over Jack's dating a girl she considered "too young." Because
of that conflict, Ruby, sometime in late September—in the period between
Rosh Hashanah and Yom Kippur, known to observant Jews as the Ten Days of
Repentance—contacted Rabbi Silverman to see if the clergyman could broker a
peace between him and his sister. Perhaps Ruby felt that he or Eva—or maybe
both of them—needed to do some repenting.

It's hard to imagine that Eva, after so many years in the nightclub business,
would object to Jack dating someone because of her age, unless, perhaps she
was concerned that it would end up with Jack somehow getting arrested. By
the same token, perhaps her protective instinct toward young women, from
the days when Candy Barr would show up at the Singapore Supper Club, was
still in play. In any case, that is what has been claimed as the cause of Eva and
Jack not speaking during this period. (Perhaps shoving Eva out of that car, as
well as that time he slugged her, also factored into the friction between them.)

Also in late September 1963, Ruby became acquainted with a crew that
had come to town to produce a show called *How Hollywood Makes Movies*
for the Dallas State Fair. The crew borrowed some props from the Carousel
to use in the production. Larry Crafard, who would play a significant role in
Ruby's story, came to work at the production and soon thereafter for Ruby at
the Carousel. In keeping with the Carousel's use as a crash pad, Crafard would
even move into the nightclub on October 20.

Also at the state fair, Ruby had opened a booth to sell novelties. That venture only lasted one night, but since he'd already paid the rent on the booth,
he had some of his Carousel employees come by to demonstrate an exercise

novelty item—the twist board—that he was hawking. Also at the fair, Ruby came across oil baron H. L. Hunt's *Lifeline* radio show's booth and picked up some pamphlets, but "the extreme right-wing literature of the *Lifeline* was a shock to Jack. . . . The particular leaflet Jack picked up . . . was *Heroism*, a radio script which espoused a neo-Nazi philosophy, complete with its message of anti-Semitism and a call for the impeachment of Earl Warren." These pamphlets would be found in Ruby's car after he was arrested for shooting Oswald.

On October 28 Jada took, not for the first or last time, a step too far on Jack Ruby's stage. As fellow (and rival) Carousel stripper Tammi True—real name, Nancy Myers—described it to Ginger Valentine in August 2013, on the *21st Century Burlesque* website,

> [Jack] ran the spotlight and it was on a post, out there in the club behind where the customers sat. And I was standing there to see what she did, because he just thought she was won-der-ful. During her show she reached down and grabbed her G-string and pulled it over to the side—that's what we called a flash—and Jack almost had a stroke. They'd close ya down back then for that. That was a no-no. So he turned the spotlight off real fast. And I said, "Yeah Jack, you're right. She's got a lot of class."

Sometime in October, despite his financial issues and his putting the Carousel up for sale, Ruby took Eva to look at a property he was considering buying for a new club. Where he would come up with the money for such a venture is unknown. Perhaps the sale of the Carousel? This seems to indicate at least a certain optimism and a desire to plan for the future on Ruby's part.

Of great interest to Ruby, as well as the entire Jewish community of Dallas, was that, in 1962 and 1963, at least four significant antisemitic events occurred in the city. These included a thwarted attack on a synagogue by two kids, one of whom was brandishing a swastika armband; a cross-burning at a Holocaust survivor's home; swastikas painted on a synagogue; and, in April 1963, on Stanley Marcus's Neiman-Marcus department store and on the windows of Marcus's own home.

Dallas, in large part thanks to its Jewish community, especially legendary rabbis like Levi Olan, the emeritus rabbi of Temple Emanu-El, had been dragged kicking and screaming into an era of desegregation. That community's hand had been forced to some degree by the fact of Jewish ownership of many of the city's retailers. That prominent position made them targets of African American protestors at the stores' fitting rooms and lunch counters. It also made the city's Jewish population highly visible targets from *foes* of integration when the stores introduced more equitable policies. The city's contradictions—like that of many cities in the country—were becoming ominously clear. Dallas could neither stay ensconced in a fantasy of a golden past, nor could it easily rush headlong into an idealized future.

And, as if to underline the city's duality, Dallas's right wing was preparing an enthusiastic reception for a man who embodied the internationalism they hated.

Adlai E. Stevenson, the United States ambassador to the United Nations—and possibly the most famous liberal Democrat since Franklin Roosevelt—was coming to town.

10 | GATHERING STORM

ON OCTOBER 23, the day before Stevenson's scheduled talk, General Walker held a "U.S. Day" rally at Dallas Memorial Auditorium, the theme being the very opposite of the ambassador's upcoming "U.N. Day" celebration in the same venue. After denouncing liberals far and wide, Walker assaulted the United Nations, condemning the organization as being a breeding ground for Communism and anti-Americanism. He denounced the man coming to celebrate United Nations Day the very next day, calling Adlai E. Stevenson, "a symbol of the communist conspiracy."

In the audience, seemingly keeping tabs on Walker, was the young man who most likely tried to kill him several months earlier: Lee Harvey Oswald.

The next day, right-wing demonstrators heckled and harassed Stevenson during his address. The demonstrators congregated after he had finished speaking, taunting and insulting him until, finally, one assaulted him with a picket sign, which barely missed poking the ambassador in the eye.

Dallas was indeed the center of national conflict and animosity, caught in the crosscurrents of its dual identities as a southern city mired in old ways yet simultaneously existing as a center of finance and, to some degree, culture, moving slowly into the modern era, trying to sidestep the violence and acrimony that was engulfing other large cities.

89

On November 2, South Vietnam's President Ngo Dinh Diem—whose sister, Madame Nhu, had been openly critical of the Kennedy administration's handling of the civil war in her country (and who had made an infamous shopping trip to Dallas)—was assassinated during a coup, with tacit US approval. US military "advisors" in Vietnam now totaled sixteen thousand as the war continued to escalate. There were those who felt that Kennedy was intent on reducing that military commitment.

But Kennedy's efforts in Vietnam and on crime and on civil rights would be limited if he only served one term. So, in late 1963, a year before the next presidential election, he was trying to shore up Texas, a hotbed of Democratic Party infighting. Kennedy felt that he had to personally go to the Lone Star State to twist arms and flash smiles until he got the state's Democrats to at least pretend to get along. Though Kennedy had won Texas in 1960, he had notably lost Dallas. He couldn't let that happen again.

A trip to the city was scheduled, with Texas's own, vice-president Lyndon Johnson, accompanying the president. Tops on their agenda was getting Governor John Connally and the governor's political—and personal—adversary, Senator Ralph Yarborough, to act as if there was some unity in the Texas Democratic Party, especially when it came to reelecting Kennedy.

Unlike Jack Kennedy—and unlike Lee Harvey Oswald, for that matter, who had recently moved to Dallas in the midst of tumultuous events in his life—Jack Ruby had no ambitions to change the world. He seemed to just want a better version of the life he had now. Ruby seemed to like running his club and being father figure to an assortment of oddballs while pursuing side gigs, some of them likely criminal in nature. All he needed now was some way to actually make money and get out of debt.

That was no small ambition. Despite the help from his family, especially his brother Earl, Jack was struggling to survive. And he was still obsessed with what he thought was discrimination against him from the performers union. Jack Ruby's political interest seemed to begin and end with which local politicians he needed to ingratiate himself with in order to stay in business. If, as some believe, he was a player in Dallas's underworld, then one would assume he'd have liked to achieve more success in that arena too.

A complication in his life was the ongoing emotional roller-coaster relationship with his sister Eva. When they had recently feuded, Rabbi Silverman had, at Jack's request, facilitated a reconciliation between them. Somewhere during this period, Eva had gone into the hospital for a hysterectomy, and it seems that Jack was her main caretaker, looking in on her and calling her multiple times a day, bringing her food, keeping her company. Indeed, though Jack would sometimes refer to Sheba as his wife and his other dogs as his children, the closest thing in his life to a marriage-like situation seemed to be his tempestuous relationship with Eva.

———————

Anti-liberal, anti-JFK sentiment was in evidence all over Dallas. As the date of Kennedy's visit approached, an IMPEACH EARL WARREN billboard was erected, and a WANTED FOR TREASON: JFK leaflet was distributed, both most likely created by associates of General Walker's. All this was very upsetting to Jack Ruby, whose activities would become remarkably bewildering from here on.

On November 21, as part of the Texas junket, President Kennedy was speaking in Fort Worth, all while news of the so-called Bobby Baker scandal, involving corruption in Lyndon Johnson's orbit, was breaking in Washington. The ramifications endangered Johnson's career, putting him at risk of prosecution and possible jail time. *Life* magazine was poised to break the story. The scandal was bad enough that it led Kennedy to consider dumping Johnson from the ticket.

This set of circumstances would fuel the idea of Johnson being involved in a possible plot to get rid of Kennedy so that he could quash the entire scandal, as well as become president, which Johnson had long desired. (Interestingly, Kennedy's Republican opponent from just a few years before, Richard Nixon, was in Dallas, on business as a lawyer for Pepsi-Cola, along with actress Joan Crawford, a Pepsi spokesperson and board member. Nixon seems to have left town just a few hours before Kennedy arrived. Some conspiracy theories, unsurprisingly, speculate about Nixon's possible involvement in the assassination.)

———————

Up until November 20, Jack Ruby's behavior doesn't seem to have been much stranger than his usual eccentric, sometimes inexplicable life patterns. But starting on that day, we see the actions taken, or believed to have been taken, by him take a turn toward the bizarre, perhaps even sinister, depending on the observer's point of view. What follows are some of the reported activities of Jack

Leon Ruby during those surreal November days in Dallas. Some of them contradict others, and never has the truism that eyewitness accounts are the most unreliable evidence been more applicable. Whether due to the effects of phenmetrazine (brand name Preludin) or other prescription drugs, an unquenchable desire to be everywhere, his active participation in a conspiracy of some kind, lack of sleep (he got just fourteen hours of sleep in four days) or just plain nuttiness, here's what Jack Ruby more or less did from November 20 to 24, 1963:

Late Wednesday night, November 20, to early morning, Thursday, November 21: at 1 AM, Ruby, along with "underworld characters," was at a party at the apartment of Frank Tortoriello. Gloria Fillmon (a.k.a. Gloria Rettig) may have been with him. What this party was for, what was discussed, is unknown.

But at 2 AM, Carousel stripper Karen Carlin, who performed under the name "Little Lynn," became ill and passed out at Nichols Garage (no relation to Alice Nichols, as far as is known), next door to the Carousel. Ruby stayed with her for the next two or three hours, then went home to bed. Or maybe Lynn was with Larry Crafard. Or maybe she wasn't sick at all. What you think happened depends on who you believe. Crafard claimed that at 3:45 AM, Ruby and a woman named Gloria had him join them for a very early breakfast at a regular Ruby haunt, Lucas B & B Restaurant. Ruby then, without seeming to stop to sleep at all, spent the day dealing with various aspects his clubs' business.

At noon, Ruby called John Newman at the *Dallas Morning News* to reserve space for his ads for the weekend. He would have to go in person to place the ads and pay for them, as his credit was overextended—cash only for Jack Ruby. At about the same time, Ruby was reported to be in the office of Dallas County assistant DA Ben Ellis, passing out cards promoting Jada's appearances at his club—so perhaps she was playing out her contract despite Jack's efforts to fire her. Ruby reportedly told Ellis, "You probably don't know me, but you will."

By 4:30 PM, Ruby was back at the newspaper office, dealing with his weekend ads again.

Beverley Oliver, a singer and stripper in clubs, including Abe Weinstein's Colony Club, claims that she, Jack, and businessman (and possible mob associate) Lawrence Meyers met up at the Cabana Hotel that night, where Jack introduced her to Meyers. Then, the three proceeded to Campisi's Egyptian, where they had dinner. Oliver left them to meet a date, but she claimed that Ruby and Meyers were there well past midnight. The intended subtext of Oliver's recollections is that the men were plotting nefarious things.

Oliver made a dramatic claim regarding Ruby and this period. Oliver would assert to have been the "babushka lady" seen in the background of the Zapruder film and to have herself shot film of the assassination. She claimed that the film was then confiscated from her before she could have it developed and that she never even actually saw the film, which some have suggested could help solve the riddle of from where exactly the bullets that killed Kennedy were fired. Oliver further states, in her book *Nightmare in Dallas*, written with Coke Buchanan, that on or around November 8, 1963, she met a man in the Carousel Club who Ruby told her was "Lee Oswald. He's with the CIA." This is one of numerous unproven accounts of Ruby and Oswald supposedly having known each other before November 22.

It does seem definite that around 10 PM, Ruby had dinner with business partner Ralph Paul at Campisi's. There, Ruby discussed with co-owner Sam Campisi—rumored, like his brother Joe, to be mob-connected—the next day's JFK visit and all the political turmoil in the city. Some speculate that planning for a conspiracy was going on.

A 2017 photo of Campisi's Egyptian Restaurant, an old-school checkered-tablecloth Italian restaurant, looking pretty much as it did on November 21, 1963, when Jack Ruby and some associates dined there. (Its previous incarnation was as an Egyptian restaurant, hence its name.) *Photo by Lorie Shaull, courtesy of the photographer, https://flickr.com/photos/11020019@N04/37058566276*

According to Ruby himself, he and Paul had dinner at the Egyptian, after which Ruby returned to the Carousel, where he worked until 2 AM, and then went home to bed. Both Meyers and Paul have contradictory and inconsistent memories of the evening. Some people say that Joe Campisi was also at the restaurant. Meyers did recall that Ruby arrived at the Cabana Club, a nightspot in the hotel where Meyers was staying, and that Ruby did visit with him in the Bon Vivant Room there.

There is disagreement as to whether Meyers—a traveling salesman—was simply in Dallas visiting, or whether he was involved in something more sinister. And if he was, did that something involve Jack Ruby, Lee Harvey Oswald, or John F. Kennedy?

As was his wont, Ruby was active through the night, reportedly being seen in the wee hours at Lucas B & B again, possibly with Larry Crafard. Crafard recalled they returned to the Carousel around 4 AM.

Sometime before returning home, Ruby once again passed the IMPEACH EARL WARREN billboard, and saw a WANTED FOR TREASON: JFK leaflet, both of which again upset him. Even later the same night, he saw the anti-JFK ad run in an early edition of the *Dallas Morning News*, with the headline WELCOME MR. KENNEDY, signed by "Bernard Weissman," that would so enrage him.

As it turned out, Weissman *was* a real person, a member of a small group of former GIs led by a friend of his with whom he shared a conservative bent, Larry Schmidt. They called themselves the National Indignation Committee. The group was evolving toward a worldview that embraced antisemitism, and Weissman—who was indeed, as Ruby feared, Jewish—would soon have second thoughts about belonging. It seemed as if he *was* being used by the group, employing his Jewish name in the ad specifically to deflect possible charges of antisemitism. Associates of General Walker seemed to be pulling the group's strings.

Busy as he was, though, sometime Friday morning, Ruby found time to call Dallas journalist Gary Cartwright and his roommate, Bud Shrake, who had both attended a Carousel performance where Jada went too far. As Cartwright recalls,

> Ruby called our apartment and asked if we'd seen Jada. Shrake said we hadn't.

"I'm warning you for your own good," Ruby said. "Stay away from that woman."

"Is that intended as a threat?" Shrake inquired.

"No, no," Ruby apologized. "No, it's just that she's an evil woman."

And by around 7:30 AM Friday the twenty-second, when Jack's roommate George Senator left for work, Senator recalled that Ruby was asleep. So Ruby must have arrived home sometime before that, getting at least *some* rest.

He would need it. He had a long couple of days ahead of him.

11 | MURDER MOST FOUL

IT WAS NOW A LITTLE LATER on the morning of Friday, November 22.

It was then that Ruby took the time to do a favor for Connie Trammell Penny, the Carousel Club patron to whom he had shown his dachshunds. Penny had moved to Dallas. That morning,

> Ruby called asking if she had decided to go to work as a stripper. She said no.
>
> Connie had scheduled a job interview with [H. L.] Hunt. Connie didn't have an automobile and Ruby agreed to meet her at her apartment and drive her to [the interview at] the Mercantile National Bank. . . .
>
> The appointment was at 11 a.m. . . . The interview ended about 1 p.m. She read in the Dallas newspapers about Hunt owning a bowling alley . . . he was converting . . . into a teenagers club. She thought she could gain employment at the club in public relations . . . according to the Warren Commission report.
>
> Ruby parked his car . . . and accompanied Connie to the elevator in the bank, but did not accompany her upstairs.
>
> "This is the last time that Mrs. Penny has seen Ruby," states the commission report.

H. L. Hunt was the source of the financing of the WELCOME MR. KENNEDY ad signed by Bernard Weissman in that morning's *Dallas Morning News*.

By around noon, Ruby was at the *Morning News* office, finalizing his weekend ads. *Dallas Morning News* reporter Hugh Aynesworth recalls that, on Friday the twenty-second, Ruby

> headed for our second-floor ad department to visit with Don Campbell, an ad salesman. . . . Campbell departed the office at 12:25, leaving Ruby to work out his usual tiny notice for the weekend papers, usually a one-column ad, no more than three or four inches deep.
>
> John Newman, another *News* ad salesman, walked into the department about this time . . . and noticed Ruby . . . reading the morning paper. "Look at this dirty ad," Ruby exclaimed in disgust as he pointed at the black-bordered announcement that Weissman and Schmidt had placed in the *News*.
>
> Newman would recall Ruby saying . . . he couldn't imagine a Jew promulgating such a message of hatred. "We've seen too much of that already," he said.

Regarding the ad, Ruby had said to Eva, "If this Weissman is a Jew, they ought to whack the hell out of him." We can assume he meant that other Jews, not anyone else, should punish Weissman.

Earlier that morning, President Kennedy's plane approached Dallas Love Field. Although the trip from Fort Worth was short and could have been easily driven, the spectacle of the flight and the greeting by an adoring crowd, including photogenic children, would have been irresistible to a campaigning politician.

At 11:30 AM, the plane landed, greeted by an enthusiastic crowd on this sunny day. The open-air motorcade into downtown Dallas soon got underway. Prominent Dallas citizens, including Rabbi Hillel Silverman, were waiting for the president and his party at the majestic Trade Mart, where the motorcade was scheduled to bring him to speak. Governor John Connally and his wife were in the same limousine as the presidential couple.

Despite no lack of picket signs demonizing the president, the crowd was, for the most part, enthusiastic and affectionate. "It is clear by now," write

Bill Minutaglio and Steven L. Davis, "that they are experiencing the largest, friendliest crowd of the entire Texas trip. . . . This is not what they expected in Dallas. Kennedy's aides are not just relieved, they are nearly giddy with delight."

Along the motorcade route—which had been printed in the *Dallas Morning News* a few days earlier—immigrant clothing manufacturer Abraham Zapruder was setting up at a viewing site next to a grassy patch not far from his Dealey Plaza factory, positioning himself to film the motorcade with his new, top-of-the-line Bell & Howell 8mm movie camera. Zapruder had fled antisemitism in Poland and established himself in the garment industry, now running his Jennifer Juniors company at the nearby Dal-Tex Building, Although working in the *shmatta* industry was perhaps not the career he ideally would have chosen for himself, he had created from it a prosperous life. Eager to see the young president, he had almost not even taken the camera with him, until he was reminded to do so by his assistant, Marilyn Sitzman, who was helping steady her boss, who had vertigo, on his precarious perch atop a slab of concrete. It wasn't every day that a president came to Dallas. If he wasn't going to shlep the camera out for that, when would he?

What happened next is beyond history, beyond memory, something so shattering—something fulfilling Kennedy's own morbid prediction of an attempt on his life—that choosing the words to express it, to either try to coin some new way to say it or unearth an existing, elegant evocation of the moment, is daunting. Perhaps the words of broadcaster Walter Cronkite summed it up most succinctly:

> In Dallas, Texas, three shots were fired at President Kennedy's motor-cade in downtown Dallas. The first reports say that President Kennedy has been seriously wounded by this shooting.

Even as the echoes of those shots faded, the roots of controversy were being sown. Where *exactly* were they fired from? Were there three or four bullets fired? Who fired them? Did they all come from one spot, or were there multiple shooters? What motive or motives could the shooter or shooters have?

But before all those questions and countless more would blossom, there was practical business to deal with: saving the president!

The motorcade sped up, racing toward Parkland Hospital, several miles away. Not only had Kennedy been shot, but Connally was also wounded, blood flowing over his handsome off-white Western suit.

Soon after the shots were fired, as Jack Ruby sat in the ad department of the *Dallas Morning News*, "someone ran into the room, shouting, 'The president's been shot! The president's been shot! I just heard it on the radio!'"

> Everyone gathered to watch the news on the television in promotion director Dick Jeffrey's office. . . . Ad man Dick Saunders watched Ruby together with the others as the story unfolded.
>
> "He sat there staring unbelieving at the television set," said Saunders of Ruby. "He was virtually speechless, quite unusual for Jack Ruby."
>
> Ruby watched the unfolding tragedy for about 30 minutes, then he grabbed a telephone. His first call was to Andrew Armstrong, his assistant at the Carousel Club. "We're going to close the club," several ad salesmen overheard Ruby tell Armstrong.
>
> Next, Ruby called his sister, Eva Grant, who seemed as devastated as her brother by the news. "My God, what do they want?!" she screamed into the receiver.
>
> As Ruby put down the phone, he said to Newman, "John, I will have to leave Dallas."

When asked by the Warren Commission what he meant by that, Ruby replied, "I don't know why I said that."

One reason Ruby might have decided to *not* leave town was revealed in a conversation he had about Eva with their sister Eileen that night. As her children recalled,

> "Jack called and he was crying. He was upset, and he wanted to come to Chicago and be with the family for the weekend," one of Eileen's daughters said.

Eileen told him that he should not come to Chicago, urging him to stay and take care of another relative [Eva] who was ailing after a recent surgery.

"I know she felt guilty about that 'til the day she died," one of her daughters said.

Not only did Ruby not leave town, he also made it his business to—for whatever reasons—be *all over* town, engaging in a whirlwind of activity.

12 | FRENZY

THE PRESIDENT HAD BEEN SHOT.

In Dallas.

In Jack Ruby's town.

Ruby went into immediate, frenzied action. It seemed as if he'd long been preparing for such an event.

But before charting his strange quest, before mapping his actions over the next forty-eight fateful hours—before observing how he came to be at a crossroads of history—some understanding of his possible motives for those actions, what endgame he may have had in mind, is necessary.

Even with motives attached, though, much of his behavior that weekend remains inexplicable. When it comes to Jack Ruby, simply detailing his actions—much less the reasons behind them—is a confounding task. Ruby had a hair-trigger temper and little impulse control. Ascribing logic and planning to Jack Ruby can feel like a fool's errand.

Of course, an argument could be made that Ruby was simply "crazy," unfocused, temperamental, unpredictable, unstable, erratic, neurotic, psychotic, immature, flaky, and corrupt and that his actions regarding virtually everything in his life were based on no plan or strategy at all. And yet, it can't be denied that, for all his seeming bumbling incompetence, he did manage to maintain a succession of entertainment businesses, whatever their ultimate financial conditions might have been, and to sustain a network of friends, relatives, and colleagues, whatever level of respect or admiration he might have elicited from them. Most important—however he managed it, whatever help he might have had—he succeeded in getting close to and assassinating a man who arguably, if not in demonstrated fact, *should* have been the most well-guarded person in the world.

———————————

And so, upon hearing of the attack on the president, and after spending some minutes in apparent shock and paralysis, something roused Jack Ruby into action, as if, indeed, he'd long been preparing for it, as if he were some kind of sleeper agent in a paperback thriller.

The question of course is, what kind of event was he preparing for? Was it general catastrophe, always in the back of the mind of a high-strung Jew who'd seen antisemitism in many shapes and sizes, from Nazi rallies in his native Chicago to a cross-burning in the front yard of a Dallas Holocaust survivor? This would be in line with viewing Jack as a "lone nut."

Or was it a specific attack targeted on the president, probably the result of a planned assault by right-wing extremists?

Or could the event have been a well-planned, orchestrated conspiracy of other interests to kill Kennedy, of which he was not a part?

Or was it perhaps a well-planned, orchestrated conspiracy to assassinate the president, to which he was somehow, willingly or unwillingly, connected?

Ruby's activities, based on his own testimony (which can be expected to be self-serving), plus the testimonies of numerous people—some more credible than others, many of them contradicting each other or simply lacking in plausibility—can be interpreted as fitting any of those theories.

Whether you subscribe to the lone-nut interpretation of Ruby's actions or take a more conspiratorial point of view, pretty much every account of Ruby's activities in the forty-eight hours after the shots were fired in Dealey Plaza corroborates one central notion: from the moment of the assault on Kennedy to his own assault on Oswald, Jack Ruby was running around in a manner that common parlance, if not a psychological evaluation, would say was "like a lunatic." Further, many of his actions seemed designed to call attention to himself. This wasn't someone laying low, evaluating circumstances as they developed, enacting a plan—or modifying an existing one. Could he really just have been acting on instinct, no matter what his real or imagined ultimate goal? And why did he feel he had to do anything at *all*? Was he a player in a plot—or was he starring in some movie in his head that only he could see?

Perhaps looking for logic or patterns in Jack Ruby's behavior that weekend is pointless. And yet, understanding Ruby's possible motivations seems key to understanding that weekend and, indeed, the past sixty years of history. And so we try. (It's worth mentioning that, in an era before the existence of surveillance cameras on every corner, establishing a consistent narrative of even Ruby's physical whereabouts becomes a head-spinning exercise in coordinating multiple, often contradictory, testimonies. But let's see what can be discovered.)

Whatever his motivations, Ruby seemed to suddenly be galvanized into action by the shooting of the president. He behaved like a man on a mission. For the next forty-eight hours, his actions were emphatic, though without apparent or consistent logic. Lone nut or key conspirator, here's what he did, and how he responded to what others did:

As reporters at the *News* mobilized into action and hurried off to Parkland Hospital, where the wounded president had been taken, Jack Ruby absorbed the news of the president's shooting, and he, too, soon hurried off. But to where?

Though Ruby would always deny it, reporter Seth Kantor was adamant that he had seen and spoken to Ruby at Parkland, waiting for news among the crowd of reporters. That makes sense. Ruby was known to like to be where the action was.

Some think he headed there (if he was indeed there) because he was somehow part of a larger conspiracy to kill the president, that he was going there to contribute to a purposeful smokescreen to confuse the public about who exactly had committed the murder. This would include Jack somehow possibly planting a phony bullet on Kennedy's stretcher.

But why would he lie about simply being there? He was an easily recognized figure to locals. Conversely, why would a reputable journalist like Kantor not only claim he spoke to Ruby at Parkland but also write an entire book springing from that conversation?

In any case, at 1 PM, Kennedy was pronounced dead, though the public was not immediately informed. According to Kantor, Ruby showed up at Parkland either just before or just after the news of the president's passing was announced at 1:35 PM. Most testimony has Ruby back at the Carousel by 1:45 or 1:50 PM. If he was at Parkland, whatever he did or didn't do there didn't take very long.

By the same token, Rabbi Hillel Silverman, who would become a frequent visitor to Ruby in prison, recalled the following about his own rush to Parkland:

> We were together [waiting for the president at the Trade Mart], Catholic, Protestant, Jewish [clergy], and leaders of the community.... And we sat there, and we were waiting and we were waiting and we couldn't understand . . . what was happening. And I think it was about twelve thirty or so, maybe a quarter to one, there was an announcement "There's been an accident and we're calling off the meeting." And that was the first that I'd heard of it. I was stunned; I couldn't understand what had happened.
>
> I went into my automobile and I went to Parkland Hospital, because I had heard that they brought the president to Parkland . . . which is only five or six minutes away from the Trade center.

When asked if he'd seen his congregant, Jack Ruby, at Parkland, Silverman replied, "Seth Kantor I remember was a very fine journalist. But I didn't see Ruby. I was there at Parkland and I would've noticed him if he was there. . . . He never told me that he was there. He tells me he was somewhere else."

At 1:11 PM, Lee Harvey Oswald, by most accounts, fleeing from the site of the Kennedy shooting, shot and killed Dallas police officer J. D. Tippit in the Oak Cliff neighborhood of Dallas (not far, some would point out, from Jack Ruby's apartment). And at 1:50 PM, Oswald was arrested for Tippit's murder as he hid in the darkened Texas Theatre in Oak Cliff, watching a screening of *War Is Hell*.

Jack Ruby, meanwhile, progressed with his array of activities in almost manic fashion. He was reported having been seen at many places, but only staying a brief period at most of them, sometimes leaving and returning to the same spot multiple times. Most of the places were within a relatively small section of Dallas, not far from his home base at the Carousel.

Ruby's next stop, wherever he was coming from, whether the newspaper office or the hospital, was the Carousel, where he returned around 1:45 PM, ten or so minutes after the announcement of the president's death. Employees Andy Armstrong—a Black man in a city at once deeply racist and surprisingly progressive—and Larry Crafard remembered Jack being there, weeping over the day's events, and making phone call after phone call. When news of Tippit's murder came over the radio, Armstrong reports Ruby as saying, "I knew him," although it would turn out that Ruby was thinking of another officer with a similar name.

Ruby made numerous calls to the Bull Pen, a nearby drive-in restaurant, and spoke with the owner, Jack's Carousel partner Ralph Paul. He considered himself Ruby's closest friend and, indeed, seemed to have sunk tens of thousands of dollars into Ruby and his businesses over the years, money he must have long ago figured out he wouldn't ever see again.

As Ruby told Paul, he was concerned about whether to stay open for business during this time of national and local trauma. Would it seem insensitive and unpatriotic to be hosting strippers and comedians? There were no rules for what do at a time like this. A lot of the decision would depend on what his competitors would do.

Besides the calls to the Bull Pen, Ruby made numerous other calls to friends, relatives, and business associates that day. Some think much of this phone calling was somehow related to one conspiracy or other. Were there calls connected to plans that had gone well or badly? Had Ruby been assigned to do something at Parkland? Was he supposed to somehow either have helped Oswald escape—or to have eliminated him? Or was Jack just an emotional guy trying to maintain his equilibrium with endless talking?

———————

At 2:38 PM, aboard Air Force One at Love Field, Lyndon Johnson was sworn in as president.

———————

During the afternoon, Ruby's calls included one to Carousel stripper Karen "Little Lynn" Carlin. He told Carlin she could drive in from Fort Worth to get pay that he owed her. He was described variously as being "nervous," "half-sobbing," "upset," and "crying."

One notable phone call was the one to his sister Eileen Kaminsky in Chicago, where he told her he wanted to leave Dallas and come to Chicago for the weekend. She told him he should stay put and take care of Eva.

Someone later recalled that, during the afternoon, Ruby was seen carelessly displaying thousands of dollars in cash at a local bank, while hysterically crying. Had he been paid for something? Was he supposed to be paying someone for something? Others claim to have seen him at Dallas police headquarters, trying to get into the office where Oswald was being questioned, Ruby reported as being "happy, jovial . . . joking and laughing."

Ruby's sister Eva, who lived nearby, was recovering from her hysterectomy surgery. Though she and Jack had had a stormy relationship, they were getting along now. She had become distraught over the news of the assassination and asked her brother to come by and commiserate—and also to bring some food. Jack went to the Ritz, a kosher-style deli, and bought an enormous quantity of food to bring to her. According to psychiatrist Walter Bromberg, Ruby told the doctor, "I wanted to get drunk on kosher food."

The purchase Ruby brought for his sister included "three bottles of celery tonic for each of them, a pound of smoked salmon, a pound of roast beef, a pound of smoked white fish, a pound of tongue, bread, onions, oranges, and six cakes." One might assume that this was intended to last a while for the housebound Eva.

But, according to Kantor, the siblings soon lost their appetites, as they watched TV news reports about Oswald. "That lousy commie. . . . We'll get him," Eva reportedly exclaimed.

The Warren Commission asked Mrs. Grant what Ruby replied to that. "He didn't say nothing," Eva Grant responded. "[He] went into the bathroom and threw up."

His doctor, Coleman Jacobson, reported Ruby had called him to find out when their synagogue, Congregation Shearith Israel, would be holding services that night. Not satisfied with whatever Jacobson told him, he also called the synagogue to get the information.

Together, Jack and Eva decided to close their clubs for the entire weekend, no matter what competitors were doing, although Ruby maintained an obsessive interest in their decisions, anyway. According to Eva, Jack was so distraught over the president's murder—"broken, a broken man already," she described him—that he decided he needed to go to synagogue services, though first he would return home to change his clothes. Kantor noted that "Ruby looked so bad that his sister worried about him getting killed in traffic en route to the synagogue."

By some reports, as discussed by Kantor, Ruby indeed went home to change but then, instead of going directly to the synagogue, went first to Dallas police headquarters:

> Shortly after 7 p.m., John Rutledge, a veteran police reporter for the *Dallas Morning News*, saw Jack Ruby . . . step from a public elevator onto the third floor. . . . Ruby was walking with some reporters, pretending to be one of them as they walked toward Room 317, where Oswald was being interrogated. . . . Ruby . . . said he was acting as translator for the foreign press. Eberhardt figured Ruby was acting as translator for the Israeli press or the Yiddish-speaking reporters Eberhardt guessed he heard in the bedlam of the corridor. Soon after, Victor F. Robertson Jr., city hall reporter for WFAA radio and TV . . . saw him again . . . in the corridor, attempting to enter 317, while Oswald was in there. The guard . . . turned him away.

Ruby—who later denied trying to enter the room—claimed he was armed that night, having with him "the pocket-sized revolver [the Colt Cobra] he had bought nearly four years earlier." Ruby would say different things at various times regarding whether he was carrying a gun that night.

Showering and changing clothes at either the Carousel or his apartment, Ruby then attended synagogue services at Shearith Israel, arriving at 10:00 PM, although the service had started at 8:00. Silverman recalled Jack getting there late and seeming quite upset. Silverman had instituted a popular Friday night service at the synagogue, and it was especially well attended because of the day's trauma. The rabbi recalled that

> it turned out to be a . . . grand memorial for President Kennedy. Everybody was in a state of shock and disbelief. . . . And [Jack] came

up to me . . . and I thought it was rather bizarre he didn't say a word about the assassination. He thanked me for visiting his sister in the hospital.

Ruby socialized for a while at the refreshments after services, almost as if nothing unusual had happened. He then drove through town, trying to get a sense of which competing clubs were open and which closed. He noted that Abe Weinstein's Colony Club was open, which upset him. As Weinstein's son Steven recalled,

> Jack Ruby went up to my dad's nightclub that Friday night that Kennedy was killed, and Ruby closes his club, and . . . puts an ad in the *Dallas Times Herald* that he's closing his club that night, that [whole] weekend, because Kennedy just got killed. My dad says, "Well, so it's the weekend—I'm in the nightclub business. I can't close my business." So that night Ruby goes upstairs [to my dad's club, and says], "How could you be open? How could you? How could you not have respect for our president that was killed?" And he starts going off! He took a swing at my dad! And my dad had a, what they called at that time, houseman [named Tex], which in my time we called a bouncer. And he had Tex escort him down the stairs and out the door.

Another of Weinstein's sons, Larry, recalled that Ruby didn't just take a swing at his father that day but threatened him with a gun.

Later that night, Ruby stopped at another deli, Phil's, to order more sandwiches, aiming to take them to the police on duty at the station. (He made a lot of phone calls from the pay phone at the deli, although to whom is unclear.) Was Jack's buying this food an act of generosity? Or did he plan to use the sandwiches in another attempt to get close to Oswald? In any case, Ruby was rebuffed when he called to ask about taking the food into the station.

Seemingly determined to get back onto the third floor at the police station, Ruby again took the elevator up, telling the patrolman who stopped him that he had sandwiches he had to deliver to KLIF newsman Joe Long, who was there covering events for the station. An officer who knew Ruby offered to find Long for him in the throng of reporters. But before Long could be found, Police Chief Jesse Curry and District Attorney Henry M. Wade announced that Oswald would be "put on display in the basement police assembly room. . . . Ruby got easily caught up with the movement of people going to the basement."

Therefore, Ruby was present when Oswald was brought out before the press to allay rumors that he had been beaten. Oddly, Oswald looked like he *had* been beaten—which he had been in the course of his arrest. When asked by reporters if he'd killed the president, Oswald stated that he wasn't charged in that case, that they were talking to him about Tippit, whose death he denied having had anything to do with.

And so, among the many members of the press there that night, wearing his glasses and looking for all the world like one of them, sandwiches seemingly forgotten, was Jack Leon Ruby. The photos from that night of Ruby, perched atop a table in the back of the room, look like someone pulling a prank that today would be called "photo bombing"—reveling in being somewhere he knew he wasn't supposed to be, with no apparent sinister purpose in mind.

Indeed, this has been cited as proof that there was no premeditation on Ruby's part when he killed Oswald, since he was admittedly (in some, not all, of his testimonies) armed at the time. In his notes taken while visiting Ruby in prison, Rabbi Silverman opines, "There was no premeditation on his part. He never intended to see Oswald there." And Silverman quotes Ruby as telling him, "I could have shot Oswald Friday evening, when I saw him with the newspaper reporters. I was only two feet away from him. At that time, I had no intention of doing this. No, the police did not search me when I entered that evening."

Seth Kantor takes a different point of view:

> If Ruby had considered using his gun to execute Oswald then and there, he could not have gotten off a clean shot. Reporters stood on tables in front of him and a barrier of photographers stood before Oswald.

Of course, when he did take the fatal shot on Sunday, that basement corridor was also filled with reporters blocking his way.

Surreally, during DA Wade's press conference, Ruby, from his spot atop the table, corrected Wade when he misstated the name of a group—the Committee for Fair Play for Cuba—that Oswald had belonged to. From the videotape of the press conference, it's clear that a number of reporters corrected Wade at the same time Ruby did. So, though the impression that Ruby somehow showed up the professional reporters is false, it does make one wonder how the supposedly apolitical Jack Ruby knew that Wade had misspoken *and* knew the correct name of Oswald's organization. Of course, as reported by Ruby's roommate George Senator and others, Jack was an avid reader of newspapers. It's possible this factoid stuck with him.

Still, no one seriously questioned Ruby's presence there. And why would they? He was Jack Ruby. The out-of-towners had no reason to think he was out of place there, and the locals all knew him. If anything, the latter would have thought the always-hustling club owner was there on a promotional mission to give free passes to the Carousel to the newsmen. Indeed, as Kantor recalls,

> Ruby was no longer the grim, crying, beaten man he had appeared to be earlier on Friday. . . . Ludicrously, he began shaking hands with out-of-town reporters, handing them "Jack Ruby Your Host at the Carousel" calling cards and urging them to come by for drinks and a show when the club reopened. . . . When New York radio newsman Ike Pappas had trouble getting Wade to his open telephone line to New York for an interview, Ruby went over and got the district attorney to go to Pappas. When KLIF sent Russell Knight . . . the Weird Beard . . . to interview Wade, Weird Beard didn't know whom to look for. . . . Ruby not only set him up with Wade but supplied a question to ask: Is Oswald insane? Wade responded, no.

It goes without saying that Kantor—a respected journalist who died in 1993—was in the conspiracy camp. He saw in Ruby someone who had it in his mind to kill Oswald at least as early as Friday night and who was part of some sort of larger plan. Kantor felt that members of the Dallas police force were in on the plan, possibly to simply allow Ruby to get close to Oswald and somehow use him as their instrument of vengeance against Oswald for his murder of one of their own: Tippit.

Though the DA would try to minimize it, it does seem that he did, at least casually, know Jack Ruby. The relationship was more significant to Ruby, though, than to Wade. Aynesworth recalls an interaction Ruby and Wade had that night, as the strip club owner greeted the DA:

> "Hi, Henry," he said, "don't you know me? I am Jack Ruby. I run the Vegas Club." . . . Bob Jarboe, an Associated Press photographer . . . found that every time he got the D.A. centered in his photo, it seemed Jack Ruby would pop out of nowhere and put his chin on Wade's shoulder, ruining the shot.

Whatever Ruby's relationship with Wade, the enthusiasm and joie de vivre that Kantor observed in Ruby—some might call it mania, in part fueled by the stimulants Jack took regularly—were genuine enough. This was a man in his element, attracting and bestowing attention, seemingly independently of any possible larger plan.

———————

As his manic weekend continued, accounts of exactly what Ruby did differ, but the following is more or less what his activities were.

Around 1:30 AM Saturday, November 23, the same time that Oswald was arraigned for the murder of President Kennedy (up to then, he was being held for the Tippit murder), Ruby left the police station.

En route, he ran across, and had a conversation of disputed length with, Kathy Kay Coleman, a Carousel stripper; her boyfriend, Harry Olsen; and Johnny Simpson, an attendant at Simon's Parking Garage at the corner of Jackson and Field. Coleman, according to Ruby, at some point said of Oswald that "if he was in England, they would drag him through the streets and would have hung him."

From that meetup, Jack took the police-refused sandwiches to radio station KLIF, where the staff gladly accepted them. One employee at the station recalled Ruby as "sullen, quiet, looking at the floor." Another remembered that Ruby showed them a clipping about a speech from H. L. Hunt's *Lifeline* magazine that he was concerned about.

Ruby claimed that he went directly home after leaving the radio station. But numerous other accounts (including a differing account from Ruby himself) have it that, somewhere around 3:00 AM Saturday morning, Ruby showed up at the composing room of another local paper, the *Dallas Times Herald*, to submit a revised ad for the club's weekend schedule to staffer Roy Pryor, who had previously been a Carousel employee. Pryor related that Ruby was "happy about being able to feel like he could assist the district attorney in making that correction" about the name of the organization Oswald belonged to. He referred to Oswald as "a little weasel of a guy," and turned tearful and agitated when he talked of the now-fatherless Kennedy children.

While at the newspaper office, Ruby also showed off the twist board he'd been promoting at the state fair. As Kantor reports,

> Ruby was giving a demonstration on the twist board, with the print-ers gathered around and everyone laughing. Then he encouraged a woman proofreader to get on the board, a performance that Ruby and everyone seemed to enjoy.

Times Herald staff member Kenneth E. Griffith recalled that Ruby had been in a "very jovial mood" that early morning and had "laughingly men-tioned that he had been hanging around the Dallas city hall that night although he was not supposed to be there." He added that Ruby had claimed to have "done favors for unnamed individuals and been allowed to enter city hall that night." City hall, of course, also housed the police station—and Lee Harvey Oswald.

Griffith also recalled Ruby proclaiming that "we are trying to find out who the man really is that placed the ad in the *Dallas Morning News.*" Griffith noted that Jack had said of the name signed to the ad that "it is probably someone posing as a Jew."

Bernard Weissman was still on Jack Ruby's mind.

Sometime around 3 AM Saturday, Ruby returned to his apartment—but not to sleep. He woke roommate George Senator. Senator recalled that Ruby was "patently upset and emotionally disturbed by the shooting of the president" and would break down crying as they sat and spoke. This was the same period of time in which Ruby had been described as acting "jovial." The man's moods seemed to be all over the map.

Ruby then called Larry Crafard, who had been living at the Carousel (in lieu of actual pay), and insisted he get ready for Jack to pick him up—including getting Jack's Polaroid camera, mostly used for novelty shots of club patrons with strippers. Ruby and Senator then drove over to the club and got Crafard. The three of them drove together to the IMPEACH EARL WARREN sign on Stemmons Highway—Ruby later reportedly asked radio personality Russ "Weird Beard" Knight who exactly Earl Warren was—and had Crafard take several Polaroids of it.

Why would Ruby find it so important to get a photo of an object that was in full view every minute of every day? According to Senator, the sign and the Weissman ad had somehow become conflated in Ruby's mind. Senator recalled that Ruby "thought the John Birch Society or the Communist Party or a combination of both were behind the billboard and the ad."

Crafard insisted on being taken back to the Carousel. After depositing him there, Ruby and Senator (although some accounts have Crafard still with them) went to the post office branch mentioned in the Weissman ad to see if, despite the place being closed, they could find the box mentioned in the ad. Although they couldn't get to the box, they saw that it was filled with mail. The apparent popularity of the ad infuriated Ruby.

As Aynesworth puts it,

> Recalling that the *News* ad had included a post office box address for Weissman's and Schmidt's "committee," Ruby's next and last stop . . . was the downtown post office, where an employee refused to provide the box holder's name.

And Kantor writes,

> Ruby looked through a slot in no. 1792 [the box in the Weissman ad] and grew angry when he saw it was filled with responses. . . . Ruby couldn't get to Bernard Weissman. There was no such person in the Dallas phone book. . . . Ruby didn't know who was behind the movement to impeach Warren yet. And for all he knew it was the same

people who may have concocted a Jewish name to sign to the hateful advertisement aimed at President Kennedy.

Ruby and Senator then went back to their apartment and went to sleep. It was approximately 6:00 AM on Saturday morning. But an 8:00 AM phone call from Crafard, calling from the Carousel, jarred Ruby awake. Jack's dogs that he kept at the Carousel needed food and there was none. Ruby snapped at Crafard for waking him up but didn't address the problem. Crafard, unwilling to put up with what he saw as Jack's ongoing abuse, took that opportunity to leave town. He hitchhiked out of Dallas, with only seven dollars to his name, five of which he'd taken from the Carousel cash register, heading for his sister's home in Michigan.

But while Larry Crafard took himself out of Jack Ruby's orbit, Ruby himself was just getting started.

13 | MANIA

RUBY SLEPT FOR ANOTHER COUPLE OF HOURS, then continued his jet-fueled weekend. He went over to Eva's in time for them to together watch a special televised Sabbath morning service from New York's Central Synagogue memorializing the murdered president. The service was conducted by Rabbi David Seligson, who, in his eulogy, pointed out the irony of Kennedy having survived savage combat in World War II only to have been murdered in peacetime. He remarked,

> Our president was a victim of the violence of our times, the miscreant spirit that stalks through our land, that shoots men in the back, that blots out the lives of little children, that spits and howls at our statesmen, and that finally shatters the life of the leader of our country and the free lands everywhere.
>
> Such a man was he . . . forthright, dedicated in spirit, resolute in his hopes for a nobler America, determined to write a new charter for the oppressed and downtrodden, to ensure peace with honor. May we be worthy of his sacrifice.

Ruby later claimed Seligson's eulogy was one of the things that motivated him to kill Oswald.

On Saturday morning Ruby was also reported seen by Frederic Rheinstein, a producer and director for NBC News. Rheinstein, who was aboard an NBC mobile unit parked in front of city hall, recalled that Ruby "put his head through the open window of our remote truck." Ruby was also reported seen that morning by Philippe Labro, reporter for a French newspaper, on the third floor of Dallas police headquarters. Labro recalled that Ruby gave him a business card and invited him to have a drink at the Carousel.

Ruby was also spotted in Dealey Plaza, "walking around, talking to people. . . . It is possible that Ruby had come to Dealey Plaza because, like Dan Rather and many other people, he expected Oswald to be transferred to the county jail that afternoon." A policeman on the scene said that Ruby seemed "deeply morose, obviously troubled."

Ruby was still preoccupied with whether other Dallas entertainment venues, not just the other strip clubs but restaurants and bars as well, were going to be open or closed for the rest of the weekend. He visited a number of the open ones, at least in part to chide them for being open, but also because he seemed to just need places to go.

His first stop was regular Ruby haunt Sol's Turf Bar, across the street from the Carousel. The bar was owned by E. R. Solomon, and people recall it as "a hangout for many Dallas area ruffians" and that "there were always fun characters hanging out there." The clientele included "bookies and pressmen not interested in the Press Club across the street." Sol's was known for its authentic pizza and pastrami. It was also close to the fondly remembered Commerce Street newsstand, which sold adult publications as well as science fiction paperbacks.

At Sol's, Ruby ran into his accountant, Abe Kleinman, who recalled that he discussed the Weissman ad and its possible antisemitic subtext with Jack. There, Jack also talked to local jeweler Frank Bellocchio, who announced that he wanted to move out of Dallas. The assassination, he said, had brought to light how horrible the city was. Ruby angrily berated the jeweler, who had prospered in Dallas, for wanting to abandon the city in its time of distress. As Bellocchio recalled for the Warren Commission on June 27, 1964,

> I believe I told Ruby that much of what had happened, Dallas could take the responsibility for. . . . His attitude toward that—he was very incoherent. He was agreeing with me and he was disagreeing with me. . . . I told Jack Ruby I felt like letting my business go and moving from Dallas, and I remember Ruby telling me not to get excited, that there were a lot of good citizens in Dallas and not to hold everybody

responsible. . . . He was calming me down—yes, but at the same time,
I showed him . . . the Weissman ad.

The ad enraged Ruby, who declared it was part of a right-wing plot to
defame Jews. He also thought that the black border around the ad meant that
whoever placed the piece knew that Kennedy would be assassinated. Bellocchio continued:

> His reaction to this was that this was perhaps the work of a group
> of individuals trying to stir up trouble here in Dallas, racial trouble
> here in Dallas. . . . I assumed he meant an anti-Jewish feeling. . . . He
> was in a sense trying to pacify me.

But while pacifying Bellocchio, Ruby was working himself into a fury. He
showed Bellocchio one of the Polaroids of the IMPEACH EARL WARREN billboard and then, himself, started railing against Dallas. "He seemed to be taking
two sides," Bellocchio recalled. "He wasn't coherent." Bellocchio proceeded:

> [The photo] upset him greatly, and at this point he seemed to be
> verifying my supposition that Dallas was responsible. As I said, he
> seemed to be taking two sides. . . . I asked Ruby if I could have one of
> the pictures. He said, "No." . . . He said he had some sort of a scoop
> and wanted to see that the right persons would get the photographs.

Ruby then drove to Dealey Plaza, where he again gave guidance to out-
of-town reporters gathered near the makeshift memorial to the president that
had sprung up. There, he spoke with Dallas Police Department officer James
Chaney, who had been riding his motorcycle behind Kennedy when the bullets
struck. Ruby abruptly pulled away because, he reported, he was about to break
down crying. (This might be the same visit to the plaza Ruby was reported to
have made earlier.)

At the plaza he also spoke with radio personality Wes Wise, who recalled
that when the topic of Caroline and her brother John-John Kennedy came
up, he saw tears in Ruby's eyes. Ruby offered to cover the Oswald transfer
from city to county custody the next day on behalf of Wise's station, KRLD.
He also called Kenneth Dowe at KLIF and made a similar offer. Both men

declined. On the other hand, it was reported that, sometime that day, at the Nichols Garage next to the Carousel, Ruby was overheard by garage attendant Garnet Hallmark as he spoke to a "Ken" at Wise's station KRLD radio about the upcoming Oswald transfer, saying, "You know I'll be there."

At some point, Jack called his attorney, Stanley Kaufman, telling him that he'd put the Weissman post office box "under surveillance." Kaufman explained to Aynesworth,

> He told me he had tried to get Weissman's address at the post office, and said he was "helping law enforcement." He was rabid about the Weissman ad. He thought the black border had an inner meaning, proof that the man knew the president was going to be assassinated . . . he was really frantic.

Ruby's next stop was back at Dallas police headquarters, his purpose there unclear. He handed out at least one business card—so he wasn't sneaking around. NBC's Frederic Rheinstein claims he saw Ruby going into Henry Wade's office.

Around 6 PM, Ruby went back to the Carousel, where he told Andy Armstrong to call the dancers and tell them the club would be closed again that night. He asked Andy to stay until 8 PM. (Later he would call—probably from home—to ask Armstrong to stay until ten, but Andy refused and went home. Perhaps Ruby wanted him there to explain to any arriving dancers or customers why the club was closed.)

Ruby then spent some time back at Eva's apartment. But he appears to have been home at about 8:30 PM when Carousel stripper Karen Carlin ("Little Lynn") called him from Abe Weinstein's Colony Club. She had apparently not gotten the word that the Carousel would be closed and desperately needed the money Jack owed her, which he'd told her to come to town to get. She had driven to Dallas from Fort Worth expecting to get the payment, only to find the club was closed. Ruby became angry at her but promised he'd be there in an hour to pay her.

For unknown reasons, Ruby didn't show when he told Carlin he would. When Carlin called him again, finding him still home, Ruby called an attendant at the Nichols Garage and asked him to advance Lynn five dollars, which Jack would reimburse him for. The attendant did as he asked, and Carlin picked up the money. Jack promised Lynn he would wire her the balance the next day.

One might wonder, why not just have Carlin come to his apartment for the money? Ruby didn't like to have his dancers—who he felt often had violent boyfriends or husbands—come to his apartment or to even know where he lived. He preferred to do business with them at the club.

Around this time, Chief Curry announced that Oswald would be transferred the next morning at 10:00 AM. This was greeted with general skepticism, many thinking they would do it well before or well after that time in order to throw off anyone wishing to do Oswald harm.

Though Eva would claim that Jack had called her from his apartment a little after 10 PM on Saturday night, it seems he was also continuing his survey of Dallas nightlife. Ruby made his way to rhythm-and-blues venue the Empire Room, at the Statler Hilton Hotel. There, he chatted with manager John Henry Branch, who recalled Ruby handing out five-dollar bills to random customers that night, something he would regularly do, likely as some sort of promotion for his clubs. Jack then proceeded to the Cabana Hotel's nightclub, where he met a visiting friend, Chicago sporting goods salesman Lawrence Meyers, for coffee. Meyers, like so many of Ruby's friends and acquaintances, was rumored to have mob ties. Ruby complained to Meyers about the Weinsteins keeping their clubs open while his was closed. Ruby seemed to Meyers very upset over the assassination.

Concluding his evening's forays on his Via Dolorosa of Dallas nightlife, Ruby stopped off at the Pago Club, where, over a Coke (Ruby rarely drank alcohol), he complained to a waitress about the place being open. He then chatted with owner Bob Norton, who angrily declared that "we couldn't do enough to the person" who had killed the president. Ruby didn't respond but simply announced he was tired and was going home.

And then, sometime between 1 AM and 5 AM, after calling Eva to see how she was doing, Jack Ruby, at home, finally went to bed. He would not get much rest.

14 | ASSAULT ON HISTORY

NOW IT WAS SUNDAY MORNING, November 24.

There are reports of Ruby having been seen around 8:00 AM near the police station, where WBAP-TV employee Ira Walker recalled Ruby sticking his head into his news truck's window and asking, "Has he been brought down yet?"

Ruby himself claimed that he was home asleep then, woken by a call from Elnora Pitts, his cleaning woman, at around 8:30 AM. She was checking to see if it was okay for her to come over and clean, as she did every Sunday. Ruby told her to call before she came over. She replied that's what she was doing. The entire conversation struck her as odd, and she wondered if the person she was speaking to might not even have been Ruby, an observation of great interest to conspiracy theorists. If he wasn't home, where was he? Out stalking Oswald? And who was it who answered the phone? Whoever the person speaking was—the logical one would have been roommate Senator, but no one seems to be claiming that—he told her to call back later because he was "going out."

Whether he had been at the police station or not, Ruby was woken at home around 9:30 AM by a call from Little Lynn, still desperate for the rest of the money Jack owed her. No one has cast doubt on it being Jack to whom she spoke. Ruby told her he would drive to the Western Union office and wire her the money. He would recall that he then made himself some breakfast and that he wept as he read a column in the *Dallas Morning News* entitled "Letter to Caroline," saddened by imagining that, as the article noted, the Kennedy family would have to endure coming back to Dallas for Oswald's trial.

According to Senator, as Ruby was about to leave with his favorite dog, Sheba, he had "a strange look on his face, almost as if he were in shock." And according to Ruby's own testimony, it was then that he indirectly told Senator he intended to kill Oswald. In his testimony to the Warren Commission on July 18, 1964 (months after his trial and conviction), Ruby recalled saying to Senator something like, "If something happened to this person, that then Mrs. Kennedy won't have to come back for the trial." Ruby then dressed himself in a suit and tie.

This didn't register as important to Senator, who didn't take it seriously and seemed to not have grasped the possible subtext of Ruby's comment—that he, himself, was going to make sure "something happened" to Oswald. He understood Ruby to simply be saying that he was going downtown to wire the money to Carlin and to take Sheba over the Carousel and take care of some business at the club.

Seth Kantor makes a salient point about this series of events. It was a Sunday, and certainly Ruby was not going to church, and he knew that the Carousel would be closed that night. Nonetheless, he didn't dress in casual clothes. As Kantor notes,

> [Ruby] had on his snap-brim grey fedora, a white shirt, an all-silk black tie, charcoal brown suit and black shoes. It was hardly the kind of attire one would normally wear in Dallas on a Sunday, to take a dog down to a place of business that was closed. Instead, Ruby was dressed to blend in with the scenery of where he actually was going. He was dressed precisely like a detective and he never did take Sheba to the club.

Kantor hypothesizes that Ruby dressed formally, like a detective (or, for that matter, a reporter of the era), to camouflage himself among the crowd at Dallas police headquarters. This is part of Kantor's case for Ruby being part of a coordinated plan set into motion by a subgroup of the DPD, involving decoy sums of cash Ruby was carrying to give himself an excuse to be carrying his gun and selective use of a second, unlisted phone at Ruby's apartment to make surreptitious arrangements with police for Ruby to "coincidentally" be at the right place at the right time.

Driving away from his apartment building, Ruby, as he later recalled, stopped to chat with a neighbor about repairs being done to the place. This did not seem to be a man in a hurry. According to Ruby, he even detoured a bit to get another look at the improvised memorial at the assassination site.

By the same token, Walker and other WBAP staffers in the news truck recalled Ruby asking them again at about 10 AM, "Have they brought him down yet?"

Continuing his drive to the Western Union office, Ruby recalled noting that a crowd was gathering at police headquarters down the block from it and figured it had to do with Oswald. But he apparently took no direct action regarding whatever was going on.

Instead, after executing an illegal turn to save time—did he have some kind of deadline?—Ruby parked his Oldsmobile, leaving Sheba in the car, and walked to the nearby Western Union storefront. There, he waited patiently in line and, when it was his turn, arranged for the money to be wired. The counter clerk gave him a receipt stamped 11:17 AM. That was more than an hour after the announced time of Oswald's transfer—and even longer after the earlier transfer that many assumed would have taken place.

No one really believed that the announced schedule of Oswald's transfer was the real time. To evade just such an attack as Ruby's—or even an outright lynch mob—various plans for the prisoner's transfer had been considered, including sneaking Oswald away completely out of sight of reporters and onlookers. As Aynesworth reports,

> [Chief Curry] denied that he was put under any official pressure to display his prisoner to the press, even though it was widely rumored that Dallas City Manager Elgin Crull had instructed the chief to make Oswald's transfer "an open move, so people can see Oswald was not mistreated." . . . Late on Saturday, over the vehement objections of his senior staff, Chief Curry told reporters they wouldn't miss anything next morning if they were on hand at City Hall by ten . . . "I told them, promised them they'd see the man moved," [Curry said]. "I want them to see we haven't abused him."

At any rate, coming out of Western Union, Ruby then walked toward the crowd at police headquarters. He would later say that he saw the commotion and his curiosity led him to want to see what was happening. And why not? That Jack Ruby would have felt it was important that he see what was going on makes perfect sense.

Ruby walked over to the scene of the commotion and—unchallenged— strode down the garage ramp (or perhaps took a different door, one that might have, intentionally or not, been left unlocked and unmonitored) and into the basement where reporters were awaiting Oswald's walk through a police-lined corridor, en route to the vehicle that would move him from city custody at the police station to state custody at the nearby county jail. (Kennedy's murder was designated a state, not a federal, crime, largely because, absurd as it seems, the most Oswald could have been convicted of under federal law was five years. There were no laws specifically against assassinating a federal officeholder.)

This is where a nexus of skepticism and controversy exists, the heart of many conspiracy theories: How could Jack Ruby, armed with a .38 caliber Colt Cobra revolver, slip so easily into a building filled with police guarding the most reviled man in the country? Surely *someone* must have had a hand in allowing Ruby such easy access.

Ruby claimed that he had, indeed, been unchallenged, the ramp unattended as he approached, the assigned guard distracted by a moving vehicle he had to direct. But even had a guard been there, who would have questioned the presence of such a familiar denizen of downtown? Everyone knew Jack Ruby. They saw him all the time: on the street, at the bank, at the local restaurants, at his clubs, at this very police station.

But whether Ruby unthinkingly sauntered into the building—following some inner need to be where the action was—or whether he was alerted to Oswald's movements by someone in the building and allowed to enter by accomplices in the police department or as the result of some other pre-arranged assignment, he did indeed find himself in the basement as the police-flanked Oswald was walking through. The prisoner was handcuffed to Detective James R. Leavelle, although *not* to Detective L. C. Graves, who was on his other side.

It was then that Jack Leon Ruby stepped out of the crowd and fired one bullet into Lee Harvey Oswald's abdomen at point-blank range.

On national television.

Witnessed by millions of people.

Oswald collapsed to the ground, dragging Leavelle, to whom he was handcuffed, down with him.

As Leavelle recalled in a May 24, 2017, note to historian Gary Dunaier,

> If Graves had [also] been hooked to Oswald that day, I would not be here writing to you today. I would be in the graveyard. Graves saved my life that day. I saw what was about to happen as soon as I stepped inside the garage. Ruby was standing in the crowd of officers and reporters, holding the gun in his left hand, pressed against his left leg.
>
> I made my move and he made his. I jerked on Oswald, pulling him behind me. Ruby switched the gun to his right hand and pulled the trigger. Me pulling Oswald to the right caused the bullet to hit Lee on the left side just under the ribcage.
>
> Like I [sic], L. C. saw what was happening. With his left hand he grabbed Ruby's right wrist and with his right hand grabbed the cylinder of the pistol so it could not turn and fire. Ruby, trying to keep up with Oswald, had moved the [gun to the] left enough that now it was pointed at my left side about the same spot where Oswald was hit. He could have got off one [more] shot or possibly two. Had L. C. . . . not grabbed it as he did I would have got one, or more likely two, under my rib cage. I called L. C. Graves my HERO for the rest of my life.

Police and reporters then tackled Ruby to the floor and grabbed his gun. All the while, he kept repeating, "You all know me! I'm Jack Ruby! You all know me!"

If they didn't before, they certainly did now.

Jack Ruby's frenzied forty-eight hours had come to an end.

His—and the nation's—three years of madness were about to begin.

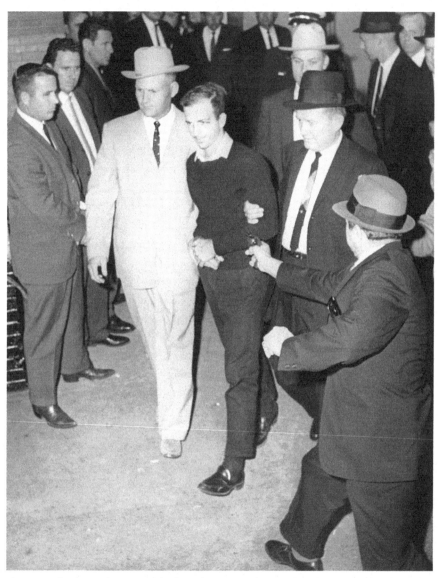

Photographed a split second before the actual firing of his history-changing shot, Jack Ruby advances on Lee Harvey Oswald. No one seems to realize, even this instant before the shooting, that the attack is coming. *Photo by Jack Beers Jr., courtesy of Wikimedia Commons*

15 | HERO OF THE PEOPLE

YOU'D THINK THAT MURDERING Lee Harvey Oswald on live television would essentially be the end of Jack Ruby's story. What could even the best lawyer do to counter that irrefutable evidence? Shoot a guy on live television, you're going to go to go directly to jail, probably get the electric chair.

But while Ruby's crime was clear, the road to his punishment (and some form of justice) would prove to be a twisted one. While to some conspiratorial ways of thinking, killing Oswald solved a problem for somebody, for most people—including Jack Ruby—it created countless problems, very few with satisfactory solutions. If Kennedy's assassination had given birth to a million questions—starting with, "Was it even Oswald who fired the shots?"—then, with Oswald's death, there was no chance of ever getting any useful answers from him. People would fill in their own answers.

Though he was interrogated by numerous agencies in the forty-eight hours preceding his death, Oswald reportedly gave no responses of substance, insisting he had nothing to do with either Tippit's or Kennedy's death. Astoundingly, there was not a single working tape recorder at Dallas police headquarters with which to capture any of his testimonies. This is one of the maddening circumstances that makes people question the entire official narrative of the assassination. Was there no reporter to borrow a recorder from? No store at which to buy one? Even in 1963, portable tape recorders were readily available, used in many homes for entertainment and amusement.

In any case, there is no electronic record of Oswald, who would die within two hours of being shot, having said anything meaningful behind closed doors.

And here was Jack Ruby, from whom avalanches of words would eventually flow, now the focus of attention.

Among the numerous theories about Ruby's motives was one that proposed that he was attempting to not merely do away with Oswald but also commit "suicide by cop." In a room filled with armed police, how could they *not* shoot Ruby after he shot Oswald? And with Ruby's life off the rails, his businesses failing, no romantic partner, no prospects—why not go out in a blaze of glory? Kill the guy who killed the president—and then get killed *yourself*. Make all your problems go away—and go down in history as a hero!

But the Dallas police were gun shy. They didn't want to risk anyone in that crowded room getting wounded or killed—Dallas's reputation had already been damaged enough. Plus, since Ruby was tackled by half a dozen or more police and reporters a split second after firing his shot, there wasn't really any time for anyone to shoot him.

There would now be endless complications in the case of the murder of John F. Kennedy. Attention that had been focused on Oswald would now be focused on Jack Ruby. There would be times when Ruby would seem to thrive on the attention he'd brought himself, other times when it seemed to be killing him. There were times when he seemed to feel like he owned the world, and times when it seemed like the weight of the world was crushing him.

Unlike Oswald, Jack Ruby would talk—and talk and talk and talk (except on the witness stand)—to anyone who would listen. And yet, because of the lack of consistency and logic in things he said, the world would get no more definitive answers from him than they got from Oswald, despite the endless torrent of verbiage that Jack would emit. Was it sound and fury, ultimately signifying nothing—or was the world too ignorant to know how to interpret his many pronouncements?

Shooting Oswald was, it turns out, just the beginning of Jack Ruby's dramatic, maddening, heartbreaking, infuriating final act.

———————

While Lee Harvey Oswald's life slipped away, Jack Ruby, stripped to his underwear, was interrogated inside an office in Dallas police headquarters. There, he was questioned by Agent Forrest V. Sorrels of the Secret Service and Sergeant

Patrick T. Dean of the Dallas Police Department, neither of the interrogations recorded. Reports of what Ruby supposedly said were later heard from testimony from the two interrogators, among other witnesses, including that he wanted to show the world that "Jews do have guts." Some would even claim that Ruby had said something similar as he was being tackled immediately after the shooting. He would also supposedly tell Sorrels that he shot Oswald "for Mrs. Kennedy's sake, to spare her and her children the agony of a trial." While Ruby's words to these men would naturally be important at his trial, *when* he said them would turn out to be equally significant.

Seth Kantor believed that, during the conversation with Dean, Ruby was actually briefed on what to say in any interviews going forward, that Dean was part of a police-backed conspiracy that gave Ruby the opportunity to kill Oswald.

In any case, while Ruby was being interrogated, his family, despite what seems like constant squabbling, went into action to save him. Whatever he had done, this was still their brother, and they didn't want to see him die. DA Henry Wade didn't share that sentiment.

And so now began Jack Ruby's odyssey through the justice system.

The entire process relating to Ruby's trial, unsurprisingly, preoccupied Ruby and his family—not to mention his lawyers—for the more than three years he lived after killing Oswald.

The trial, including various hearings before and after it, played a significant role in the evolution of America's view of itself, its feeling toward minorities, and the use of a trial as theater—which would come to a peak with the circus trial of the Chicago Eight (later Seven). Ruby's trial was filled with strange and combative things said by both sides. And, significantly, running through the proceedings was the ever-present notion that this was history being made.

For that and other reasons, the courtroom was filled with reporters and curiosity seekers every day—people started lining up for seats at 4 AM—especially the day the verdict was delivered. The historical aspect was why so many directly involved in the trial were writing or planning to write about it, from the lawyers to the judge, to Hillel Silverman, whose insightful notes shed light on fascinating aspects of the process and on Ruby himself.

Though Silverman's entry into events might have been based on some combination of concern for a congregant and a desire to be on the inside of a historic event, it does seem that he was soon swept up in becoming a participant in the trial and its preparations, sitting next to Ruby at crucial points in the process and being included in meetings with Ruby's defense team and family.

Silverman seemed, in his own way, to be as concerned with the public's image of Jews—in Dallas and in the world at large—as Ruby was. The rabbi also did genuinely seem to be concerned with Ruby, both as a person and as a symbol, and to genuinely want to keep him from being executed. (It's also quite possible, though unknown for a fact, that Silverman may have been philosophically opposed to the death penalty.) Strategizing with Ruby's lawyers and visiting him more than would seem necessary, even if he was taking notes for a book about the trial, Silverman seems to have become swept up in the events and emotions of the situation.

The rabbi had a history of intentionally, often nobly, placing himself in challenging and even dangerous situations. The Ruby case may have "cured" him of that, as he would abruptly leave Dallas within a few months after the trial, well before the appeals could be decided, venturing into high-profile Jewish institutional situations, though ones involving significantly less peril. For now, though, he was very much involved with Jack Ruby.

Jack Ruby's trial—including the preparations leading up to it—would take on a life of its own. And once the verdict was in, things would only get weirder. Let's face it, when a member of the prosecution team, when asked if he thought Ruby had organic brain damage, responds, "Well, we'll send them his brain from Huntsville [where the state's electric chair is installed] so they can find out," then you know this trial was more than a bit unconventional.

That prosecutor, assistant DA Bill Alexander, also said of Ruby that he "was about as handicapped as you can get in Dallas. First, he was a Yankee. Second, he was a Jew. Third, he was in the nightclub business."

The trial inhabited its own reality, whatever convulsions may have been taking place in the world outside. In Jack Ruby's universe, victory in court was the only game. The existence of a possible conspiracy or cover-up seemed to disappear in the courtroom, although it was always there in the background. But the trial was narrowly focused on whether Ruby was legally sane when he killed Oswald. Context was minimized by both prosecution and defense, except when either thought it might score a shot against the other side.

Nonetheless, the road to the verdict and beyond is fascinating and illuminating and crucial to the story of Jack Ruby.

For his part, Earl Ruby had been, as he so often was, working at his Cobo Cleaners in Detroit when he heard the news about his brother's deed. As he recalled,

> I'm sitting in the office, talking to a friend of mine in Chicago . . . and he says, "I gotta hang up. Somebody just shot Oswald." . . . I was with a friend. . . . We get in the car. We drive off. I turn on the radio . . . and we hear "A man named Jack Ruby has been identified as the one who shot Lee Harvey Oswald." . . . You know, I . . . pulled over to the side. . . . My friend said I turned white as a ghost . . . and from then in, really, the tumult started. That night I went to Chicago, to the home on Loyola Avenue, where my brother [Hyman] and two sisters lived. [The FBI] interviewed each of us separately.

Years later, Earl would recall that Jack called him from the Dallas jail later on the day he shot Oswald, and said, "Earl, I think we're going to get a lot of good publicity out of this," which is what Earl thought too, seemingly contradicting what he'd recalled about his initial response. "He thought they'd book his brother, and that he would be released as a hero. 'I was naïve; we were naïve,' he said." One can imagine that multitudes of different thoughts, often inconsistent with each other, would run through the mind of someone who, like Earl, found himself suddenly thrust into the middle of history-shaking events.

Eva Grant was the Rubenstein sibling who was first on the scene after Jack's arrest. She had quickly arrived for a meeting with attorney Tom Howard, who had inserted himself into the case. Howard had a storefront office across the street from the police station. A stylish dresser, he was in the habit of defending small-time clients: hoods, pimps, lowlifes—not a high-class roster. But the lawyer had a successful record of getting murder-case clients off with relatively light sentences, especially when their crimes could be considered acts of passion. As John Kaplan and Jon R. Waltz, authors of *The Trial of Jack Ruby: A Classic Study of Courtroom Strategies*, note, "Tom Howard had tried twenty-five other capital cases and in each his client had escaped the death penalty."

It's uncertain if Ruby himself was at this meeting, but it seems unlikely. One way or another, though, Ruby—considered fully competent—would have had to be part of the process of vetting and approving Howard's being hired out of the numerous lawyers who showed up, eager to represent this high-profile potential client.

As for how that first day went for the beginnings of Ruby's defense, Wills and Demaris explain,

> Five lawyers showed up Sunday afternoon trying to arrange for bail for Ruby. . . . Taking his friend Ralph Paul's advice, he accepted Howard as chief counsel, with Jim Martin to assist. Howard's strategy was clear—to go for "murder without malice," a charge on which juries are lenient in Texas. . . . Every lawyer we [Will and Demaris] talked to in Dallas believed that Howard was taking the right approach.

Having been chosen from all the contestants, Howard, after his meeting with Eva, then walked across the street to his office. There, he had a phone call, surreptitiously eavesdropped on by Hugh Aynesworth, who reported that it was a conference between Howard (in the room), Earl Ruby (calling in from Michigan), and superstar lawyer Percy Foreman (also calling in), "the most famous criminal lawyer in Texas history. . . . Percy had won something like 300 straight murder cases." Howard wanted to bring Foreman onto the case.

However, according to Aynesworth, Earl had taken a dislike to Foreman and was also outraged by his demand of $75,000 (more than $700,000 today) to join the defense. As the most financially successful of the Ruby siblings, Earl would have to shoulder the lion's share of expenses for the case, and his resources were not infinite. Earl would soon have his own idea of who he wanted on the case, and it wasn't Percy Foreman, nor any of the Dallas lawyers so eager to join the party.

Around this same time, Ruby's apartment was searched by police. The search warrant was issued by Judge Joe B. Brown Jr., the son of the man who would eventually oversee Ruby's trial. The police team was headed by homicide detective Gus Rose. As their search was described by journalist Dave Reitzes,

> Rose arrived at Ruby's apartment at about 2 PM that Sunday. . . . "I showed the manager the warrant and she let us right in," Rose recalled in an October 1992 interview. "We were there for about an hour and a half, and we searched the place thoroughly." . . . According to Rose, the search failed to turn up anything of significance. . . .
>
> "We collected a few notes and telephone numbers that had been written on pads, but that was about all we took. Once we were finished, we just locked the place back up and left again." According to Brown's posthumously published book about the trial, they also found "a copy of the morning newspaper opened to a picture of the President's assassination."

Hours later, George Senator, Tom Howard, and some other men, including a few reporters, would return to the apartment, not realizing anyone had been there. They were looking for photos of Ruby that they could publish but didn't find any. Nonetheless, as would be the case with many people connected with the Kennedy assassination, several of the men who visited Ruby's apartment would die in ways that some have linked to a possible conspiracy, despite the fact that the deaths all seemed to have plausible, if in some cases unusual, explanations.

Jack Ruby, now dressed in prison garb, was paraded before newsmen. He was smiling but seemed a bit confused. He joked with reporters, seeming to be enjoying the attention. As he was fingerprinted, he made small talk with the man doing the job, Ed Carlson, a cop he'd once saved from harm in a brawl on South Ervay Street, and joked about how, with part of a finger missing, they wouldn't be able to get a full set of prints from him.

With his actions, Ruby had relieved himself of the mundane problems that had been dogging him and had entered a hall of mirrors where—now the center of attention—the details of his life and the condition of his mind would become of importance to the entire country. While the nation mourned and feared for the future—what if the killings were part of a Russian plot or a coup d'état?—Jack Ruby was riding high.

Interestingly, plenty of people thought he did, indeed, do the right thing—what they would have wanted to do if they had the chance and the guts. He received many messages of thanks and congratulations, hailing him as a hero. For a guy who'd always wanted to be revered and admired, this was perhaps the peak of Jack Ruby's life.

Shortly after his arrest for shooting Oswald, Jack Ruby found himself in prisoners' clothes, posing for his official mug shots. That same day, he was photographed in handcuffs. Despite his grim demeanor in these photos, Ruby was reported as seeming relieved, joking with Dallas police officers and staff. *Dallas Police Department (mug shots), US National Archives and Records Administration (handcuff photo), both courtesy of Wikimedia Commons*

Some selected telegrams read as follows:

> WE LOVE YOUR GUTS AND COURAGE.
>
> WELL DONE SOLDIER. MISSION ACCOMPLISHED.
>
> CONGRATULATIONS MR. RUBY YOU REDEEMED THE STATE OF
> TEXAS.
>
> YOU ARE OUR HERO.

Jack Ruby's actions reverberate to the present day. The nation and its politics were and would be shaken. But what often gets lost in the recounting of historic events is how the lives of people related to the players can be affected. It's worth hearing what a niece and a nephew recall about their Uncle Jack's actions, and how it impacted on their lives.

Earl's daughter, Joyce Ruby Berman, who was nine in 1963, would remember:

> I was at a sleepover birthday party for the rabbi's daughter [the day Ruby killed Oswald]. My mother came to pick me up early . . . and I heard her talking to the rabbi's wife. I didn't know what was going on. So I go home, and there were cops everywhere, and I had to stay in my room.
>
> There was another rabbi's daughter [my age], and he and his wife wouldn't let this other person my age come overnight. We had moved to a suburb of Detroit just a year before, where we didn't know anybody. Then, all of a sudden, everybody knows you—my parents were on the cover of *Life* magazine! I was escorted to school by the Southfield Police Department, and we had police at our house for a few weeks, because there were crank calls, weird scary letters. My parents were worried [for our safety], since we got threatening phone calls and letters.
>
> Some kids were nice, like, "I'm sorry about what happened" . . . but some people were mean, name-calling. And there were some people who wouldn't let their kids come over to our house. I didn't quite understand that. Did they think my father was gonna kill them?
>
> Then, in middle school . . . it's in the history books. People start asking all these questions. I didn't have any certain answers . . . and I don't know anything except what my dad told me.

And when she was in college, at Michigan State,

> somebody came to speak . . . about how there was a conspiracy [involving Jack], and people that knew me gave me such a hard time. I would avoid people. I didn't want to talk about it. . . . I kind of got tired of defending myself.

Interestingly, Joyce studied criminology in college, though she didn't pursue it as a career. Earl—who recalled that her classmates would tease her with the nickname "Killer Ruby"—thought her crime studies might indeed be because of what her uncle did. Joyce is less certain of that but realizes it's possible.

Sam Ruby's son, Fred, who was twelve and living in Dallas in November 1963, recalled the following:

> There was a Civic Light Opera in Dallas. . . . We had school tickets sold for the matinee on Saturday, and that got canceled and pushed off to Sunday.
>
> It was my mom's turn to drive carpool, and she's getting dressed, and I'm watching the TV. I see the assassination [of Oswald] happen, and I yell out, "Hey, some son of a bitch shot that bastard!" My mom comes out, pissed off: "Don't use that kind of language!" And almost immediately, they said it was my Uncle Jack. And I literally saw the color drain from her face. You could see the blood draining out. . . .
>
> The phone rang, it was her best friend saying, "I just saw the news. Sit down. I'll run the carpool for you." And nobody said anything to me about it at the performance, on the way there, on the way back.
>
> In school Monday, nobody said too much, but the gym coach used to go to one of [Jack's] clubs all the time. I guess he was dating one of the strippers on and off. . . . Grady Chapman was his name. . . . Grady must have told the school bullies, "You stay away from the Ruby brothers or you will deal with me personally." . . . So nothing [bad happened to me] in elementary school. . . . When I got to junior high a couple years later, all bets were off. I was getting pounded on daily [for being related to Jack Ruby].
>
> And everybody [in school] knew it was my uncle. You've got an uncle that owns a strip club, you think you're *not* going to tell

[people] about it? And then our family life was deteriorating badly. . . . We had to raise money for lawyers for Jack, which threw us under a bus. That's something my younger brother never quite put together, why we were so poor all of a sudden. I told him about it as an adult, and he didn't quite believe me. Earl Ruby was very wealthy. . . . So my dad sold off all his laundromats to raise the same kind of money that my Uncle Earl was giving, because he needed to show up his rich brother. . . . We were living hand-to-mouth.

It was embarrassing [to be Jack Ruby's nephew]. I felt shame. I'm related to this asshole who killed the president's assassin, and now, because that guy's dead, we'll never know what really happened. I'd say the Warren Commission was pretty close, if not spot-on. But, then again, even if they had photographic proof, and all kinds of scientific evidence and DNA and everything else, there'd still be doubters, because you can always make money by starting a conspiracy theory and writing a book about it.

The entire family [Jack and his siblings] had very short fuses and very bad tempers, being raised by a seriously alcoholic father and a mentally ill mother. It's a product of a bad childhood. It's classic. Jack walks in, sees Oswald, doesn't even have a rational thought, just impulsively acted. That's my perspective on it. I mean, in my mind he couldn't have planned it out. . . . He gets there, sees Oswald, and just *boom!*

That shot dramatically ended Oswald's life. But for Jack Ruby—and his family—*boom!* was just the beginning.

16 | SEARCH FOR JUSTICE

DESPITE THE OPINIONS OF SOME OBSERVERS at the time that any competent attorney could get Jack Ruby a reasonably light sentence, DA Wade had made it abundantly clear that his goal was for Jack Ruby to die in the electric chair. Knowing this, Jack's family—with Earl taking the lead—was determined to get the best legal representation for their brother that they could. At the same time, they were also looking for someone to write—from Jack's point of view—his side of the story, hoping to sell the story to newspapers to raise funds to *pay* for those top lawyers.

With this in mind, Earl contacted his old high school classmate Mike Shore, the possibly mobbed-up cofounder, with Frank Sinatra, of Reprise Records. Shore directed them to William "Billy" Woodfield, an accomplished writer and ghostwriter, notably for Caryl Chessman, famously sentenced to death for heinous crimes, though not for murder (and eventually executed). Woodfield not only took on the ghostwriting assignment but also suggested to Earl that he engage Melvin Belli, then possibly the most famous lawyer in America, to defend his brother. Woodfield arranged a meeting between Belli and Earl in Los Angeles.

At the meeting, Belli expressed great interest in the case, saying that he "thought that a successful insanity defense was possible . . . that the case . . . offered a perfect opportunity to bring the law of insanity up to date while helping Jack Ruby." Of course, to be brought on to the case, Belli would have to be approved by Ruby himself, not just his family.

Dissatisfied with the first lawyers they had hired to defend their brother, the Ruby family enlisted Melvin Belli (seen here in a 1967 photo), perhaps the most famous lawyer in America at the time, to plead his case. *Courtesy of Wikimedia Commons*

Ruby, for his part seemed to, oddly enough, be enjoying himself. He loved the attention he was getting and seemed to think he would serve little or no time. He was allowed to entertain visitors and to make calls on a pay phone. His jailors supplied him with change to make those calls, likely in hopes of monitoring the calls for statements on either side of the conversations that would enable them to bring the most serious charges possible against Ruby (and any possible coconspirators) and, perhaps, to unearth solutions to some of the mysteries that might have died with Oswald.

Belli recalls:

> The FBI . . . made sure [Ruby] had access to a pay telephone, and they gave him a great sack of nickels and dimes. . . . He started to telephone everyone he could think of—people he had known, people he read about in the newspapers, people he thought could help him.

Needless to say, the bell had hardly stopped tinkling on the other end [of the phone] before lawmen arrived, demanding to know what the party knew about Jack Ruby, how they had conspired together, and so forth. Many of the people Ruby called had hardly heard of him.

His calls went all over the nation in a pattern so random that, I am told, those sober-minded FBI men decided that this was the most complex conspiratorial communications pattern that they had ever seen . . . before the FBI finally gave the operation up.

The first nonfamily, nonlawyer visitor Ruby requested to see was Joe Campisi, the restauranteur and likely mob boss to whom Ruby reportedly remarked about Oswald that "somebody had to kill him." Ruby also called his friend Tony Zoppi, nightlife columnist for the *Dallas Morning News*. Zoppi remembered getting the call:

I was having lunch at the Kings Club, and [someone] came over to my table, and he said, "You got a telephone call—a fellow by the name of George."

So, I said, "That's Jack Ruby."

He said, "No, no. His name is George."

I said, "I know."

Every time I'd see Jack, he'd talk a little jive talk. . . . I'd see him, and I'd say, "How are things going, Jack?"

He'd say, "Real George" . . . When things were going good, it was "George." That was an expression.

Interestingly, Zoppi was the only person to mention that Ruby would sometimes speak in showbiz argot, reminiscent of the insider language used by Sinatra's Rat Pack. Zoppi continued:

I said, "Jack, why in the hell did you do it?"

And he started to cry, and he said, "Those poor kids left without a father." . . . He was really upset. . . . "I know what it is to be raised without a father." . . . Then he said, "I didn't want Jackie to have to come down here and stand trial with that Commie rat."

These would be reasons Ruby would give many times, a story that he may have concocted with one or more of his lawyers. But here, within days of his arrest, either Ruby had mastered this alleged motive this early, or, given his crying, might have actually believed it to some degree. Of note is that this narrative is at odds with what would be the defense's contention at trial, that killing Oswald was spontaneous and unplanned.

Ruby then tearfully announced that he was going to tell Zoppi "something I've never told anyone." Instead of some kind of confession of a conspiracy or heretofore-unknown motive, Ruby instead expressed regret about his inability to carry on a personal tradition with a local orphanage. He said, "Every year I took gifts to every kid in that orphanage, and to the nuns. . . . And here it is, it's going to be Christmas . . . and nobody's going to get a gift."

Then, Zoppi recalled, in a lightning-swift mood shift that epitomized Jack Ruby,

> He was sobbing. And all of a sudden, he stopped and he said, "And I wanted to prove there was one Jew with guts." Very belligerent.

On Monday, November 25, three funerals were held.

The first was the elaborate, choreographed hagiography that was the burial of President John F. Kennedy. The second was the tear-filled burial of Officer J. D. Tippit. And the third was the small and bizarre funeral of Lee Harvey Oswald. Though history would certainly not leave those three alone, for the men being mourned, their active participation in their lives' sagas had ended.

Jack Ruby's surreal journey was just beginning.

That same day, Ruby was transferred to the county jail—without the type of violent interruption that had shattered Oswald's transfer—and indicted for the murder of Lee Harvey Oswald. Kaplan and Waltz recount the situation:

> In dramatic contrast to the efforts which had been made to accommodate the press at the time of Oswald's abortive transfer, Jack Ruby was moved without warning. An unmarked car containing Ruby and four detectives raced over the fifteen-block course from the Dallas

city hall to the county jail just before noon. . . . No crowd had time
to gather.

Ruby, they continue, "alone in a three-cell block in the county jail, became a
model prisoner."

———————

Also on November 25, Assistant DA Bill Alexander in effect tricked Ruby onto
being examined by the state's psychiatrist without an attorney for Ruby present. Alexander brought Dr. John T. Holbrook to see the prisoner, telling Ruby
that, as he had been friends with Jack for thirteen years, Alexander wouldn't
do anything to harm him. Alexander later recalled what happened:

> I said, "Jack, if you're crazy, you should be in the insane asylum; and
> if you're not, we're going to burn your ass."

Ruby asked Alexander what he would do in his place. Alexander advised Ruby
to talk to the psychiatrist.

The trap was laid. Ruby agreed to be examined. The next day, Alexander
announced that the state of Texas was going to prosecute Ruby for murder and
ask for the death penalty. Apparently, Jack had passed the psychiatric exam.

———————

Despite the fact that he had been known for pretty much his entire residency
in Dallas as "Jack Ruby," the indictment for the murder of Oswald was against
"Jacob Rubenstein." And to hear the recording of Chief Curry reading the
indictment to reporters, practically sneering the name, it's hard to not think
that the intent was to make sure that the entire world knew that it was a Jew
who had killed Oswald. This is not necessarily to implicate Curry as an anti-
semite, but rather to indicate that, in 1963, even with Jews relatively prominent
in the city, bigotry was so ingrained in Dallas's culture as to not be given a
second thought.

Interestingly, in a meeting with Hillel Silverman on January 13, 1964,
Henry Wade made a point of telling the rabbi, "I want you to know that

I did not intend to be antisemitic when I used the name Rubenstein and not Ruby."

Silverman, who frequently visited Ruby in prison, often several times a week, starting a day or two after Ruby's crime, wasn't sure if he was asked to do so by Jack or his family or just decided on his own to visit his imprisoned congregant. As he said, "I have a feeling that I took it upon myself, though he might have asked, I just don't remember. . . . And I know that he wanted to see a rabbi, or *his* rabbi, because he asked me for a Bible and . . . for a prayer book. And he wanted someone to bring him a bit of inspiration and comfort."

The rabbi made elaborate notes after his visits to Ruby. It is from them that we have some of the most intimate looks at what Ruby was going through, the evolution in his behavior, and what subjects he thought important to explore.

Like many involved in the Ruby case, Silverman was contemplating writing a book about it, which is one of the reasons the notes were taken. The rabbi, who passed away in April 2023, never did write that book (in 2013, he told me he had abandoned his plans to do so). His visits with Ruby, though, do occupy a few pages of his 2009 memoir, *The Time of My Life.*

As Silverman's notes recounted, the first time he visited Ruby, either on Monday, November 25 or Tuesday, November 26,

> I brought with me an English translation of the Bible. I asked him to read this while he was in his cell. He said to me, "Thank you, but I don't read Yiddish." I told him that this was an English translation.

It's curious that Ruby would assume the Bible Silverman brought was written in Yiddish, when most Bibles used by Silverman's Conservative Movement (and probably edited by his father, Rabbi Morris Silverman) would have been in Hebrew, not Yiddish, with accompanying English translation. Earl Ruby has noted that when he and his siblings wanted to speak privately, they would converse in Yiddish. It certainly would be plausible, though, that the American-born Jack Ruby would not necessarily be able to *read* the language simply because he was able to speak it colloquially. He also might simply have thought that the Hebrew text was Yiddish, which uses the Hebrew alphabet, neither of which he seemed able to read.

Though Silverman doesn't specify a date for his next visit, since he visited Ruby two to three times a week, we can calculate that it was within the next few days. He recalled the second visit:

> [Ruby] told me that he had read from the book of Daniel. His jailor, Stevenson, a member of the Four Square Gospel Church, is a fundamentalist Baptist. He has been telling Jack stories from the Bible and explaining them to him. Jack had read the entire book of Daniel. . . . He told me that, "Daniel also had many problems and faced them with great courage. This Book will give me courage, too."

It's generally been assumed that Stevenson was, at the most benign, trying to encourage Ruby to convert to Christianity and, at worst, trying to lull him into admitting some kind of premeditation—or possibly both.

On the rabbi's third visit, somewhere within a few days of the second—approximately a week after Oswald's murder—Silverman observed,

> [Ruby] had begun to read from the book of Judges. "I liked the story of Gideon and the Trumpets, Samson and Deborah."

Although the Bible can work as metaphor, consolation, and inspiration, and so almost any section that Ruby would cite could plausibly be interpreted in terms of his situation, it's worth noting the Bible tales he mentioned to Silverman. The story of Gideon is about a small band of soldiers tricking a much larger, more powerful enemy, using loud trumpets to make their own forces seem larger and more formidable, leading to victory. The biblical Samson was defeated by Delilah, then regained his strength and triumphed. And Deborah was a warrior prophet who led the Children of Israel to triumph in battle, which ushered in forty years of peace. All three stories are about adversity overcome and happiness achieved.

Right after his entry about Gideon, Samson, and Deborah, Silverman reported that

> Jack Ruby said to me, "The other night I saw God and a picture of my mother."

Then, immediately following that, Silverman recounts that Ruby launched into a seemingly unrelated story regarding the time he called the synagogue to inquire about services on the night of Kennedy's assassination, how the call made him angry that synagogues charge money for holiday seating, but that when it was explained to him that they need the money to continue operating, he calmed down.

If this is how the conversations early in Ruby's incarceration went—bouncing from the poetic and hallucinatory to the mundane and trivial—then it does seem a harbinger of the increasingly strange progression of Ruby's thought processes. As time would go on, based on the recollections of Silverman and others, we can almost observe Ruby's thinking becoming less and less reality-tethered, taking trips into uncharted territories, but always returning to some semblance of reality. Ruby would spend the next few years negotiating between reality and fantasy. Some may say it was all acting, that everything he said and did was planned and contrived with an agenda behind it. If that was the case, then Jack Ruby was the greatest actor that ever lived.

Ruby certainly seemed to be living on multiple planes, and this changing relationship with reality would only become increasingly pronounced. Arguably, his crime and arrest accelerated what was probably brewing in him for a while. In his mind, he was the central figure in a drama—like Daniel in the lions' den—in a world where he believed that the fates of entire peoples were determined by *his* actions, where he was simultaneously guilty of multiple, serious crimes and innocent as a lamb.

While Silverman doesn't state—as perhaps Ruby did not—whether Ruby saw "God and a picture of my mother" in a dream or in a hallucination, it certainly seems as if much of Jack's mental energy was being spent on things that only he could see and understand.

During that first week, before Melvin Belli arrived in Dallas, Ruby asked to see former Carousel entertainer Breck Wall. Despite their earlier falling out, they had, indeed, made up. As Wall recalled, after Kennedy was murdered, Ruby had said to him that "the man who shot the president deserves to be killed."

Wall thought he was just "rambling on and on," not making an actual threat. Wall recounted that, on the Saturday after Ruby shot Oswald—six days after the killing—he received a call about Ruby from Sheriff Bill Decker, telling him, "Jack is extremely depressed . . . majorly . . . and we're really concerned about him. He keeps talking of you and it seems like you're the only one that can sort of cheer him up. . . . Would you come down and visit with him?"

The police sent a car for Wall and drove him through the crowds of people clamoring to get into the prison, presumably to get a glimpse of Ruby. Wall was taken to see Ruby in what the performer described as not a cell but "a tank, and there was a little glass that I could see him through and talk through a perforated hole." He continued:

> There was someone [a guard] in there with him. . . . And the minute [Jack] saw me . . . he had a big smile on his face and he was happy— as happy as someone could be, under the circumstances. . . . And he asked me if I would be . . . not publicity director but [do] PR, I guess. . . . He had gotten so many telegrams and what have you . . . people were thrilled that he did it, and then people were furious he did it. . . . He had gotten . . . about 500 letters and wanted to know if I would answer them and represent him, like a spokesman. . . . I told him I wasn't qualified . . . that he should pick somebody else. And he said, "No, because I trust you . . . and I know that you'll represent what I say."

Ruby also, according to Wall, told him, "I was right to kill Oswald."

Wall declined the offer to direct his friend's publicity, despite his warm feelings for Ruby. "We had a type of friendship that, when you see each other, you start laughing right away," he recalled. "He certainly wasn't like a brother, because you couldn't have Jack as a brother, but he was . . . kind of a joke buddy. . . . He liked me and enjoyed me . . . we had that kind of friendship. I was the last person he talked about before he died."

Andrew Armstrong, the African American Carousel bartender, also visited Ruby regularly to ask advice on managing the still-open nightclub. He reported,

"Jack talked as if it would be no time before he was back running things." Indeed, a lawyer who reached Ruby even before Howard did opined, "He never expected to spend a night in jail." And that, weirdly, was almost the case, thanks to Judge Joe B. Brown Sr., who would end up being the judge in the Ruby case.

Brown "had been taking his turn supervising the grand jury in a four-judge rotation when Oswald, and then Ruby, was indicted, so he would automatically try the case." Like Belli and Ruby, Brown loved the spotlight. That passion of the judge's would eventually be critical in determining Ruby's fate.

For now, the largest problem that Brown posed was that he was the judge in Candy Barr's marijuana case, where Jack Ruby's close friend Barr had been sentenced to prison despite the best efforts of her lawyer, one Melvin Belli. Belli and the judge had butted heads during that trial. Bill Alexander had been the prosecutor in the case, as he was now, with Wade, in Ruby's.

But Belli hadn't arrived in town yet, and the players in Dallas's legal world were often friendly and casual about legal matters. So when Tom Howard—before being replaced by the Ruby family—requested Ruby's release on bond, the judge readily granted a writ for it. Amazingly, it seemed, briefly, as if Jack Ruby would be set free pending trial, as if he was a well-intentioned guy who had simply gotten a little carried away after some Saturday night drinking.

But Bill Alexander was on the job and got Brown to change the writ to a "dry writ," one that requires a hearing before the prisoner can be set free. The hearing was scheduled for December 23. Ruby would stay imprisoned at least until then.

Even regarding Brown's appointment to the case there is controversy. As Kaplan and Waltz note,

> Judge Joe B. Brown had the duty of assigning the judges . . . for trial. In the case of *State v. Jack Rubenstein* . . . to no one's great surprise, he executed the prerogative of assigning it to himself. . . . Despite the reported urging of his good friend Henry Wade that "this case is too big for you," Judge Brown would not reassign the case.

On November 29, President Johnson announced the formation of what has come to be called the Warren Commission, a group tasked with discovering the facts surrounding the murders of John Fitzgerald Kennedy and his presumed assassin Lee Harvey Oswald. The commission, it was predicted, would investigate and report, and the public would soon breathe easier, knowing the incontrovertible facts about everything and everyone connected to those shattering events.

17 | INTO THE MAZE

RUMORS OF POSSIBLE CONSPIRACIES were spawned the moment JFK was shot. And so, on November 29, partly in hopes of setting such speculation to rest, President Johnson appointed Chief Justice Earl Warren to head up the President's Commission on the Assassination of President Kennedy. The group was created to investigate the killings of Kennedy and Oswald, charged by the president to "satisfy itself that the truth is known as far as it can be discovered." That Earl Warren would head the investigation was strangely resonant, as one of Ruby's obsessions was about a possible threat to the man.

The commission was staffed by men who were or would become prominent, some who seemed to have an agenda going in. For instance, Allen Dulles, former head of the Central Intelligence Agency until he was fired by Kennedy in the wake of the Bay of Pigs, was a commission member. It was highly unlikely that he would shed light on any alleged participation in a conspiracy to murder the president from within the government.

Besides Warren and Dulles, the other commission members were:

- Senator Richard Russell Jr., Democrat of Georgia
- Senator John Sherman Cooper, Republican of Kentucky
- Representative Hale Boggs, Democrat of Louisiana, House Majority Whip
- Representative Gerald R. Ford, Republican of Michigan; future US president (1974–1977)
- John J. McCloy, former president of the World Bank

More than 550 witnesses would testify before the commission, and also to the FBI, which was also investigating. Though Jack Ruby had spoken to the FBI soon after shooting Oswald, nothing he reportedly said to them revealed anything of great significance. And, as his lawyers insisted, he would not testify before the commission until after his trial.

That the commission was composed only of white men was perhaps not so unusual for 1963. More troubling for historians and scholars over the decades was that the commission was composed of government insiders, men who could credibly be accused of having a don't-rock-the-boat agenda, or worse, starting with Dulles, who had a history of conflict with President Kennedy.

Of course, some of the theories regarding who might have wanted the president dead involved Lyndon Johnson himself. Johnson, the ultimate political operator, had been bitter about losing the Democratic nomination to Kennedy in 1960 and was now on the verge of being *indicted in connection* with the unfolding Bobby Baker scandal. Even if possible subterfuge on Johnson's part regarding investigating the assassinations could simply be attributed to his fear that Kennedy's murder might be linked to the USSR and could have triggered a nuclear war (as opposed to the more nefarious theory that it was part of a coup led by Johnson), it does seem as if the composition of the commission was almost designed to cast doubt on its ultimate findings. Of course, it was pretty much inevitable that *any* group Johnson appointed would be distrusted simply because *he* had appointed it, especially by those who thought that he might have been behind the assassination in the first place.

To add to the complexity of the Warren investigation, before it was convened, J. Edgar Hoover's FBI had already started investigating the assassinations. Those agents involved, in effect, ended up as investigative agents for the Warren Commission. But Hoover's goal was to do a short, sweet investigation, conforming to the narrative of both Ruby and Oswald as unstable independent operators. The commission's findings would, ultimately, be much the same, but would take much longer to reach.

Unsurprisingly, the FBI's original haste has led to many conspiracy theories involving the agency, and in the short term led to conflicts between the FBI and the commission. There were also divisions within the commission itself as to what its priorities should be, especially regarding the passionate conviction on the part of younger staff members that truth, not political expedience, was paramount.

The Carousel Club had reopened under the direction of Ruby's business partner, Ralph Paul, although, as the *New York Times* reported, "the strippers have been back on the job, what zest they had for their work somewhat muted. . . . Most of the tables were empty . . . with dancers, musicians, waitresses, and bartenders going through the motions."

Meanwhile, Jack Ruby was adjusting to life in prison, entertaining visitors and strategizing his defense with his siblings and lawyers. As Melvin Belli would recall of Ruby's incarceration, it was in a remarkably clean prison, upstairs from the courthouse where Ruby would be tried. Belli describes the cell as

> a square room, its only furnishings a toilet bowl and a mattress on the floor. [Ruby] kept his clothes . . . folded on the mattress. A small window at the rear of the cell led to some sort of ventilator shaft. . . . No prisoners were allowed in sight of Ruby's cell. Sheriff Decker . . . was taking no chances. There was a table in the hallway across from Ruby's cell, and a guard sat there night and day, making sure that Ruby came to no harm.

Belli's behavior at his first meeting with Ruby was in keeping with the lawyer's general modus operandi, but certainly not what the Ruby family or Tom Howard was hoping for. Kaplan and Waltz report the following:

> The Ruby family had expected that Melvin Belli would slip quietly into Dallas for the interview [with Jack] and were somewhat upset by the fact that the San Franciscan's arrival received a great deal of publicity and that Belli had wanted a photographer [from *Life* magazine] to accompany him into Ruby's cell to take a picture of him with the prisoner.

At the prison, though, Belli and Joe Tonahill—a tall, three-hundred-pound Texan, who cut quite the intimidating figure, and who would be part of the defense team—met Ruby, not in his cell but in a ten-foot-by-ten-foot interview room. Belli recalls Ruby as wearing white jail coveralls and being "a distraught little man with a face like a ferret . . . burning with intensity . . . his dark eyes brilliant as if he had taken an overdose of Benzedrine. He was clean-shaven and neat. . . . He gave an incredible performance [for us]."

Belli felt Ruby out, trying to see just what his client was all about. Ruby spoke nonstop for three hours and would have gone on longer had Belli and Tonahill not grown fatigued, while Ruby was "stronger than ever." Belli took away from this conversation that "clearly there was something wrong with Jack Ruby." The lawyer also notes:

> There was one weird trait. Unfailingly, at the mention of a member of President Kennedy's family, tears would start to course down his cheek. . . . It was too spontaneous to be an act. I am convinced of the sincerity of this affection, although I am just as convinced . . . that the affection could not have been a preconceived motive for the killing.

Belli believed that when Ruby shot Oswald, he had been triggered into a fugue state in which he acted automatically, which was one version Ruby had been telling of his story, a version that seemed to have been forgotten. Ruby now seemed to be buying into the idea that he had killed Oswald so that Jackie Kennedy and the Kennedy children wouldn't have to return to Dallas to testify at Oswald's trial. Belli believed that either Ruby himself or someone else had devised that story (which, if true, would have made Ruby's act premeditated), and Ruby had latched onto it because he needed to believe his actions *did* have motivation.

Belli observed about Ruby overall, "On and on he chattered; and amid the scramble of words the lack of concentration, of perception, was startling." Indeed, Belli was very concerned that Ruby would sabotage his own defense. But there was nothing Jack Ruby liked to do more than talk.

Still, as Belli told Wills and Demaris, something was compelling to him about Ruby's case. "I try to be clinical," he told them, "but I guess I'm at my best when someone's kicking the shit out of some poor little Jew boy. Then I can take them all on." These words, spoken after the trial and verdict, were at odds with how Belli would view the perceived use of the term "Jew boy" during the course of the trial. (Apparently, Texas musician Kinky Friedman was paying attention to the Ruby trial, and a decade later would dryly call his country-western band the "Texas Jewboys.")

Ruby seemed glad to see Belli from the first meeting and was glad to hire him as his lead attorney, agreeing with his kid brother's selection. When the three-hour conversation was over, Ruby told Belli that he wanted to see him alone the next time. Was there something Jack thought he couldn't share with Howard and Tonahill? (A bright young attorney named Phil Burleson—an expert in local Texas legal minutiae—would also become part of the defense team.)

The next meeting (not the private one with Belli that Ruby had requested) lasted *eight* hours, and, again, the lawyers tired out before Ruby did. With the expertise of a lifelong schmoozer with virtually unlimited phone access, Jack told Belli that an acquaintance in Chicago had told him good things about the lawyer. Belli introduced Ruby to lawyer Sam Brody of his office. Ruby pegged Brody as Jewish—"a landsman." Ruby asked if Belli was sure having a Jew in the case was a good idea. "We already have one," Belli replied. "You."

According to Belli,

> [Ruby's] main jail activities seemed to be keeping himself clean and keeping in shape. He took as many hot showers as he was permitted . . . [in a] communal lavatory that had been cleared for his use, and he would shower while the guard watched. He was a health fanatic and was very concerned about his diet. He used to exercise in his cell.

He also notes that

> Ruby read very little, except for his Bible. He had been a voracious newspaper reader outside, but in jail he read few of the stories about him. He did say he got angry at his favorite columnist, Dorothy Kilgallen, when she wrote that he was a gangster, so apparently the stories made some impression on him.

Kilgallen would become a persistent footnote to Ruby's story, both in life, and then in her—to some—mysterious death.

As time went on, Belli noticed that DA Wade and his staff seemed to know more about Ruby than they should have. Fearing that the information might be coming from Stevenson, the guard who talked religion with Jack, Belli asked Ruby what he had told the guard. "I told him everything, Mel," Ruby replied, seeming to not understand the problem.

What he meant by "everything" was, in part, the story about wanting to spare the Kennedy family from having to return to Dallas for Oswald's trial. Belli was now even more convinced that Ruby's need to believe what the lawyer saw as an invented story was a sign of Ruby's much deeper psychological problems. He felt that Ruby "kept trying to convince himself, or someone had tried to convince him, that he really could fill in the blanks" in his memory. The blanks were what Belli believed to have resulted from Ruby's lapse into a fugue state when he shot Oswald. This was to be the basis of the lawyer's defense strategy.

But whatever strategy there was, it risked being torpedoed if Ruby couldn't keep his mouth shut. As Belli notes,

> Ruby turned out to be a demon information dispenser. He spent a good bit of his jail time scribbling memos to us, usually on the most inconsequential things. . . . But this erratic man had the habit of writing things that, improperly interpreted, could cause him all sorts of trouble if they got out.

Dan Abrams and David Fisher put it this way in their book *Kennedy's Avenger*:

> While Ruby was silent during proceedings in the courtroom, he was practically rambunctious speaking to the media. He gave daily press conferences before the sessions began, at every break, and when done for the day. . . . Belli and Tonahill urged him to hold back . . . but Ruby couldn't resist. . . . Jack Ruby had become a celebrity.

On December 4 Dr. Holbrook showed up in Ruby's cell again, but this time, Belli was on the case and told Ruby not to speak with him. Holbrook came with a battery of psychological tests, which Ruby refused to take. But according to Belli, "By then, [due to] my own suspicions about Ruby's mental soundness aroused through my conversations with him, I was arranging to bring in some of the nation's leading doctors to test him." What those doctors would find would startle Belli and lead, before long, to his decision about how the case should be handled.

Belli called in Dr. Walter Bromberg and Dr. Manfred S. Guttmacher to examine Ruby during the week of December 22, before Ruby's first bail hearing, and Dr. Roy Schafer on December 29–31, after it, to do the same. All found that, to one degree or another, Ruby was legally insane. Also, in a change-of-venue hearing, he would try to get the case moved out of Dallas, where he believed Ruby couldn't get anything resembling a fair trial, the city too traumatized by what had happened there.

In the period before the change-of-venue and bail hearings, Robert B. Denson, private investigator for the defense team, had made some findings and recommendations that he thought of utmost importance. Denson's investigations, though, had in part led Belli to erroneously believe that Judge Brown would eventually grant a change of venue, which would lead to some strategic missteps on Belli's part. Denson felt that Brown "is extremely sensitive to political pressures, especially from wealthy and influential persons. He is a vacillating figure whose personality can be capitalized on. . . . Although he could change overnight, it appears at present that Judge Brown will favor change of venue."

Denson thought that, if a change of venue was granted, San Antonio would be a good alternative trial city:

> San Antonio, being largely Mexican and Catholic, is a city having some rather strong minority groups. Burlesque operations and coexistence with vice are a part of its accustomed way of life. . . . There is a marked tolerance for actions triggered by emotional outbursts.

Likewise, he opined that Beaumont, Texas, would be a good place to get the trial moved to because "Beaumont supports an unusually large prostitute population and open vice has always been the rule there. . . . They are also notorious for light murder sentences."

On December 23, Jack Ruby's first bail hearing began.

"'I feel wonderful,' Ruby announced to onlookers as he was led into the courtroom by guards." He seemed to believe that bail would be easily granted and he would soon be out on the street.

The defense strategy, including its request to have bail granted, was to show that Ruby's attack on Oswald was unpremeditated. Key to that narrative was the fact of his presence, on the morning of Oswald's murder, at the Western Union office, seemingly in no hurry, as he wired money to Little Lynn. The dancer herself was scheduled to testify at the hearing on Ruby's behalf.

Unfortunately, for her and for Ruby, as Lynn was being searched before entering the courtroom, a gun was discovered in her purse.

Denson, who accompanied Lynn, said that she didn't know the small, 6.35 caliber Italian pistol was in her purse. As Elmer Gertz, author of *Moment of Madness*, recounts, "It had apparently been there for a long time, and it had no firing pin and no ammunition." She would be allowed to testify but, "so far as the public and the court were concerned, the tiny gun in her purse had destroyed the credibility of her testimony."

But this was not enough to dampen Ruby's spirits. As Belli recalls,

> After the first bail hearing . . . he welcomed us to the interrogation room upstairs with a jovial commentary on which prosecution witnesses he would like and which he wouldn't. As it turned out, he had them pretty accurately spotted.

However, Belli also notes,

> As the hearings moved along, he began to get confused, and his demands for attention, always heavy, began to mount. . . . To the end, he maintained that the people in the police department and the district attorney's office were his friends.

Belli was requesting bail for Ruby, though he knew it was highly unlikely to be granted, on the premise that, in addition to Ruby's presumed lack of premeditation, Jack would need more detailed mental examinations, which he couldn't get while in prison. To Belli, this was the most important reason for making the effort to get Ruby out on bail.

The lawyer also felt that he might be able to gain some important insight into the prosecution's intended strategy during a bail hearing. This was the point at which Belli's strategy took over from Tom Howard's. Belli was not going to try for a "murder without malice" strategy. He felt that he could get an acquittal for Ruby with an insanity defense.

Interestingly, during the hearing, when Joe Tonahill made a motion seeking to have both sides agree that Oswald had acted alone and that Ruby and Oswald had no prior relationship, Wade responded, "We ain't agreeing to nothing." This statement, unsurprisingly, fueled numerous conspiracy theories.

Belli was unsuccessful in getting bail for Ruby. Judge Brown denied it "for the present," and another hearing was scheduled for January.

Although Belli saw Ruby as being jovial after the first bond hearing, Hillel Silverman had a different experience of him. As would become more and more common, Ruby had taken to speaking to the rabbi (and others) in a strange word-goulash. Of one conversation with Ruby shortly after the first bond hearing, Silverman wrote,

[Ruby said:] "I am more sympathetic to the American public." I assume he had [made] reference to the psychiatrists labeling him as emotionally disturbed. He added, "Yes. I am more sympathetic, but they see I am not a martyr or a patriarch."

Suddenly, he exclaimed, and this was the first time he voiced the sentiment, "I hope I didn't hurt the Jews."

Silverman recorded in his notes that, in between the two bail hearings, on January 13, he met with Wade, which was when Wade told the rabbi that "I did not intend to be antisemitic when I used the name Rubenstein and not Ruby." Silverman believed that Wade was sounding him out, since he would be cross-examining the clergyman at Ruby's hearings and trial. Wade asked Silverman if he would testify that Ruby was insane. Silverman recalls, "I looked at him skeptically and non-committedly said, 'In my role as clergyman, I shall testify to his character. I am not a psychiatrist.'"

Wade then told him that the prosecution would try not to inject the "Jewish issue" into the trial, but there was no getting around the facts that Ruby had attended services on Friday night and that Ruby had told people at the court-house on Friday night that he was "an interpreter for the Jewish newspapers." Wade maintained that, even though he had come to the phone when Ruby beck-oned him, he "did not recognize him nor had he ever spoken to him before."

Silverman wrote:

> I reported to Jack what Henry Wade had said concerning his remark that Friday evening, "I am an interpreter for the Jewish newspapers." Jack Ruby denied ever making that statement, though it seems to me that his denial was not strong enough. Obviously, he was covering up.

That day, when Silverman met with Ruby, he found him playing cards with Stevenson. Ruby showed the rabbi a note Stevenson had written to him weeks before concerning faith in God. The note contained the words of Psalm 27, which Ruby had copied over and kept in his wallet. "He continually recites this to give him faith and courage," Silverman recalled.

Psalm 27 contains these lines:

> *Do not reject me or forsake me, O God my Savior.*
> *Though my father and mother forsake me, the Lord will receive me.*

The specific verses Ruby found especially meaningful in his favored Book of Daniel were these:

> *My God hath sent his angel, and hath shut the lions' mouths, that they have not hurt me.*
> *Forasmuch as before him innocency was found in me; and also before thee, O king, have I done no hurt.*

During Ruby's second bail hearing held on January 20, 1964, Belli called the prominent psychiatrists who had examined Ruby to testify. Dr. Roy Schafer testified that Ruby apparently suffered from an organic brain disorder that he called "psychomotor epilepsy" and that people with this condition "if emotion-ally distraught, are typically subject to uncontrollable and explosive behavior."

Dr. Walter Bromberg agreed, noting that he was convinced that when he shot Oswald, Ruby was in a "fugue" state, "where consciousness is impaired and acts are committed without conscious thought."

Kaplan and Waltz note, "The whole of the second bail hearing was disorderly as the prosecution and defense traded jabs and insults. . . . Its most disorderly moment took place during the cross-examination of Dr. Bromberg" by Bill Alexander. Alexander, responding to a statement Bromberg had made about Ruby getting overly excited when discussing sports as a boy, asked whether it wasn't true

> that a Jewish boy like that [Ruby] discussing baseball scores with
> somebody from Chicago, would do it with different mannerisms and
> gestures than maybe a couple of colored gentlemen of African descent
> in South Dallas.
>
> Melvin Belli leaped to his feet and shouted, "I didn't get that—
> 'Jew boy'—is that what he referred to?" . . .
>
> It is . . . likely he [Alexander] was trying to upset the defense and,
> if so, he succeeded. Throughout the trial, Belli—still quoting Alexander as saying "Jew boy"—brought up the incident again and again.

The defense then called Dr. John T. Holbrook, the psychiatrist Alexander had maneuvered to examine Ruby before Belli became involved in the case. Belli was able to get Holbrook to agree that "before any final diagnosis . . . could be made, the performance of additional neurological tests was vital."

Also testifying was Rabbi Silverman. He averred that "Ruby was so emotional and unstable . . . that the rabbi had pondered seriously whether to recommend psychiatric treatment for him." And then, as if underlining Silverman's testimony,

> Ruby displayed a variety of moods throughout the . . . hearing. Paying close attention to . . . the witnesses, Ruby would nod his assent
> to favorable statements but would gaze at the floor, appearing nervous and agitated, when the prosecution scored a point. Ruby seemed
> buoyant, cocky, and self-assured during the press conferences which
> preceded each court session . . . smiling cheerfully.

But when asked during one of those press conferences about Bromberg's mention during his testimony that Ruby had gone to Cuba to make money selling merchandise to the Castro regime,

> Ruby became agitated, shouting that it was a fabrication. . . . Then a newsman asked about his feelings when he learned of President Kennedy's assassination. Ruby broke into tears and wept openly until the defense lawyers ended the conference.

But the day after the psychiatrists' testimony, the hearing was abruptly terminated. Judge Brown reported that both sides had agreed that Ruby would receive a full battery of neurological tests, which was what Belli was after all along. The doctors slated to supervise the tests were Dr. Robert L. Stubblefield, chairman of the Department of Psychiatry at the University of Texas Southwestern Medical School in Dallas; Dr. Martin L. Towler, of the Titus Harris Clinic in Galveston; and Dr. Holbrook.

The defense, having gotten what it wanted, withdrew the bail motion. For his part, Wade was pleased that Ruby was staying in jail, where the state wanted him. However, as Kaplan and Waltz spell out,

> The prosecution, now forewarned that the defense was preparing to employ the relatively rare defense of insanity produced by organic brain damage, was able to concentrate all of its pretrial efforts on gathering evidence to counter Ruby's claim.

Belli then requested the change of venue, believing that, though the entire world had witnessed Ruby's murder of Oswald, nonetheless, because of all the negative attention brought specifically to Dallas, it would be impossible to find objective jurors there. As Belli told the *Dallas Morning News*, Ruby was in danger "because of a conspiracy in Dallas to deprive him of a fair trial."

February 10 was set as the date for the change-of-venue hearing; Judge Brown mandated that jury selection would proceed in the meantime, to find out if an impartial panel of Jack Ruby's peers *could* be assembled. Jury selection would begin on February 3, a week before the venue hearing.

In the meantime, behind the scenes, there was conflict about how Ruby's legal expenses would be paid for. Part of the problem was that the money anticipated for the foreign newspaper rights to *My Story*—a series of serialized "tell-all" articles, ghostwritten for Jack by Billy Woodfield—was not coming in as Ruby's family and lawyers had hoped.

Silverman had a ringside seat to this infighting when he went to visit Ruby on January 23. He reported that "Jack was tremendously upset and emotional about his altercations with his lawyers. At great length he explained to me that Eva Grant had become very angry in her conversations with Belli concerning the fee that was to be paid to him and the other lawyers."

Belli was writing a book—and producing a documentary—that he anticipated would help fund his services. Reported details vary on what he and others would exactly get from the Ruby family. According to Ruby, though, Belli had written a letter to him pledging that "I will stay with the case no matter what I receive." (Only Tonahill unambiguously agreed to not worry about payment, in part because he was wealthy enough not to care.)

Complicating things even more, on January 27, researcher Robert Denson complained to Silverman that Eva had told him that Jack wanted accomplished Dallas attorney Charles Tessmer to replace Tom Howard (who was still attached to the case), with whom he had become disenchanted, especially after realizing how Howard had allowed him to be played by Alexander and Holbrook in the early days of Ruby's imprisonment. Denson also told Silverman that Belli wanted, for *his* book about the case, all the material that Denson had been researching, which incensed Earl, since it was he who had been paying Denson's salary. Denson told the rabbi that "I am . . . giving Earl all of the material that I have been collecting" so that Earl could give it to Billy Woodfield to use in writing Jack's "tell-all" articles.

The first of those articles, published in numerous newspapers on four consecutive days, hit newsstands on January 28, the same day Ruby was scheduled to go for the mandated neurological tests.

Melvin Belli was not pleased.

18 | THE POWER OF THE PRESS

WHILE *MY STORY* WAS CAUSING a worldwide sensation, Ruby, on his way to the Dallas Neurological Clinic for the scheduled tests, told the press, "I have never talked with anyone about my background or this case." He was, in effect, denying any involvement in *My Story*.

In fact, he had indeed participated, but could not be considered even coauthor of the articles. According to Kaplan and Waltz, even after Belli had been hired,

> the negotiations in connection with the writing and marketing of Jack Ruby's life story continued between William Woodfield and Earl Ruby. An agreement was eventually hammered out . . . and the contract was finally prepared by Larry Schiller, a business associate of Woodfield's.

This was neither the first nor last time Schiller's name would be associated with Jack Ruby. On assignment for the *Saturday Evening Post*, Schiller was in the room when Ruby shot Oswald, helped photographer Jack Beers develop one of the famous photos of the event, and would be involved with Ruby's last days. He also would be the researcher for Norman Mailer's take on the JFK assassination and Ruby's role in it: *Oswald's Tale*.

Kaplan and Waltz continue:

> Members of the Ruby family provided the information on Jack's background, while the material on Ruby's activities after the [JFK]

assassination . . . was provided by Joe Tonahill. . . . On the basis of this information, some rough notes written by Ruby . . . and a very brief meeting with Ruby . . . Woodfield then wrote his story.

Woodfield's supposed interview with Ruby was based on Tonahill's notes taken during Ruby's December 25 questioning by the FBI. Belli's associate Sam Brody cleared the articles for publication.

(Ruby had also been questioned by the FBI on November 25, the day after he shot Oswald, without any legal representation. In none of the FBI interviews, whether through planning or sheer luck, did he give testimony that would negate the possibility of an insanity plea.)

On the website of auction house Alexander Historical Auctions, a 2008 description of an auction of "notes, drafts and edited versions" of *My Story* points out that "Belli edited the notes, excising crucial passages that may, if published, have proven prejudicial to Belli's 'irresistible impulse' defense." These deletions included a phrase [of Ruby's] pointing to a possible predisposition to murder: "I can't help but wondering if Oswald might still be alive if everyone hadn't been so 'certain' of his guilt." The auction house's cataloguer notes in an aside, "This seems to show that in shooting Oswald, Ruby was acting as an 'executioner,' simply killing a man already condemned to death."

And, in the section where *My Story* describes Ruby's supposed memory of his killing of Oswald, the original manuscript contains the information "I lost my senses. . . . I pulled out my gun and took a couple of steps. . . .They could have blown my head off. I only shot him once . . . I guess I intended—I don't know what." The cataloguer here notes:

> The final initialed and approved version of *My Story* does not include the damning phrase "I guess I intended," and also changes a key phrase to: "I *must have* pulled out my gun."

The edits seem as if they were intended to emphasize that Ruby's actions were spontaneous, not planned, and so were in keeping with Belli's defense strategy.

———————————

Although the results of the tests performed on Ruby on the day of the series' premier installment's release would not be revealed until the trial itself, *My Story* was an immediate sensation.

The first part of the series avers that Ruby sold "millions of salt and pepper shakers" for Earl's company when they were in business together, his show business dreams led him to Dallas to operate nightclubs. He spoke of resentment at reports that described him as a "loser," a "hanger on," a "small time operator."

Further, he wants people to know that he was not, nor had he ever been, "a gangster, a racketeer, a hoodlum or an underworld character." Also, he maintains, "I am not a white slaver, a panderer, a homosexual, a sex deviate or a narcotics user." He denies that he was a Communist or a radical right-winger, and insists that he had not known Oswald and had not been employed by anyone to "silence" Oswald.

In the series' second and third parts, Ruby and Woodfield give an account of the forty-eight hours encompassing the two murders, adding the interesting information that, on Sunday the twenty-fourth, "I was up early. I was sad. I took my Preludin pills (diet pills) and a cold prescription. The diet pills helped me with my diet but they aggravate me. They make my problems worse and I have doubled my dosage four or five days before."

In the article Ruby recalls that he observed a crowd at one of the city hall's basement ramps and became curious. He walked down the ramp and was passed by a police officer whom he knew. "I thought I'd see what was happening. I thought they had already transferred Oswald." But then Oswald "came out all of a sudden with a smirky, defiant, cursing, vicious Communist expression on his face. . . . I lost my senses. There was no one standing by me. . . . I must have pulled out my gun and took a couple of steps. . . . I must have been crazy. I only shot him once." The next thing he knew, he was being pinned to the floor by police, to whom he said, "You don't have to beat me—my brains—out. I'm Jack Ruby. What am I doing here? What are you guys jumping on me for? Why am I here? I'm Jack Ruby. I'm not somebody that's wanted."

So, here, the article emphasizes the defense's eventual assertion that Ruby was unaware of where he was and what he had done. It was only when he was taken upstairs by the police that, the article claimed, he realized what he had done. "I said, 'My God, my God!'"

In the fourth part of the series, billed as a face-to-face interview with Ruby by Woodfield (but likely taken from Tonahill's notes), Ruby stated, when asked if he had a history of mental illness, "Well, I've been hit on the head a few times, but . . . there's no history of mental illness." Then he added: "I get shocked and saddened by violent death. I have to do something." To demonstrate this, Ruby cited a couple of examples, including one situation where, after a Dallas detective was killed while working on a narcotics assignment, he contributed money to the detective's family, closed the club and took his employees to attend the funeral. Kaplan and Waltz observe,

> In both cases, one of the facts which had most affected Ruby was that a husband and father had been killed, leaving a widow and fatherless children. The case . . . is perhaps even more significant. Though *My Story* did not mention it, the killer . . . was never prosecuted, for lack of evidence—a fact which Ruby on several occasions remarked had caused him to lose faith in the inevitability of justice.

Despite the edits made by Belli (or Sam Brody or both), some information in the printed articles about Ruby's supposed state of mind was unlikely to have been pleasing to the defense team, as it made Ruby seem at least to some degree aware of what he was doing ("I only shot him once").

Though the articles weren't published in Dallas (the defense didn't offer it to the *Morning News*, which had been printing ongoing stories painting Ruby in a negative light, and the *Times Herald* turned it down), they had "an instantaneous effect in that city." Wade claimed that Woodfield had never been to see Ruby and that the series was something that "Ruby's attorneys got together." Belli claimed the DA was lying.

Belli later disowned the series, speaking of Earl Ruby as having been behind it, getting a "lucrative contract for Jack's 'exclusive story,' a troublesome treatise." And, of course, Jack himself had said, "I have never talked with anyone about my background or this case."

Unfortunately, the revenue generated by the articles was not anywhere near as great as the Ruby family had hoped. Earl's pockets were deep but not unlimited. As Kaplan and Waltz note,

> The only real asset Ruby and his family had was his life story. It was barely enough. The total amount realized from the sale of *My Story* was approximately $45,000 and Ruby's share was some $30,000. Of this, $11,000 was paid to Melvin Belli; Tom Howard received $4,000.

Various other parties received another $13,500, leaving $1,500 to fund the defense, and much of that went to "miscellaneous." (The wealthy Joe Tonahill declined compensation until all the other defense expenses were paid.) Accounts differ over how much Belli was paid, or whether he was paid at all. But in any case, the articles clearly didn't translate into much money for his defense.

Whatever he was or wasn't paid, it's easy to see why Belli—whether or not he was actually involved with the creation and distribution of *My Story*—would look back on it as a folly perpetrated by his client's family. Even with the deletions, the series, while aiming to paint Ruby in the most positive possible light, had dropped potentially incriminating tidbits, nuggets that could sabotage Belli's plans.

———————

When Silverman visited Ruby in prison on January 30—the day the third part of *My Story* appeared—Ruby showed him the letter from Belli in which the lawyer stated, "I will not take a nickel from [you] and will stay with you until our case has been seen through all of the courts." Also that day, Ruby spoke to Silverman (and his assistant, Rabbi William Fertig) about the psychiatric tests he had undergone on the previous two days, and about the newspaper series. Silverman wrote:

> He complained that the back of the neck pained him because of the fluid [he had had spinal fluid removed for testing]. . . . Ruby explained that when he returned to the jail after the first day [of tests] . . . he was shocked by the tremendous throng of newspaper men and photographers. . . . One of the newspaper men asked him if he had written the confession that had appeared in the Houston paper.

While the articles were intended to be anything but a confession, clearly some saw them as exactly that. And although he seems to have been fully aware that his life story was being sold to raise funds, Silverman reported,

> Jack denied writing this, "When the man used the word 'confession' it was as if I am admitting my guilt. . . . Now what will people think when they read the article in the newspaper? . . . Maybe it is good, for they will see that I am really crazy."

It seems Ruby simply couldn't keep straight whether he actually believed he had lost his mind, temporarily or permanently, and also, regardless of what he believed, what *impression* his lawyers wanted him to make at any given time.

February brought the dual ordeals of jury selection (scheduled to start on February 3), which would determine if finding an objective jury in Dallas was indeed possible, and the change-of-venue hearing. The outcome of jury selection was then supposed to be used as evidence in the change-of-venue hearing, scheduled to begin on February 10, the idea being, apparently, that a jury could be found—or not found—over the course of a week. It should come as no shock that this would not be the case. Jack Ruby's future would be determined by an unusually long jury-selection process combined with change-of-venue hearing, and by an amazingly short trial, followed by an even more astonishingly short jury deliberation.

Seth Kantor describes Judge Joe Brown Sr., who presided over jury selection, thusly:

> With only a grade school diploma Brown enrolled in a short-cut law school at 23 and emerged . . . with a law degree. . . . After some 20 years as justice of the peace [in Oak Cliff], Brown was elected to the criminal district court bench, where nearly a third of his verdicts later reviewed by the state appeals court were overturned. . . . The most notorious episode of his judicial career took place . . . at the marijuana trial of Candy Barr. He recessed the trial . . . and invited her into his private chambers. There she posed for pictures for him.

While jury selection was still going on, the change-of-venue hearing began, punctuated by the appearance of another gun—but *not* with a bang. A female spectator was searched on her way in and found to be carrying a water pistol! It would not be the last on-the-premises weapon that would play a role in the drama of Jack Ruby's murder trial.

Security was tight at the venue hearing, in the sense that everyone entering was searched, as the water-pistol discovery demonstrated. On the other hand, dozens of reporters waited outside Brown's small courtroom, and at breaks, they would surge into the courtroom and fire questions at the hearing participants:

> It was a bizarre spectacle: a man who was on trial for killing an accused killer in the midst of a large crowd was surrounded by a large crowd with no security. . . . And while Jack Ruby sat silent when court was in session, when reporters surrounded him during these breaks he seemed thrilled to be the center of attention.

The prosecution and defense each presented numerous witnesses over the three days of the hearing. Belli and company were trying to prove that Dallas was no place for a fair trial. Wade and his team were out to establish that, given that the entire world had seen the live or recorded murder on TV, Dallas was as likely a place for the killer to get a fair shake as anywhere else.

The head of the prestigious Neiman-Marcus department stores and a leading liberal force in Dallas, Stanley Marcus, testified at Ruby's change of venue hearing that he had "great reservations whether either the defense or prosecution can get a fair trial in Dallas."
Photo by Jun Miki, courtesy of Wikimedia Commons

Starting with jury selection and the venue hearing and then through the trial, there was a continual edge to the antagonism the dueling legal teams showed toward each other. Wade's team would often raise objections to questions before Belli or Tonahill had even finished asking them. This prompted Tonahill to say to the judge, "Never in my life have I ever seen such rudeness by prosecuting attorneys. I don't know whether it's rudeness or a desire to suppress the truth. I think it's a combination of both."

The hearing, jury selection, and trial itself would be marked by extreme behaviors, in some ways presaging the theatrical aspects of the 1970 Chicago Eight trial. Belli later referred to the Ruby hearings and trial as a "hog-calling contest."

And, though, in his posthumously published memoir, Judge Brown repeatedly asserts that he would much rather not have been involved with the trial, his actions belied those statements. Abrams and Fisher note, "As it later became known, Judge Brown did not want to move the trial unless he went with it. This was the case of his career and he was not going to give it up."

In the change-of-venue hearing, the defense brought on Costine Droby, chairman of the Dallas County Bar Association, who told the court that "Jack Ruby couldn't get a fair trial in Dallas County," that the region overall felt that Ruby "must be convicted to clear Dallas's name." Droby went on to describe the situation as "so dangerous that, when it appeared he himself might represent Ruby, anonymous callers had made threats on his life."

The defense also made much of columnist Tony Zoppi's testimony that renowned singer Tony Bennett lamented the JFK and Oswald assassinations, saying, "This is unbelievable that a thing like this could happen in Dallas." Zoppi observed that, overall, "the city was being vilified around the country" because of the two murders.

Belli's team also pointed out that the very fact that Judge Brown had hired a public relations consultant to help him deal with the unprecedented pressures of the case indicated that the negative attention being brought on the city was so great that it was obvious the venue would have to be changed.

The venue hearing concluded, on Friday February 14, with Brown not ruling at all but, rather, echoing the prosecution's argument that "the true test of whether the state and defense can get a fair trial rests on the prospective jurors. The decision rests until examination of jurors."

Over that weekend, significant events relating to the trial occurred. To begin with, Judge Brown announced that the trial would be moved to the much larger courtroom of Judge J. Frank Wilson, thereby providing room "to seat the entire press contingent." This prompted Tonahill to crack, "We asked [Judge Brown] to move the trial two hundred miles and instead he moved it two hundred feet."

In addition, Tom Howard finally resigned from the defense team. Not only was Howard concerned that Belli's tactics would lead to a harsh sentence for Ruby, but he was also afraid that the rest of the team would somehow find a way to blame *him* for such a defeat. Howard was not the only one who didn't like what Belli was doing. As Kaplan and Waltz noted:

> The entire Ruby family . . . did not like the way things were going. Jack's family considered Belli inaccessible and too preoccupied with other things to talk to them about the case. They sensed also that [Belli's] antics . . . were harming Jack's chances before the eventual jury and they had observed what appeared to them as a succession of prosecution victories and defense defeats. . . . Jack, his brother Earl, and his sister Eva decided they wished Belli to have the aid of a criminal lawyer more experienced than either Phil Burleson or Joe Tonahill. Specifically, Jack . . . wanted to bring Charles Tessmer, probably Dallas's most prominent criminal lawyer, into the case.

The family was hoping to use Tony Zoppi, who knew Tessmer, as an intermediary, but when Zoppi told Belli of the plan, "he was greeted by such a burst of invective that he decided to have nothing further to do with bringing Tessmer into the case." Belli chided Ruby that he was confident that his strategy would prevail, and that if Ruby wanted to replace him, he would be glad to resign. Belli did not, and Tessmer was not brought on board.

How did all this impact Jack Ruby?

Hillel Silverman visited him on February 16, after the change-of-venue hearing was suspended, and noted that "Jack is most nervous, agitated and concerned" and that, after he is returned to his cell after each day of the hearing, "he becomes despondent . . . one night the past week he was not able to sleep at all."

Silverman added that Ruby confided to him that "the newspapermen make him extremely nervous since he is not accustomed to public speaking. 'I don't want the public to see that I am weak.'" Silverman commented, "This seems to be an obsession with him that he has to put on a façade of strength and hardness." The rabbi continued:

> In order to help him regain his confidence, I repeated to him the story of Daniel and the Lion's Den, which he had read in the Bible that I had given him. I told him that he must find the courage of a Daniel since he was being thrown to the lion's den. He was terribly concerned about his family. . . . "I am not afraid of [sic] myself, but of the disgrace to them." . . .
>
> Suddenly Ruby informed me that he wanted very much for me to go to Washington and arrange for him to take a lie detector test. He had even asked Belli if this could be arranged and of course, Belli discouraged it.

Belli didn't want Ruby to testify *anywhere*, fearful of what his client's unfiltered responses might do to the case. Silverman continued:

> Ruby, for the first time . . . seems to be concerned about the possibility of a death penalty. He had even asked Belli if he could make some kind of a "deal" for a life sentence. "I don't care for myself. It is for my family and for the Jews. . . . They are after me and all the Jews." . . .
>
> Ruby is more jittery and incoherent than ever before. I strongly suspect that within a week or two he will "crack up" completely and be sent off to an institution.

19 | A JURY OF HIS PEERS

MORE THAN TWO MONTHS had passed since Ruby's murder of Oswald. By this point, the vision that Ruby might have had of himself as a hero who would be quickly released and become an admired figure had pretty much faded away. Now he was truly at the mercy of the justice system. For better or worse, he—and his family—had thrown their lot in with Melvin Belli, offbeat theories and all.

Whatever had impelled Ruby to kill Oswald—impulse, conspiracy, grandiosity—seemed to have evaporated. Whatever brought him to this place in his life and in history seemed less and less relevant. Perhaps, as some have theorized, he was enacting some kind of grand strategy of his own, or perhaps Belli's, invention. Ruby's repeated requests for a lie-detector test and inquiring about making a deal certainly could be seen as evidence of Ruby as, if not a player in some larger plan, then a pawn who still had a few tricks up his sleeve. Or he could, of course, have been merely delusional.

Rabbi Silverman noted on February 16, "I brought him a Sabbath Prayer Book that he had requested. . . . I showed him the prayers he should recite on Friday nights and Saturday mornings." The rabbi added,

> When I left Ruby's cell and passed by Sheriff Decker's office, he showed me a calling card from a missionary by the name of Michaelson. . . . Michaelson has a radio program and requested permission to see Ruby. I told Decker that, under no condition, should any other minster or missionary receive permission to see Ruby unless I

approved it first. I can just see the publicity from a missionary that he had converted Ruby to Christianity.

It's not clear why Silverman would think Decker could enforce his instructions, especially when Stevenson, who was there so much of the time, seemed to be constantly trying to move Ruby toward Christianity. Apparently, over time, the rabbi and the sheriff had become comfortable enough with each other that they could have this kind of conversation.

———

On February 18 jury selection began. Belli, operating under the assumption—fostered by private conversations with the judge—that Brown would, sooner rather than later, order a change of venue, was relatively careless with his juror exclusions and spent a lot of time and energy disparaging the city of Dallas. His reasoning, many believed, was that if he could alienate potential jurors into disqualifying themselves with angry responses, he would demonstrate that a fair trial for Jack Ruby was not to be had there. As Kaplan and Waltz put it, "The only thing [Belli] wanted more than a favorable jury for Jack Ruby was no jury at all." Still, he did have to at least go through the motions of jury selection, the *voir dire*.

Over the close to three weeks of jury selection, the opposing parties and the judge would be presented with 162 prospective jurors. And, as Belli recalled, "of the 162 questioned, four were Catholics, two Jews, all the rest varying shade of Protestant, and of these latter, eight were Negroes." Belli and Tonahill were outraged that the few Black prospective jurors were treated with near-disdain, the prosecution lawyers addressing them by their first names, while addressing white potential jurors as Mr., Miss, or Mrs. (Ms. did not exist yet.) Their objections actually caused the prosecutors to change the way they spoke to the Black candidates for the rest of the proceedings, though none would land on the final jury.

———

On Thursday, February 20, 1964, the first juror, Max Causey—who would also be the foreman—was picked. As Causey recalled of the moment he was selected, "In my thirty-five years on this planet I had never been exposed to a more devastating shock than at that moment. I suddenly felt as though the ceiling and all the upper seven floors of the building had collapsed on my head." Clearly, the historic import of the trial was not lost on him.

On the fourth day of jury selection—with only one juror having so far been picked—Belli finally realized that Brown had no intention of moving the case. "If I made one mistake in the case," Belli was reported as saying, "it was in trusting Judge Brown."

Belli recalls the situation:

> There was not a one of the twelve finally seated whom I wouldn't have challenged in the unusual circumstances of this case, but our task was not to pick a good jury; that was impossible. Rather it was our task to head off the dedicated hangmen, those whose minds were completely closed to us.

The prosecution had an important advantage over Belli in that, being on its home turf, it was able to, in those pre-Google days, access information about the backgrounds and predilections of the potential jurors that Belli could not. DA Wade "regarded picking a jury as his single greatest strength as a trial lawyer and [the prosecution] not only possessed greater access to reliable local information, but were in a far better position to interpret what intelligence they obtained."

There was at least one potential juror Belli liked a lot, and who made the cut. That was J. Waymon Rose. Belli recalls,

> Rose made me sit up by volunteering an anecdote about a football player who, sitting on the bench and watching an opposing player break into the clear toward a touchdown, had been so overcome by emotion ("so carried away," Rose said) that he had dashed onto the playing field and tackled the runner.

Belli thought Rose would be open to the defense's concept of Ruby having acted on instinct, without premeditation.

And there was the surreally amusing moment when an attractive blond housewife named Dixie Valetto, after being questioned, stopped on her way out of court to shake hands with Ruby. "Can we get any more like her?" Belli asked. The judge eliminated her for cause.

As for how Ruby was reacting to all the drama—and tedium—of jury selection, we have Silverman's recollections of his visits during the period of jury formation. For instance, on Sunday, February 23, the day before the second week of jury selection was to begin, Silverman noted that Ruby was "terribly distraught and disturbed. . . . He seems to have lost a great deal of weight, his face is drawn and his glance unsteady."

It seemed that Ruby was still concerned about a gun (he remembered it sometimes as four guns) that he had shipped to Cuba on his friend Lewis McWillie's behalf in 1958 or 1959. He had not told the FBI about this, and told Silverman, "This will link me to the underworld and reflect on all of the Jews." He seemed to be afraid that the FBI would find out, possibly from Tom Howard, who he believed was still owed money by the family, and that Howard would tell Wade. Ruby confided in the rabbi, "I am a 'meshugeneh [sic] martyr' and now it has backfired."

Silverman noted, "For the first time in many weeks I have the feeling that he is holding back and hiding something."

When Silverman visited again a few days later, he found Ruby still despondent but not "as dejected or morose as he was on my previous visit . . . on occasion, he actually smiled." While still concerned about the McWillie gun business and that he would be seen as being part of the Chicago underworld, Ruby "seemed to be more disturbed about the question of 'pre-meditation.'" Ruby told the rabbi—while drawing him a diagram of his travels on the morning he killed Oswald—that he thought about killing Oswald when he got into his car to go to the Western Union office, then forgot about it, then thought about it again as he left the place. He seemed worried that Belli was asking him to lie somehow and that he needed to tell the truth or else "they will cut me to bits. Once I tell a lie there is no stopping." Ruby again expressed to Silverman the desire to take a lie-detector test.

In this era, lie detectors—polygraph machines—were often depicted in popular culture as being virtually infallible, though the reality was far from that. This may well have been the source of Ruby's growing obsession with being questioned while hooked up to a polygraph.

Ruby expressed to Silverman that he felt that he had divulged too much to Stevenson and that Stevenson would testify against him, or that he might have given information to Wade. In addition, Silverman recalled that Ruby said, "again and again," "I can't let this happen to my people. I don't care what happens to me—but they are out to get me and all my people."

The rabbi visited a day or two later, on February 26, at Eva's request, because she observed that Jack was very depressed. Silverman noted that "I have never seen Jack so despondent and distraught. . . . Not only did he not smile but he evinced no animation whatsoever." Ruby was still preoccupied with the gun-running episode that he was afraid would become known. "Now the world will see that I have [underworld] connections. This will be terrible for the Jews. Wade and his staff are all out to get us."

Silverman noted that, for the first time, Ruby seemed to express some kind of "distorted remorse, not for his deed, nor for Oswald's family, nor for depriving America of information about Oswald. He merely said, 'I have unleashed terrible hatred. Now everyone hates Dallas and hates the Jews. . . . This will be terrible for all the Jews everywhere. And it's all my fault.'" Silverman continued:

> Once again, he expressed the wish to take a lie detector test in Washington. I asked him, "What good would this do?" "Then people will see that I had no connections." I asked him, "You mean connections with the Communists?" "No, certainly not. Connections with the underworld."

In 1964, in the heart of the Cold War, fear of being thought to have anything to do with anything or anyone labeled *Communist* was rampant. That would certainly be at play in this situation, where Oswald's political leanings and activities were being discussed in conjunction with Jack Ruby. The "Communist" epithet was constantly used throughout Ruby's trial by both sides.

In this entry, Silverman notes once again, "It seems to me that Jack is hiding something of the past which he is terribly afraid will crop up in the trial."

Belli's dual task of picking a jury while demonstrating that a nonprejudiced jury couldn't be found was made even harder when Brown was briefly ill and was replaced for one day by ultraconservative Judge J. Frank Wilson, as no-nonsense and by-the-book as Brown was casual and informal.

Wilson proceeded to terminate the change-of-venue motion (which, on his return, Brown reinstated and then, himself, denied) and pressured Ruby's lawyers, who had used up their preemptory challenges—challenges needing no explanation—into finishing their selection of jurors. Under Wilson, a juror was allowed who was the aunt of the Dallas Police Department's public relations officer. The officer, Art Hammett, "was deeply involved in the effort to relieve the Dallas PD of responsibility for allowing Ruby to slip through security and murder Oswald."

And then the proceedings were disrupted for a day by the very public March 2 appearance on the scene of Maurice A. Melford, director of the National Epilepsy League. Melford was concerned that the defense case—that Ruby was suffering from psychomotor epilepsy when he shot Oswald—would make epilepsy, once believed to be a form of demonic possession, even more misunderstood than it already was. Melford handed out informational packages that stated that the close to two million Americans with epilepsy "are also on trial. . . . Because the public knows so little about epilepsy and because so much of what it believes is based on ignorance, superstition and myth" and that arguments made during the trial "can further prejudice the public."

Melford's literature quoted epilepsy expert Dr. Frederick Gibbs: "You don't have to worry too much about a patient in a psychomotor seizure. You will read in novels and see in movies all kinds of dramatizations, spiced-up stories about what psychomotor epileptics do: murder, criminal activities, etc. This is nonsense." Ironically, Gibbs's research would end up being a significant part of Belli's defense of Ruby.

Because Melford had alerted the prosecution (but not the defense) that he was coming to town, Belli moved to have a mistrial declared, but Brown denied the motion. As Belli feared, Melford would end up supplying experts to testify on the prosecution's behalf.

The last juror was picked on March 3, and the trial was set to begin the next day. The final jury was made up of two engineers, an accountant, a book-keeper, a research analyst, a corporation vice president, a secretary, a postman, two salesmen, an airline mechanic, and a telephone company employee. Belli observed, in a compliment wrapped around an insult, that "the intelligence level of our jury is well above what you would expect from a cross-section of Dallas residents." Interestingly, Texas law did not provide for alternate jurors. If any member of the jury was unable to serve for the entirety of what was expected to be a lengthy trial, the trial would be invalidated.

Assistant DA Bill Alexander recalled, "Belli picked a perfect jury—perfect for us. He wanted people who could understand his fancy psychological talk, so he chose people who were educated, middle-class, never been to clubs like Jack's, couldn't sympathize with his world. . . . . Belli's tone deaf. From the first juror I knew Jack would get the death penalty."

While Belli and company were certainly beyond competent, they had selected a tough road to travel, perhaps because of hubris on Belli's part, per-haps because it was abundantly clear that Wade was not interested in anything less than the death penalty and that Judge Brown seemed generally inclined to lean toward the prosecution's side. (The fact that he was negotiating with a publisher to write a book about the trial, a book that would benefit from dramatic events that his rulings could effect, wouldn't necessarily favor either side, but it would come back to bite the judge.)

Later on March 3 Silverman joined Belli for dinner at Dallas's upscale Cipango Club. Also present were Tonahill, Burleson, and Drs. Guttmacher, Stubblefield, and Towler. The dinner was a strategy session for the trial, due to start the next morning. Silverman observed that Belli

> wanted to draw Stubblefield, who is Judge Brown's advisor, to his side. . . . [Belli] was attempting to formalize his psychiatric approach to Ruby's defense. . . . Belli appeared most disturbed about the Epilepsy League literature. . . . I broached the subject of Ruby's possible suicidal tendencies. Belli pounced upon this thought and asked Guttmacher if Ruby might not be committed to a mental institution on the basis of suicidal tendencies. I suspect Belli will follow this logic more closely in the next few days.

The odds did seem stacked against Ruby, and not simply because he had murdered a helpless victim on live television. Belli seemed to be staking his case on a theory even the most sophisticated jury would find hard to accept, given the narrow legal definition of insanity.

And, as if Ruby's crime on live TV before millions of witnesses wasn't enough, Wade was, as Kaplan and Waltz see it, "fully prepared to cope with any surprise witnesses the defense might . . . produce. . . . [The] investigation . . . had been perhaps more thorough than any before . . . with efforts of the Dallas police being supplemented . . . by the FBI as well as several other federal investigative agencies. FBI agents had . . . followed [Ruby's] entire life history."

Even with so much in their favor, though, the prosecution team, until the very last day of the trial, couldn't believe that Belli was *really* hanging his defense on psychomotor epilepsy. They would wait for him, despite their regular ridicule of him—including referring to the slightly overweight attorney as "Mr. Belly"—to pull some kind of brilliantly conceived rabbit out of his hat and, as he had so many times before, prevail on behalf of his client.

Belli would certainly try.

20 | JAILBREAK

WITH THE PRELIMINARIES OVER, the Jack Ruby trial itself would begin. Melvin Belli's theories would now be put to the test.

The trial, as had the hearings, would take place on the second floor of the Dallas County Criminal Courts Building. The eleven-story building, erected in 1915, was an all-in-one justice edifice. As Abrams and Fisher describe it,

> this "state of the art" model for the "administration of justice" had included both men's and women's segregated jails . . . a chapel, a hospital, and operating room . . . a barber shop. And, on the top floor, a hanging room.

From the first day, the trial was unlike any before and, with the possible exceptions of the Chicago Eight trial and the O. J. Simpson trial, unlike any since. Here was a case filled with eccentric personalities inside and outside the courtroom, a case that was being covered by worldwide media and that refused to be conducted quietly. The animosity each side held for the other was a guarantee that things would not go smoothly. As Elmer Gertz observes in *Moment of Madness*, "From beginning to end there were constant displays of bad manners, bad tempers, shouting matches, interruptions, rudeness, by attorneys on both sides." For the many inside the courtroom writing or contemplating writing a book about the proceedings, there was certainly no lack of material.

To all this, add what defense investigator Robert Denson had observed in a memo to the defense team:

> Reliable sources report . . . that the Dallas Police Department is exceptionally bitter toward Ruby, the Chief of Police has "passed the word: that any officer giving information or testimony for Ruby in any respect will be either dismissed or severely disciplined." . . .
>
> Sources in the Jewish community also report that most Jewish people are extremely unhappy with Ruby. They feel they have been embarrassed and humiliated, not only by Ruby, but by Bernard Weissman, who caused the article entitled "Welcome Mr. President"* to be published in the *Dallas Morning News*.

One of Belli's regular lunch companions during the trial was reporter Dorothy Kilgallen, best known as a panelist on popular TV game show *What's My Line?* Kilgallen, a *New York Journal American* columnist, would claim to have inside information from an interview with Ruby that would blow the case open. (*What's My Line?*'s host, John Daly, was married to Earl Warren's daughter.) Belli also socialized with Oswald's eccentric mother, Marguerite, who seemed to view the trial as a way to prove that her son was the victim of a conspiracy.

The first day of the trial began with Judge Brown formally rejecting the defense's motion for a change of venue. Then, numerous other motions from Belli's team—including a demand for a mistrial because of the activities related to the National Epilepsy League; a demand that the jurors selected while Judge Wilson was presiding be removed; and a demand that the trial be adjourned while a sanity hearing would be held for Ruby—were also denied.

It then came time for the defense to formally enter a plea. Texas law permitted only a declaration of "guilty" or "not guilty." "Not guilty by reason of insanity" was not permitted, the idea being that insanity was one of the numerous ways a defendant could be found not guilty. Nonetheless, Belli wanted to make his argument clear to the jury, and so the following dance with Judge Brown ensued:

---

* Actually, the article was called "Welcome Mr. Kennedy to Dallas."

JUDGE BROWN: Mr. Ruby, how do you plead to the indictment?

JACK RUBY: Not guilty, Your Honor.

MELVIN BELLI: For and on behalf of the defendant, Jack Ruby . . . he now pleads . . . not guilty by reason of insanity at the time of the alleged offense. . . . I ask Mr. Ruby to repeat that. "Not guilty, and not guilty by reason of insanity."

JUDGE BROWN: All the Court is interested in, Counsel, is whether he pleads guilty or not guilty.

JACK RUBY: Not guilty.

Those two sentences that Ruby uttered when entering his plea would be the only words of his spoken during the proceedings that would appear on the trial transcript.

Dorothy Kilgallen (left), famous as a reporter and as one of the regular panelists on the popular TV game show *What's My Line?*, claimed to have gotten an exclusive interview with Jack Ruby that would reveal secrets about the Kennedy and Oswald assassinations. With her in this 1952 photo are fellow *WML* panelists Bennett Cerf, Arlene Francis, and Hal Block, and show host John Charles Daly, who was married to Chief Justice Earl Warren's daughter. *CBS, courtesy of Wikimedia Commons*

Ruby, as described by Maurice Carroll in *Accidental Assassin*, presented this first day of his trial as "a pale pudgy guy who nibbled nervously on his fingers as he sat at the defense table." The reporter added that "Ruby, a chunky guy with a pointy nose and a receding hairline, had an apologetic manner that suggested that he had no business intruding into a world of first-class talkers like Belli."

Carroll continued:

> While the legal gladiators battled . . . Ruby sat silently by, occasionally passing notes to his lawyers. On the spectator benches, it was hard to get much sense of him. He was a spectator, too . . . he sat, pale and hollow-eyed, watching the legal show.

Indeed, Belli was the flamboyant star of the trial—it's what he was known for doing—though the other lawyers were not without their flair for the dramatic. Reporters joked among themselves that the trial was "The Joe B. Brown show. Starring Melvin Belli. And, in his farewell performance, Jack Ruby."

That opening day, the prosecution went first, to present its case. It was given to Bill Alexander to make the state's case and call witnesses to back up its contentions: that Jack Ruby had murdered Oswald with malice, *and* that the killing was premeditated. The prosecution was intent on showing that Ruby had, in essence, stalked Oswald on Friday and Saturday, trying to get as close to him as he could, with the idea in mind, even then, to kill him.

Belli, for his part, spent much of the day trying to establish that Ruby was "a pretty volatile individual" and a strange guy in general. Wade, too, was trying to paint Ruby as weird, but his interest was not in establishing that Jack was prone to blackouts and epileptic seizures and worthy of compassion but, instead, that he was a vicious and violent guy, someone capable of premeditated murder.

Belli kept trying to establish that a friendship had existed between Wade and Ruby, although Wade claimed to have never met Ruby before the Friday-night press conference at the police station. This tactic, according to Kaplan and Waltz, was more to annoy the DA than to establish any specific point. It could be thought that it might also have been a way for Belli to try to throw Wade off his game. One can imagine that, on appeal, it might be argued that

Wade had let embarrassment over a possible relationship with Ruby somehow make him more eager to punish the guy.

Much of the day was devoted to the testimony of James Leavelle, one of the two Dallas police officers who had flanked Oswald as he walked through the police station basement. Leavelle, a homicide detective, had famously been handcuffed to Oswald as he was shot by Ruby. Leavelle recalled that while he was trying to save the wounded Oswald, Ruby had proclaimed, "I hope the son of a bitch dies!" Belli contended that "Ruby, having fired the fatal shot during a psychomotor epileptic attack, did not realize he had shot Oswald until he was told about it." Belli advanced the idea that Ruby had made that statement about hoping Oswald died in response to shouts of "Oswald is shot!" without realizing "that he himself had shot Oswald."

The second day of the trial advanced the state's premeditation argument.

Detective L. C. Graves—who had been on Oswald's left side but not handcuffed to the prisoner when Ruby fired—testified. He was the one who first lunged at Ruby and grabbed his gun, keeping it from firing again, despite Ruby's still trying to pull the trigger.

Graves and other officers in the room were questioned as to what Ruby had said and, equally important, *when* he had said it. If Ruby had made incriminating statements within a short time of the killing, then those could be admissible in the case against him. If too much time had elapsed, when he conceivably could have been aggressively questioned without a lawyer present, then his words would be inadmissible.

Among the statements that Ruby was alleged to have made were: "I intended to shoot him three times." "I hope I killed the son of a bitch." "You rat son of a bitch, you shot the president."

All these would have indicated that Ruby was in full control of his behavior, knew what he was doing, and had planned it out beforehand and with malice. In Belli's favor, most of these alleged statements by Ruby were not included in the officers' original reports. The implication Belli tried to draw from that was that the statements were invented after the initial reports to falsely demonstrate that Ruby had awareness and intent.

Belli added that when Ruby, upon being pinned by the police, kept repeating, "You all know me. I'm Jack Ruby," the inappropriateness of his words "might reflect a lack of comprehension . . . that he had just killed a man."

Nonetheless, after a day of parrying, things Ruby had supposedly said were left in the record. Belli attempted to rattle witnesses, especially Detective Thomas McMillon. According to Kaplan and Waltz, McMillon's seeming inability to understand Belli's questions, and insistence on the accuracy of his own testimony, instead rattled *Belli*. As Kaplan and Waltz see it,

> The day had been a complete debacle for Melvin Belli . . . he had made a number of errors in his cross-examination . . . the day had left Belli completely unnerved. . . . And as attention increasingly focused on counsel, the defendant, Jack Ruby, was gradually forgotten.

Belli might well have been suffering from the shock to his ego that Dallas was providing. Wills and Demaris note that

> the jury selection seems to have drained all the energy from Belli. "By the end," says Tonahill, "I had to steer him out on the street to keep him from being run over by a cab. . . . Jack's sister told friends that Belli looked like a man who had just suffered a stroke."

Ruby must have sensed the overall loss of energy around Belli and the failures of the day. In Silverman's notes for that evening, March 5, he reports that Ruby started out upset that his friend and business partner Joe Slatin had been arrested in connection with a mysterious restaurant fire and was afraid that would somehow affect the outcome of Ruby's own trial. The rabbi observed,

> Ruby was most distraught and as despondent as I have ever seen him. . . . He went into a tirade as to how everyone is against him. "Rabbi, teach all the children in the Synagogue that they should lead decent lives so they should never have to be subjected to what I'm going through. . . . I don't mind if I am placed in an institution now. Anything would be better than this."

Silverman observed that Ruby had become wary of Stevenson, calling him a "*momzer*" (Yiddish for "bastard"). Regarding the day's events in court, Ruby "stated unequivocally that he never said 'I intended to shoot him three times.' He said that the police officer was lying on the stand."

Every time Silverman tried to leave, Ruby insisted he remain. "He wanted to continue to talk about his fears and apprehensions. The only smile that I was able to elicit from him was when I said, 'Jack, when you smile you are handsome.'" Ruby replied: "Really, Rabbi?"

———————

The third day of the trial arrived. In many ways, it would be the most important day of the proceedings. It would certainly be among the most memorable.

The day began with the jury being shown two film clips of Ruby killing Oswald, one from United Press International, the other from a local Dallas station. No American murder trial had ever used this type of evidence before. Both films were run in slow motion, then in stop action, frame by frame. It was the first time both Judge Brown and Jack Ruby had actually seen the footage.

Then, the prosecution's next witness, Captain Glen D. King of the Dallas Police, testified that he went into the jail office shortly after Ruby was arrested. There, he claimed to have heard Ruby say, "You didn't think I was going to let him get by with it, did you?" It was also mentioned that Ruby had a large quantity of money with him when he was arrested, implying that he was going to use it to finance some kind of getaway and that he therefore *must* have planned everything out in advance.

Then came the testimony of Sergeant Patrick T. Dean of the Patrol Division of the Dallas Police. Dean testified that about ten minutes after the shooting of Oswald, he had accompanied Secret Service agent Forrest Sorrels to the fifth floor of the building, where Ruby was questioned, and that Ruby had said that he had thought about killing Oswald two nights earlier, when he had seen Oswald paraded out for the press. According to Dean, Ruby said "that he saw no reason for a lengthy trial or to subject Mrs. Kennedy to being brought to Dallas for it . . . that he would kill [Oswald] if he got the chance . . . to show the world that Jews do have guts."

Wade offered into evidence two reports made by Dean. Belli attacked them on the grounds that they contradicted each other. One report said that the

interrogation of Ruby took place about noon, but Dean had testified in court
that it took place about 11:30 AM, less than ten minutes after the shooting.
This difference in time was crucial. Dean's testimony could only be admitted
if Ruby's statements were made within minutes of his shooting Oswald.

After numerous objections and overrulings, Dean testified that "[Ruby]
said . . . something to the effect that he had thought about this two nights prior,
when he had seen [Lee] Harvey Oswald on the show-up stand."

Belli objected. Overruled.

Dean continued that Ruby was so upset "because this man had not only
killed the president but had shot Officer Tippit. . . . It would be inevitable that he
[Oswald] would receive the death penalty that he didn't see any sense for a . . .
lengthy trial." Several Belli objections and Brown overrulings later, Dean continued:

> [Ruby] said that . . . two nights prior . . . is when he first thought that
> if he got the chance he would kill him. And also that he guessed that
> he wanted the world to know that Jews do have guts.

With that, Belli pounced:

> "Jews," Belli yelled, "J-e-w-s, was it, officer?"
> Dean answered him, "Yes, sir."

Belli had made his point that there was something more than incidentally
prejudicial that Jack Ruby was facing in that courtroom.

Dean reasserted that Ruby had said all this "some ten to twelve minutes
after the shooting." But his written statement, brought in as evidence, had said
it was half an hour. The wrangling between the parties over the time frame
went on and on. Which was correct? Perhaps neither! If the time frame was
forty minutes or more between the shooting and when Dean heard Ruby say
what the officer claimed he said, then a mistrial could have been declared.
Belli and Tonahill *demanded* one. Judge Brown did not grant it. They didn't
expect him to, but the conflict in Dean's statements "would be at the center
of the appeal if Ruby was convicted."

The prosecution rested. It was now Belli's turn to make his case. That is
when things got extremely strange. As Maurice Carroll put it in *Accidental
Assassin*, "Just as the defense case began, came an incident that dashed all of

the Dallas establishment's careful preparations to show the world that Dallas was able to conduct a dignified and orderly trial."

The dayroom on the sixth floor of the men's jail—in the same building as the trial—was where the madness that would mark the trial became amped up. As reported by Jack Langguth in the *New York Times*, prisoners, some doing time for armed robbery

> escaped from the Dallas County Jail today, fleeing past the door of the courtroom where Jack L. Ruby is on trial for murder.
>
> One of them carried a pistol carved from soap. Brandishing it, he terrified a striptease dancer who was waiting to testify in Ruby's defense. . . .
>
> Four of the men were caught shortly after their escape at 3:30 P.M. The three others remained at large. A clerk, Mrs. Ruth Thornton, was held hostage for a time. She was later freed.

The backstory, according to the *Times*, was that

> commandeering an elevator, [the prisoners] made their way to a jail entrance on the second floor. Snatching keys from a jailer, they fled into the courthouse corridors.

In one of those corridors, Little Lynn—nine months pregnant—had been waiting to testify. Apparently, she had left her gun at home this time and had not thought to carve one from soap for herself. She was standing outside the courtroom with Belli's wife and "became hysterical when she saw one of the prisoners rush by with the bogus gun."

> "He's after me! He's after me!" [Lynn] screamed. Then she slumped to the floor. Sheriff's deputies revived her.
>
> The sheriff said the artificial weapon had been realistically carved in soap, painted with black shoe polish and held together with syrup. Its barrel was a black pencil.

The convicts apparently didn't have much of a plan beyond the escape itself. At least one escapee was less fierce then perhaps he'd wanted to believe and was caught by "Leon Davis, a 22-year-old messenger for the Columbia Broadcasting System."

Clarence D. Gregory, the escapee holding the dummy gun, "had grabbed Edna Biggs, a clerk in the probations department, and held the soap pistol in her ribs." She wriggled free, but Gregory grabbed another hostage and, with her, fled past the photographers and TV cameramen, into the parking lot. There, Gregory was surrounded by sheriff's deputies and "disarmed" by one of them. The remaining prisoners were soon apprehended, as well.

Of course, given all the publicity surrounding the trial, numerous reporters, photographers, newsreel camerapeople, and curiosity seekers were hanging around outside the courtroom. The convicts were actually banking on that as part of their escape, figuring—correctly—that police wouldn't shoot them for fear of accidentally hitting a member of the press or someone in the crowd outside.

While the *New York Times*'s headline about the escape was straightforward—7 Flee Dallas Jail, Passing the Door of Ruby Courtroom—the headline on the tabloid *New York Daily News* was not so demure. It read: OH, DALLAS! Jailbreak Panics Ruby Trial; It's Captured in Pictures!

Carroll, who would cowrite Belli's *Dallas Justice* and was at the time a *New York Herald Tribune* reporter covering the trial, noted in that paper, "Dallas, which looked tragic when the President was assassinated and stupid when . . . police let Ruby . . . shoot the alleged assassin, managed with this latest business to look simply silly." He reported that Dallas's newly elected mayor, Earle Cabell, simply reacted to the courthouse fiasco with the observation that "you can't win them all."

21 | HEARTBREAK

WITH THE JAILBREAK STEMMED, the nine-months-pregnant, nineteen-year-old Karen "Little Lynn" Carlin did finally testify. The point of her testimony was to establish Ruby's alibi of wiring her the money she needed, his time spent casually waiting in line at the Western Union office, the randomness of the events around that transaction, and the time that it took. But Wade was able to use her words to paint Ruby as a sort of predator, a creep who preyed on teenagers like her, turning them into strippers or worse.

The day also saw testimony by defense witness William G. Serur, a salesman who testified that Ruby had once asked him to sell and bring him replacement seat covers for his car. Serur came over as Ruby was feeding his dogs. Jack had cut his hand on the dog food can. Blood was all over the hand and the largest dog was licking it off. Serur advised Ruby that giving the dog a taste for blood was a bad idea. Ruby replied, "These are my children, and I respect them just like you respect your kids."

Needless to say, Serur found this odd, as he did the interior of Ruby's Oldsmobile. "They [the seats] were all eat[en] out [by the dogs]. All the upholstery was all over the back floorboard and . . . the front floorboard. . . . You could see the springs protruding." Serur had also found similar destruction done by the dogs to Ruby's apartment. Serur had accomplished what Belli needed him to do: establish how eccentric (but harmless) Ruby was.

Wade, however, used Serur to insinuate for the umpteenth time that Ruby might be gay, the witness saying that in the twelve years he had known Ruby, he had never seen him in a public place with a woman. He even got Serur to admit to having traveled with Ruby to postrevolution Cuba for two or three weeks, the subtext being not that they were lovers but that perhaps Jack was a Communist. And, finally, Wade was able to largely discredit anything positive Serur might have said by getting him to admit that, despite being married, he attended the Carousel Club almost every night, tainting him with the disrepute of Ruby's seamy business.

Another defense witness, oilman William E. Howard, testified about Ruby's sudden and violent temper, and to the fact that Jack would often be seen beating someone up for no good reason, that he was "unpredictable." On cross-examination, Wade got him to admit that Ruby "had a large ego, that he loved to be in the limelight" and that he was "pretty tough." The implication was that he was tough enough to maybe kill somebody who looked at him the wrong way.

And with that, the proceedings ended for the weekend. On Monday, Belli would be bringing out his big guns—the medical and scientific experts he believed would make the psychomotor epilepsy defense come alive for the jury. Who knows? Maybe he could pull it off.

On Saturday night, March 7, Hillel Silverman visited Ruby, having been told by Eva that Jack was eager to see him. "As always," Silverman wrote, "he was disturbed, this time about the impression he had created when one of the police officers quoted him as saying, 'I did it in order to show that the Jews have guts.'

> Ruby denied having said this and . . . denies having told a police officer that he had planned this from Friday evening. "Nor did I say to him someone had to do it and you couldn't. . . . Nor did I try to pull the trigger three times."
>
> "You see, Rabbi, this is a conspiracy. They are all out to get us and they will succeed."

Ruby told Silverman that Belli had come to see him that afternoon and had shown him a clipping from a Houston newspaper playing up the issue of "Jewishness." He told the rabbi that he had watched the replays of his murder of Oswald in the courtroom because "I didn't want to give the jury the impression that I am not interested in these films." He then added, "They even doctored the film to show that I had stepped out from the crowd." That Ruby apparently believed the films had somehow been altered indicates where his mind was headed.

Ruby also thought that Serur had "overdone it" when talking about his "unnatural love" for dogs. But, despite the prisoner's obsessions and concerns, Silverman noted that "this evening, Ruby seems to be in far better control of himself" and that he had asked to see the rabbi "only to make sure that I was not offended by what he was quoted to have said about the Jews."

The trial reconvened, as scheduled, on Monday, March 9. The testimonies would be from a mix of expert witnesses brought by Belli and character witnesses enlisted by him to essentially declare that Ruby was a hotheaded but lovable guy, even kind of crazy, but *not* someone capable of planning out a murder with malice.

Among those who testified to that effect was a doctor who worked for the Dallas Health Department who emphatically contradicted Sergeant Dean's reported timeline for questioning Ruby after the shooting, bolstering the argument that even if Ruby had said what was claimed, he said it way outside the time window in which it could be used against him.

Also testifying was, amazingly, Jack Rubenstein's childhood friend, former welterweight boxing champion and war hero Barney Ross. Ruby was "far more animated during his testimony than at any previous time," note Abrams and Fisher, "leaning forward to make certain he heard every word."

Ross spoke of how, when they were teenagers, Ruby would "go into a tantrum and scream" if his friends didn't take his advice when betting on sports. Ross also noted that after a tantrum "he wouldn't step on a fly or a caterpillar, that's how quiet he would become."

He also noted that Ruby's friends didn't think he was emotionally capable of holding a job, that "he understood his own trouble, and that's why . . . he was on his own all the time." When both sides were finished questioning Ross and he left the witness stand, he stopped at the defense table, warmly shaking hands and exchanging whispered words with his old friend (whom he did admit having seen only a few times since World War II).

Ruby's roommate, George Senator, testified for the defense that Ruby "was in grief" over the assassination of President Kennedy. He recalled that when Ruby left the apartment to send the money to Lynn, "he had a moody look . . . [a] very faraway look . . . a look I had never seen before on him. . . . He was mumbling and he was pacing the floor forth and back, and I just couldn't make out what was going on."

Senator's testimony was useful to both sides. Ruby's emotional response to the assassination could have shown that he had been hatching a plan *or* that he was just off his rocker. Or both. On cross-examination, Wade again insinuated the possibility that Senator and Ruby were lovers. And, when Senator stepped down from the witness stand, he was greeted publicly by a pair of IRS agents who wanted to speak to him about his problematic tax situation. This could not have been encouraging to anyone else planning to testify on Jack Ruby's behalf.

Patricia Ann Burge Kohs, who had danced at the Carousel under the name Penny Dollar and who at the time of the trial was serving time on narcotics charges, also testified. She was perhaps not what would generally be considered a great character witness—except in *this* case, where the aim was to show just how crazy Jack Ruby could be. She was there to testify that, in her presence, Ruby committed an act of violence without seeming to be aware of what he was doing. She asserted that one night, at closing time at the Carousel, Jack had an argument with a cab driver who had come upstairs to find a passenger who had called for a taxi. She said,

> [Jack] knocked him [the driver] down the stairs and out through the door. . . Jack was beating his head on the sidewalk. . . . And then he stopped all of a sudden, and he said, "Did I do this? Did I do this?" . . . He acted like he didn't know that he had done it.

During her and Senator's testimonies, Wade and Alexander did their best, even when objections to that theory were sustained, to insinuate that Ruby only ever attacked men who were smaller than him and women; that he was not only violent but a bully—a guy who'd like nothing more than to shoot a small, unarmed, shackled man and then claim to be a hero.

The defense then introduced a tape recording of the on-the-spot radio broadcast, by reporter Ike Pappas of New York's WNEW radio, of Ruby's shooting of Oswald. Pappas himself then testified. He noted—and the tape, made with a highly sensitive microphone, confirmed—that Ruby hadn't said any of the incriminating things attributed to him during the moment—and the moments immediately after—he shot Oswald. On cross-examination, Wade was not able to rattle the reporter.

Later that day, Belli began to present the true core of his defense: expert witnesses, people who were undisputed stars in the fields of psychology and neurology. However, as Carroll noted,

> At the outset, the prosecutors insisted that Belli wedge his medical case into the legal straitjacket [and Texas law] about whether Ruby knew right from wrong, the so-called legal definition, and Belli argued that the real test was what his whole medical package showed, not whether each doctor could fit into that legalistic box. . . . It was as if his defense was a separate case. . . . Belli . . . [wanted to] get to the sort of thing that had made him famous as a negligence lawyer, detailed medical testimony.

In retrospect, the strategy seems almost magical thinking on Belli's part. And yet, it's possible it *might* have worked, which is why the prosecution enlisted its own experts—eight of them—to rebut Belli's.

The expert witnesses Belli brought in included Drs. Roy Schafer of Yale University, Martin Towler out of Galveston, and Manfred Guttmacher (perhaps the most famous of the witnesses) of the institute named for him.

One witness he *wished* he'd had was Dr. Frederick Gibbs, who had engaged in pioneering research of the electroencephalogram (EEG), upon which much of the other experts' testimony was based. (Invented by Hans Berger in 1924, EEGs measure electrical activity in the brain and are specifically used to detect and investigate epilepsy.) Gibbs was "the first to convincingly record and report EEG findings in epilepsy and states of altered consciousness."

But Gibbs had declined to testify—which didn't stop Belli from using him and his research in making his case with the experts he *did* have on hand. Belli recalls in his 1976 memoir,

> The brunt of our defense—in fact our only defense—was that Jack Ruby was incompetent when he killed Lee Harvey Oswald. . . . From the experts, I was hoping for a medical diagnosis of a *functional*

psychosis, which could lead to a simple insanity plea, one that any juror would have to acknowledge and say, "Well, okay, he's crazy."

Schafer concluded, based on his own tests of Ruby and of EEGs done by others, that Ruby had "organic brain damage" and that it was most likely psychomotor epilepsy. He added that Ruby was a person of great emotional instability, confirming what the non-medical witnesses had attested to. Schafer had no opinion regarding whether or not Ruby knew right from wrong at the time he shot Oswald.

The trial then adjourned for the day. The next day, Tuesday, March 10, testimony by Belli's expert witnesses continued.

Dr. Towler, who had given Ruby the EEGs, gave Jack's medical history, which included many fights and brawls and a number of head injuries. He reported that Ruby had told him he experienced spells during which he felt an intense sense of uneasiness, the feeling that his head was cracking up.

Towler opined that Ruby had an abnormal condition, a seizure disorder of the "psychomotor variant" category, and that a person having one of these seizures is "behaving as an automaton" and doesn't "know what he is doing." Towler, like Schafer, did not venture an opinion on Ruby's condition at the time he murdered Oswald. During Towler's testimony, Belli and company theatrically presented the EEGs as evidence, "six hundred feet of spidery black lines on white chart paper that folded out like an accordion."

Belli added that the EEGs were sent to the famous Dr. Gibbs at the University of Chicago, the man who had helped develop the test, and he confirmed Towler's reading.

Dr. Guttmacher had examined Ruby and believed that he "was not capable of distinguishing right from wrong or of realizing the nature and consequences of his act at the time of the slaying of Oswald." He chalked a lot of Ruby's mental processes up to heredity, and thought that he displayed paranoid thinking.

Guttmacher noted that people like Ruby did not feel guilt over killing Oswald but believed he was an "exterminator" and that Oswald was a "rat." He added that he thought Ruby was unable to tolerate anxiety, and was very unstable, and that the lights and commotion in the police station basement triggered his actions. Ruby, he believed, was "a mental cripple and was carrying on his shoulders an insufferable emotional load and . . . he cracked under it momentarily."

What Guttmacher was *not* willing to say, unfortunately for Belli, was that Ruby had been in the throes of a psychomotor seizure at the moment he shot Oswald. He would only say that Ruby had undergone "a very short-lived psychotic episode."

Surreally, during this testimony, Ruby was absorbed in a book he was reading: Guttmacher's tome *The Mind of the Murderer.*

The prosecution then brought on its *own* experts. Dr. Sheff Olinger, a staff doctor at the Dallas Neurological Clinic, where Ruby had been examined, testified that all Ruby's tests, with the possible exception of the EEG, had turned out normal, but that even an abnormal EEG "would have no significance." He stated that a diagnosis of psychomotor epilepsy couldn't be made on the basis of an EEG alone, and that it was unlikely Ruby would have had his first seizure at the age of fifty-two.

Likewise, Dr. Robert L. Stubblefield, chief of psychiatry at Parkland Hospital, testified that he thought Ruby would have known right from wrong at the time of shooting Oswald. And Dr. John T. Holbrook, who had had examined Ruby the day after the shooting, was of the opinion that Ruby was sane at the time of the shooting and that it wasn't possible for Ruby to have killed Oswald if he was in a fugue state.

Dr. Peter Kellaway, an EEG expert from Houston, stated that an EEG alone never provides a diagnosis, that there was no way to know the source of the abnormality in Ruby's EEG, and that psychomotor variant is not a disease, but a name given by Dr. Gibbs to a particular pattern in EEGs.

Court then adjourned for the day.

The next day would start with a bang—this one, fortunately, only metaphorical.

As he tells it, Belli had gone for a haircut at a barber shop near the courthouse:

> The barber had just placed the towel around my neck when I heard someone say, "—and they got those Jew psychiatrists out from Maryland."
>
> "Yeah," said another voice, "those slick Jew psychiatrists with their slick Jew lawyers."

This was simply Nazi stuff. I swept away the towel and the barber stepped aside as I leaped and gave the Nazi salute. *"Achtung!"* I yelled. *"Achtung! Heil Hitler!"* And I goosestepped out of the shop while those locals stood there with their mouths open.

That day, another prosecution witness, Dr. A. Earl Walker, a professor of neurological surgery at Johns Hopkins University, testified that Ruby's EEG was not necessarily abnormal and that there was no basis for a diagnosis of epilepsy.

By this point, it seemed to be a he-said-she-said situation as far as the experts' testimonies. The jury members had their pick of doctors with impressive credentials whom they could believe or not.

Aside from the medical experts, a testimony of possible significance came from police detective E. H. "Billy" Combest, who was standing about three feet from Leavelle and was looking at Ruby when the shot was fired. Combest recalled that Ruby's lips were moving, but he couldn't make out what he was saying. But he—Combest—had shouted, as Ruby lunged forward, "Jack, you son of a bitch, don't!" Maybe it was *Combest*, not Jack Ruby, who had used the phrase "son of a bitch." And if that quote was wrongly attributed to Ruby, perhaps the damning testimonies of what Jack had said and when could be considered suspect.

That day, March 11, Rabbi Silverman—who would testify the next day—spoke to private investigator Denson. Denson was fed up with the way Belli was conducting the trial and was quitting. He felt Belli was overly concerned with publicity for himself, that he "had not even bothered to read all the material which Denson had prepared." Denson was angry that "every night in his [Belli's] hotel, television people were shooting a picture. He is spending time with them rather than speaking with the witnesses in preparation for the trial."

Silverman visited Ruby that day, finding him "less despondent" than he had anticipated. Ruby was concerned about how Silverman would portray him in his testimony. Silverman wrote,

> He was disturbed that Dr. Guttmacher had made mention of many personal things which "place me in a very unfavorable light." . . . He asked me how I would answer . . . "Why did you not recommend that Ruby see a psychiatrist?" He did not want me to bring up the subject of his dogs. He asked me, "What if they mention my love for Kennedy

and then accuse me of being a homosexual?" I assured him that I did not want to offend him on the stand, but that I would say certain things for his own good. He apparently accepted my explanation.

Now it was Thursday, March 12. The trial was winding down. Among the significant witnesses that day was Dr. Walter Bromberg, director of a private psychiatric hospital in Mount Kisco, New York, testifying for the defense. He had examined Ruby in December and January. Bromberg testified that he believed "Ruby was mentally ill and did not know the nature and quality of his acts at the time of the shooting," that he "was emotionally unstable, and had an epileptic personality," and that his "actions were of an automatic nature, not voluntarily controlled." The specific term *psychomotor epilepsy* was never uttered by Bromberg, though.

The prosecution proceeded to fairly thoroughly discredit Bromberg by implying, based on the most negative possible interpretations of work he'd done in the past, that he was in favor of allowing convicted sex offenders complete freedom to mingle in society.

Hillel Silverman then took the stand as a character witness. If Jack Ruby was, for all his pride in being Jewish, seen by many Jews as an embarrassment and worse, Silverman was the diametric opposite—spiritual yet rational, a modern figure representing the gravitas of an ancient people with a history of persecution.

As he had at the bail hearing, Silverman mentioned that on the Friday night of the Kennedy assassination, Ruby "seemed to be in sort of a trance . . . and rather than mention the terrible thing that happened that afternoon, he suddenly thanked me for visiting his sister in the hospital the previous week, which struck me . . . as being very, very odd."

Silverman also recalled that two months before the assassination, Ruby had phoned him, upset that Eva wouldn't attend high holiday services with him. When Silverman asked Eva why that was, she told him that Jack "had shoved her, pushed her, and actually struck her." And yet, when the rabbi asked Ruby about this, Jack claimed he had no memory of any such event.

Silverman also spoke of Ruby's strange relationship with his dogs. He then said that he considered Ruby "very unstable, very emotional, very erratic."

And, responding to a question by Tonahill, he expressed the opinion that "at the time of the shooting he [Ruby] did not know the difference of right and wrong." Silverman added that "I have found that on many occasions Jack has been most emotional; very rational one moment, very logical, very precise and then suddenly would begin to cry . . . and then suddenly come right out of it and would return again to emotional stability. . . . He will suddenly stop in his conversation, with a blank slate, again, almost a trance."

The rabbi added, "It is also my opinion that during these last few months, and at this moment, he doesn't know the difference between right and wrong." This would be the only testimony in the entire trial on the topic or Ruby's *present* state of mind.

Wade treated Silverman politely, as if to show that, despite Belli's opinion, the prosecution was not prejudiced against Jews—at least not any Jew who wasn't named Jack Ruby. The prosecutor simply confirmed that, despite his belief that Ruby was mentally ill, Silverman had never suggested to Ruby that he see a psychiatrist. It seems that the point being made here by Wade was that, if Silverman was *really* concerned about Ruby's mental health, he would have suggested he see one.

In the middle of these testimonies, though, fireworks again erupted.

First, and seemingly out of the blue, Joe Tonahill announced that the near-legendary Dr. Frederick A. Gibbs—the pioneering researcher of the EEG, who had up to now declined to testify—had changed his mind and would be in court the following morning! Even Belli hadn't known that Gibbs would actually show up.

Though DA Wade and Judge Brown made a show of declaring that Gibbs's pending appearance was too little too late and that the trial "had to" end that day, they really had no choice but to allow this figure—praised throughout the proceedings by both sides—to have his say. Neither prosecutor nor judge wanted to risk the jury feeling they'd been denied hearing a crucial piece of testimony.

And then, before adjourning for the day, the defense called Alice Nichols, Ruby's former girlfriend, to testify. Belli had indicated to the jury that her testimony would not be that important. As Kaplan and Waltz note, though:

> In a sense, this was a great shame because . . . hers was one of the most dramatic interludes of the trial. One had only to look at the woman on the stand to know that Jack Ruby had ruined her life . . . having wasted about ten years . . . with someone she loved but who would not marry her.

Nichols testified to Tonahill that when she spoke to Ruby on the day of the JFK assassination, he had sounded upset. She also said that she didn't recall him ever mentioning suicide to her, even during his period of profound business failure, when he "was very despondent . . . lost quite a bit of weight and he looked very bad." She didn't feel that, even then, he was in danger of taking his own life. On cross-examination, Wade revealed that he had spoken to her previously:

> WADE: And I believe I asked you if you had any opinion as to whether or not he was sane or insane and I believe you told me, "I never did feel he was insane. I never could see any indications of insanity"?
> NICHOLS: That's right.

Nichols's opinion was most likely why Belli, though probably hoping her presence would humanize Ruby in the jury's eyes, had also tried to minimize in advance the specifics of her testimony.

Seth Kantor points out, though, that, despite the fact that they had broken up years ago, "the day John F. Kennedy was killed, Alice Nichols was one of the first people Jack Ruby wanted to turn to." He continues:

> Joe Tonahill recalls the heartbreak in Ruby's face as Mrs. Nichols was called to the witness stand and passed by the defense counsel table where Ruby sat, without even looking at him.
> But Robert B. Denson recalls something else. . . . He remembers that when Alice Nichols finished her testimony, and passed

by again, Ruby pushed his chair back, stood and bowed gently toward her.

As she left the courthouse, Nichols found herself at the mercy of some twenty photographers, flashbulbs going off in her face, "and this additional stress was enough to destroy her brittle composure. She broke into tears and struggled to get away . . . out of the courthouse." Finally, about half a block away, she "permitted herself to be surrounded by her pursuers, who snapped picture after picture as she sobbed and shouted incoherently."

And then it was Friday the thirteenth. Dr. Gibbs did indeed take the stand. Belli recalled that "some . . . said he resembled Henry Fonda. . . . He was tall, with a square jaw, deep-set flickering eyes, his dark hair grey at the temples . . . the scientist personified."

At home in Chicago, Gibbs had been following the trial, growing more and more annoyed as the prosecution attacked his findings regarding Ruby. He felt he had to appear. An innovator in EEGs, he had first named psycho-motor epilepsy in a 1952 book. It was clear to him that Jack Ruby suffered from the malady.

"Jack Ruby," Gibbs testified, "has a particular, very rare, form of epilepsy. . . . The pattern occurs only in one-half of one percent of epileptics, and is a distinctive and unusual epileptic pattern."

Unfortunately, there was one thing Gibbs would *not* say.

When Bill Alexander asked him if he thought Ruby knew the difference between right and wrong, and the nature and consequences of his act, at the moment he fired at Lee Harvey Oswald, Gibbs's response was not what anyone thought it would be.

As Jury foreman Max Causey wrote in his memoir:

> Dr. Gibbs's answer absolutely floored me, because I felt certain that he would offer his opinion to support the defense. [But] he stated, without hesitation, "I have no opinion." . . .
>
> Needless to say, I had expected more from this great man. Perhaps I had expected too much.

And with that, testimony in the case came to an end. It was a little after 10 AM on Friday, March 13, 1964.

———————

Silverman visited Ruby in his cell shortly after this, at 12:30, just before Judge Brown was to charge the jury—that is, instruct jury members how they should weigh the evidence to come to a verdict. Silverman reported that Ruby "was not as despondent as I had anticipated. He was terribly concerned about the testimony of Dr. Gibbs that morning. He felt that it was very unfavorable to him." Silverman noted that Belli thought the opposite, despite Gibbs' lack of opinion on that point crucial to the defense. Silverman then observed,

> Ruby was terribly concerned that [Alice] Nichols was forced to testify the afternoon before. He did not want her to think that he had caused her to testify.
>
> He was terribly concerned about the verdict of the jury. "Under no condition do I want to fight for an appeal. I can't go through this again."
>
> He was not at all offended by my testimony the day before.

The rabbi related that Ruby mentioned he had prayed that morning and referred to a prayer for forgiveness he found in the prayerbook. "What will you do, Rabbi," he asked, "if the verdict is bad?" Silverman's notes make no mention of a response.

They would know the verdict soon enough.

22 | PLEADING FOR A LIFE

THOUGH THE OFFICIAL ARGUMENTS in the Jack Ruby murder trial were over, steps still needed to be taken before the jury would determine his fate.

First, Judge Brown would charge the jury. Then, the opposing sides would give summation arguments, distilling for the jury the reasons why their side was right. After that, the judge would give yet another set of instructions to the jury, which would only *then* deliberate and reach a verdict.

Though the summations would, as required, recapitulate the arguments already made, they also, in this strange trial, would end up being compressed, high-potency versions of the previous days' chaos, supercharged with emotion and laden with personal attacks from both sides. All that was missing was Jerry Springer as moderator.

In a Texas trial, the charge to the jury would be written by the prosecution, then vetted by the judge, and, if necessary, amended by him. Only then could he show it to the defense. On finally seeing the version provided by Judge Brown, the defense's Joe Tonahill angrily noted that it pointed the jury toward "a directed verdict of guilty of cold-blooded murder." And his fellow defense team member Phil Burleson realized that it was nearly identical to a charge from a recent murder trial where an insanity defense had been rejected by the jury and the defendant sentenced to death.

In response to the charge, Burleson wrote a thirty-six-page document containing 134 objections to it. This, and wrangling between the lawyers, delayed getting the charge to the jury. Belli pleaded to have the closing arguments begin the next day, Saturday, but Wade wanted to keep things going through the night, worried that the jury—with no alternates—might somehow not make it intact to the next day.

Brown sided with the prosecution and announced that the trial would resume at 8:00 PM that night. He also announced that TV cameras, which he had reluctantly banned from the trial up to now, would be allowed for the reading of the verdict but were then to be immediately turned off, because of anticipated tumult, no matter *what* the verdict would be.

Spectators started arriving and taking seats well before eight o'clock. "This final session," Abrams and Fisher noted, "had been transformed into a social event. Spectators dressed for an evening out piled into the courtroom."

The jury was called back in, and the judge delivered the charge *and* the defense's objections to the jurors. The main issue to be decided, Brown told them, was Jack Ruby's mental state when he committed the crime. As the *New York Times* put it, "The jury, if it finds Ruby sane and guilty, may choose from a wide range of penalties, from death in the electric chair to a suspended sentence. The jury [however] must acquit Ruby if it believes he was insane at the time of the killing."

Next were the final arguments.

In his summation, Bill Alexander charged that "American justice is on trial" and that Ruby had denied Oswald the protection of the law, had appointed himself to be Oswald's "judge, his jury and his executioner!" He declaimed, "You denied him the very thing that your demand through your lawyer the loudest." Alexander also charged that Ruby "wanted to become famous and make money" out of killing Oswald. "He is nothing but a thrill killer seeking notoriety!" Alexander even implied that perhaps there had indeed been a conspiracy behind Ruby killing Oswald, stating that "the Lord knows what secret—" Before he could go on, Belli objected and, for once, Brown sustained the objection.

For the defense, Phil Burleson spoke first, emphasizing that, even if the jurors believed Ruby was sane when he shot Oswald, if they also felt that he didn't act with evil intent or malice, he should receive a light sentence. Ruby had acted on impulse, he argued, with no advance thought or planning. In effect, this was the traditional defense for an emotion-triggered, unpremeditated murder. Burleson, at least, wasn't giving up on making sure that—apart from the bells and whistles of Belli's psychomotor epilepsy defense—the jury remembered that they still had the option of judging the killing a crime of passion.

Joe Tonahill made things personal when he accused Wade of demanding "that you do something to Jack Ruby to make up for this great political opportunity that Mr. Wade might have had to prosecute Lee Harvey Oswald!" Of Bill Alexander, Tonahill bizarrely noted, "Have you watched his . . . tarantula-like eyes and seen the terrific pleasure he would derive if you would give [Jack Ruby] a death sentence?"

By the time Tonahill finished, it was after 11:00 PM. Now it was prosecutor Jim Bowie's turn. Named after the legendary hero of the Alamo who was famous as a knife fighter and who was further immortalized in the 1950s *The Adventures of Jim Bowie* TV series (complete with a memorable theme song), Bowie got in some sharp digs of his own, coming across as eccentric—or maybe just trying to stay awake after the arduous day—as he "bounced around the courtroom on the balls of his feet, whirled his arms out of sync with his words and would suddenly crouch or do several deep-knee bends." Bowie characterized Tonahill's oration as "the oldest defense . . . if you can't defend the defendant, prosecute the prosecutor."

Seizing on Belli's various statements relating to real or perceived antisemitism directed at Ruby, Bowie observed that Ruby saw himself as "the martyr, the hero . . . the anointed one, the Messiah" who claimed he killed Oswald "for the Jewish race? . . . As if the Jewish race needs any assistance in being brave. . . . He never did if for any race. . . . The suffering that race has had is horrible. And it didn't take a Jack Ruby to do anything for them. They have done plenty for our community, for the country and this state, that they don't need his assistance."

Bowie finished a little before midnight. It was then the exhausted Melvin Belli's turn. As Belli would recall, "I felt like Alice in Wonderland falling down the hole. My feet didn't seem to touch the floor."

While Belli, of course, refuted the prosecution's case, he largely appealed to the jury's emotions.

"The cry goes out . . ." he declared. "'Who would do a thing like this?' The village character . . . the village idiot, the village clown . . . The man who is always around the police station bringing the coffee . . . the donuts, the sandwiches, who can be sent out for the cold beer. Publicity . . . he seeks? . . . I suppose [that] . . . we'd all like to engrave our initials in some oak tree, that we'd like to be . . . in Dorothy Kilgallen's column . . . be engraved at Mr. Rushmore. . . . I think it's a part of our craving to seek after some bit of immortality.

"This poor sick fellow . . . and you know he's sick in your hearts, every one of the twelve of you . . ." the lawyer continued. "Acquit him, not guilty by reason of insanity. . . . Give him a just and fair verdict compatible with modern science. That's what the world wants to see in justice from this community." Belli was asking them to prioritize the insanity-by-way-of-psychomotor-epilepsy argument, to essentially ignore Burleson's crime-of-passion/murder-without-malice argument.

Belli later justified his approach by insisting—reasonably—that Wade had won death sentences in twenty-four of twenty-five murder cases he had tried. There was essentially nothing to risk by focusing on the esoteric epilepsy defense when any appeal for mercy or lenience would likely have been subverted by Wade's prosecutorial expertise. Belli also later asked, rhetorically, "Would it have been moral to take this sick man, this mental cripple and have him grovel, 'I'm just a Jew boy and I'm sorry. Please forgive me.' I don't believe that demeaning Ruby in that way would have been right tactically any more than morally."

Henry Wade was the last lawyer to present, going on at 12:45 AM Saturday morning. This landmark, highly publicized case, when focus and precision were of utmost importance, was going on way past the hour when even the most motivated lawyers and jurors could function optimally.

Wade touched on the possibility of conspiracy, noting that Ruby's lethal deed had robbed not only Oswald of his life but also the country "of the right to see whether anyone helped him or not." (Wade later recalled receiving a call from a Lyndon Johnson aide on the night of Kennedy's assassination, cautioning, "Any word of a conspiracy . . . by foreign nations . . . would shake our nation to its foundation . . . whether I could prove it or not . . . I was to charge Oswald with plain murder." Was he saying that, given his druthers, he would have approached the case differently?)

But the meat of his argument was what it had been all along.

"Ladies and gentlemen, what would you want the history books to say about you?" the DA asked. He insisted that to "turn this man loose, you would set civilization back a century; you would set it back to barbarianism; you would set it back to lynch law, and say that 'anybody that I have decided should be killed, I can kill.' . . .

"I ask you . . . to show Jack Ruby the same mercy, compassion, and the same sympathy that he showed Lee Harvey Oswald."

Wade finished a little after 1:00 AM Saturday morning. Instead of giving the jury its final instructions then, however, Judge Brown sent them back to their quarters to get some sleep and declared that their deliberations would begin later that morning.

———————

And so, at a little after 9:00 AM on Saturday, March 14, the jury's deliberations commenced. To add another dose of surrealism to the proceedings, outside the courthouse, high school bands were tuning up for the St. Patrick's Day parade that was scheduled to start in a few hours, three days early so people off from work for the weekend could enjoy it. Seeing the parade preparations going on, Jim Bowie quipped, "Dallas is sure crowding its luck holding another parade for an Irishman."

After voting for Max Causey as foreman, the jury quickly decided that Jack Ruby was sane.

A little later, the jury's members agreed that Ruby was guilty of murder *with* malice. As Kaplan and Waltz note, "The single factor mentioned most often [in the jury's deliberations] was that Ruby had shot a manacled, defenseless man."

They next concluded that the only possible sentences were either life imprisonment or death. They ruled out any possibility of a lighter sentence, although a life sentence would make Ruby eligible for parole in ten years.

After several ballots were taken by the group—Causey trying to slow the deliberations down just to make sure there wasn't undue haste—a sentence was agreed on.

It had taken the jury all of two hours and nineteen minutes to decide Jack Ruby's fate.

Causey sent word to the judge that the group had arrived at a verdict. None of the lawyers, though, had expected one before the afternoon. Some had left the building, and Judge Brown himself had gone home to rest. By the time all parties were assembled, an hour had passed.

At that point, the jurors were allowed to enter the courtroom. A single TV camera—disallowed to be used until now—with feeds to all three major networks, was switched on for the verdict to be read.

"Is this your verdict?" asked Brown. The jurors all affirmed that it was. Causey wrote the verdict on a form and handed it to the judge.

Belli sensed that it was unlikely such a speedy decision was good news for his client. He whispered to Ruby, "It's bad. Take it easy. We expected it all along and we tried this case for the appeal court. We'll make it there."

Judge Brown read the verdict aloud:

"We the jury find the defendant guilty of murder with malice as charged in the indictment and assess his punishment as death."

The verdict was unsurprising.

The verdict was shocking.

23 | CONDEMNED

JACK RUBY SHOWED NO VISIBLE EMOTION at being condemned to death.

Melvin Belli was less stoic. After a second or two, as Ruby was being led back to his cell, his lawyer leaped to his feet and cried out:

> May I thank the jury for a victory for bigotry and injustice!
>
> Don't worry, Jack—we'll appeal this to a court outside Dallas where there is justice and due process of law!
>
> I hope the people of Dallas are proud of this jury that has made Dallas a city of shame forevermore!

As the jurors left the courtroom, reporters flooded in. Brown made his way to Belli, who refused to shake his hand. "I can't shake hands with you, Judge," Belli said. "You've got blood on your hands."

"I'm sorry you feel that way about it, Mel," Brown said to him. "Come back and see us again."

Brown would later admit to being taken aback by the death sentence. It "shocked even me," he admitted. The editor of the *Dallas Times Herald*, A. C. Greene, said, "The town's a little bit shaken. The verdict was almost as shocking as Ruby's own shooting [of Oswald] had been." The overall feeling seemed to have been that Ruby would be sentenced to life, avoiding a more extreme fate.

As jury foreman Max Causey later wrote, "Perhaps twelve other jurors . . . might possibly have reached a different verdict, but to each of us, the defense

215

counsel had completely failed to establish a reasonable doubt in our minds Jack Ruby did not know right from wrong and the nature and consequences of his act at the time he shot Lee Harvey Oswald." He added, "There should have been more latitude within the law as it would apply to an unstable person than there was."

Soon after the verdict, Belli and his team visited Ruby in his cell. He was "calm but distant," as if he didn't completely understand the impact of the verdict. "Just think," Ruby reportedly said. "If they can do this to me, think how many others they've railroaded in Dallas." More than the verdict, he seemed upset that the police officers he thought of as friends had testified against him.

When the verdict was read, Hillel Silverman had been at a bar mitzvah reception at his synagogue, Shearith Israel. He received word of the decision during that celebration. "I was completely shocked and stunned," he wrote." It took me hours before this sank in."

Eva called him early in the afternoon, hysterical. He was able to calm her down and made arrangements to meet with the family and Denson at 9:30 PM, after he was scheduled to visit Jack.

Indeed, after evening services, Silverman visited Ruby at 8:45 PM. He recalled saying to himself, "It is all over and no one gives a damn about Jack. He is all alone and is atoning for Oswald."

The rabbi was surprised to find Ruby in "reasonably good spirits. . . . I had expected that he would be extremely depressed or would be climbing the walls. He shed no tears, nor did he utter any complaint. . . . He looked better than he has in weeks." He reported Ruby telling him, "It is a great relief now that it's over" and then, bizarrely, "It is a conspiracy. They are out to get me."

Silverman noted that he relayed a message to Jack from Earl that hundreds of calls were flooding in, people asking what they could do to help. Silverman also wrote that he was informed that Ruby's jailors "had become much more sympathetic and friendly with him because of the verdict. They were patting him on the back." The rabbi was told that as soon as he returned to his cell after the verdict, Ruby had gone to sleep for over an hour, and when he awoke said, "It was the best sleep I've had in a few weeks." Silverman reflected,

"Undoubtedly the implication of the verdict has stunned Jack and really not sunk in."

The clergyman then went to his meeting with Eva, Eileen, Earl, and Denson. Eva told him that Jack had joked with her that afternoon, "Where I'm going, I won't need shirts." The family informed Silverman that they were about to fire Belli. They told him that the defense had cost them many thousands of dollars and they were desperate for money to continue. Silverman wrote, "I was impressed by the way the family was sticking together despite the tragedy."

The rabbi recalled that Earl told him Jack had strangely asked a few days before: "When will the trial begin?" Earl also reported to him that, that very afternoon, Jack had said, "I want to take a lie detector test to show I didn't kill him." Was Jack now remembering his widely witnessed murderous act as not having happened?

In short order, Belli was, indeed, fired by the Ruby family. Nonetheless, like pretty much all the many lawyers who had served in Jack's defense, he refused to completely go away.

Over the following three years, until Ruby's death in early 1967, there would be endless hearings and examinations and depositions and news stories relating to Jack Ruby. Through it all, his lineup of lawyers would constantly be shifting, the lawyers continually squabbling among themselves, all leading to regularly changing advice to Ruby and his family. The height—or depth, if you will—of the internecine fighting between his lawyers came when one fired another only to be informed by the other man that, no, *he* was doing the firing of the first one!

Much of this infighting was due to the multiheaded beast that was the Ruby family—including Jack himself—wanting to have much more say going forward in the various motions and appeals than they'd felt they'd had in the trial itself. They believed they'd been ignored and badly used by Belli and didn't want that to happen again.

By the same token, with their funds virtually exhausted, there was in theory a limit to how controlling they could be. But the case kept attracting lawyers like the proverbial moths to a flame, lawyers who, for the most part, didn't seem to care if they made much or any money representing Jack Ruby. Perhaps the challenge of trying to procure freedom for a man who'd murdered a shackled victim—and changed the course of history—in front of millions of witnesses was more exciting to legal minds at these top levels than was any possible payday.

In the meantime, the Warren Commission was steadily going about its work. A significant portion of the commission's investigations, of course, was focused on Jack Ruby. Did Ruby and Oswald have a previous relationship? Was Ruby acting on behalf of anyone when he committed the killing?

Leon Hubert and Burt Griffin were the commission lawyers assigned to investigate Ruby's background, connections, and possible motives, a task they took seriously. They had many questions, including about the number and nature of Ruby's Cuba trips.

Hubert and Griffin also wondered if Ruby might possibly have known Oswald, if only because they had discovered that the housekeeper at Oswald's rooming house had a sister who had met with Ruby several times, including on November 18, 1963, to discuss an investment with him. In a memo to J. Lee Rankin, the commission's general counsel, Hubert and Griffin emphasized, "We believe that the possibility exists, based on evidence already available, that Ruby was involved in illegal dealing with Cuban elements who might have had contact with Oswald."

Griffin and Hubert pushed for more investigation into Ruby's activities, including interviewing Jack. Earl Warren hadn't wanted to interview Ruby until his trial was finished, so that anything said or done before the commission wouldn't in any way prejudice the trial's outcome. Ultimately, Griffin and Hubert were blocked from investigating such questions of conspiracy.

Griffin was not pleased with that decision, although, years later, he came to a different understanding of why he and Hubert had not been allowed to go further. As he told the Select Committee on Assassinations of the US House of Representatives in 1976:

> The evidence seemed overwhelming that Oswald was the assassin and the conspiracy questions that remained were entirely speculative. They were based upon political or underworld acquaintanceships but

devoid of any concrete evidence on any participation in a murder or in the planning of a murder. . . . No witness . . . has come forward with information showing that any specific person assisted or encouraged either Oswald or Ruby in their murders.

And I would like to point out a major success which Warren Commission critics tend largely to ignore . . . that the civil liberties of Americans were conscientiously protected by the Commission and the Commission did not become an official witch hunt [like the recent-in-1963 McCarthy hearings of the 1950s] that destroyed the reputations and lives of innocent citizens.

Interestingly, in a 2018 interview with the Columbus Underground's Jesse Bethea, Griffin noted,

After Oswald shot at [General Edwin] Walker and missed, there was a wave of antisemitic violence in Dallas because the supporters of Walker were convinced that Jews were the ones that shot at Walker. So there's this ironic connection between all of this kind of stuff. . . . This whole business about Ruby fearing antisemitism, there are a lot of valid reasons why Ruby would feel that way.

As Bethea summarized, "To Griffin, the influences of antisemitism on Jack Ruby's behavior that week in 1963 make more sense than an assassination plot. They were also understated in the final Warren Commission report, spawning hundreds of conspiracy theories."

Of course, in 1963 and 1964, Griffin did not have the benefit of hindsight regarding any of these topics.

Another commission lawyer, David Belin, also thought having Ruby testify posttrial for the commission was important. Although he wasn't on the team assigned to investigate Ruby, commission lawyers were given the flexibility to step outside their assigned zones. Belin had become friends with Hillel Silverman during a recent study trip to Israel that they'd both been on. Because of his relationship with the rabbi, Belin had become especially interested in Ruby.

With the trial over, it was now more likely that Ruby and his handlers might agree to have him testify before the commission. But it was by no means a sure thing. Ruby's brain trust couldn't agree whether or not it was a good idea.

With this in mind, in mid-March, Belin and commission senior lawyer Joe Ball flew to Dallas to begin investigations in the city and to meet with Silverman. The rabbi reiterated that he believed that Ruby was not part of any conspiracy and that Ruby and Oswald had never met each other.

At Belin's next meeting with Silverman later in the month, Belin broached the subject of a lie-detector test. Belin told the rabbi, "I believed that Ruby would never convince the world . . . of his innocence of any conspiracy unless he undertook a lie detector test." But he knew the commission would likely never ask Ruby to take a polygraph—Earl Warren himself didn't believe they were credible—unless, Belin continued, Ruby "made it a condition precedent to giving any testimony before the Commission."

Belin convinced Silverman that he was right, and Silverman informed him that Ruby had actually repeatedly requested such a test. But Ruby's lawyers had refused to allow him to testify before the commission with or without a lie detector, fearing he might say something incriminating that could sabotage his appeals.

Silverman reiterated to Belin that he strongly felt that "Ruby was innocent of any conspiracy, and he felt that in the long run, the most helpful thing would be to have this innocence of conspiracy accepted throughput the world." (Or, as Silverman told me in 2013, "He was really too stupid to be part of a conspiracy.") Belin recalled that Silverman "agreed that there could be no better way" to prove Ruby innocent of conspiracy "than through a lie detector test."

The next day, when Silverman visited Ruby, Jack "agreed immediately to appear before the Warren Commission." No mention seems to have been made of the lie-detector aspect. "Burleson, Eva, Earl, and [Ruby's business lawyer] Stanley [Kaufman] all thought it was an excellent idea. Hubert Winston Smith wanted to think it over." (Smith, a doctor as well as a lawyer, had been Belli's medical advisor on the case and was now on board for the new legal team. He would soon leave the case, though, when his employer, the University of Texas Law School, threatened him with termination if he didn't.)

Earl Ruby, the family's point man in the continuing quest for Jack's freedom, was a fellow Detroit-area Hebrew school parent with lawyer Sol Dann. Through that relationship, Dann became the family's main scout for new lawyers. For a short time, it seemed the legendary Percy Foreman, who had almost joined the defense early on, would now come onto the case. But Foreman resigned sixteen hours after he was hired, unwilling to take instructions from the Rubys or from Kaufman—who was now also in the mix. In his resignation letter, Foreman told Jack Ruby, "You have my sympathy and best wishes."

Tonahill and Burleson were still involved with the case, filing various motions, in effect trying to convince Judge Brown to remove himself from the case or otherwise admit he was guilty of judicial misconduct. While the chances were nil that he'd do either, the motions did get those objections on the record.

Silverman visited Ruby in his cell on March 25, 1964, two days after Foreman's departure. He found that Ruby "looked terribly depressed and confused." He observed that, in the conflict with Foreman and hiring of Smith, "Ruby seemed to [had] have little to do with these decisions."

With Passover only a few days away, Silverman brought Ruby matzah and a Haggadah, the prayer book followed during Passover seders. The clergyman assured Jack that by next Passover he would be free. As he was leaving, Silverman reported, Sheriff Decker "begged me to speak to Eva. He related that when she visits [Ruby] she upsets him tremendously and loud arguments in the waiting room evince [sic] between them." Decker, himself a colorful Dallas character, seemed—like so many others—to genuinely care about Jack Ruby.

Of course, the sheriff was also determined that Ruby would come to no harm under his supervision. "If anything should happen to Ruby while he was with the other prisoners, I would never forgive myself," he told Silverman. Ruby was, supposedly, under twenty-four-hour suicide watch.

———————————

On Friday, March 27, a few hours before Passover was to begin at sundown, Silverman visited Ruby again, bringing more requested Passover food, though anything in glass containers was banned "lest he mutilate himself with them."

Silverman noted that "Jack was delighted" with the items he was brought. Nonetheless, Silverman observed that Ruby seemed "quiet and depressed."

And by Friday, April 17, Silverman observed that Ruby "has deteriorated so rapidly that I have the feeling he is on the verge of a complete mental breakdown. He was disturbed and distressed, at times completely incoherent." Silverman recorded that "he feels that . . . they will throw him in the 'hole' and torture him. He pleaded with me to see the Governor and other individuals in order to forestall a 'blood purge' against the Jews."

Then, on Friday, April 24, after having received two urgent calls from Ruby himself, Silverman came to visit. "He has deteriorated tremendously since I last saw him," recalled the rabbi. "I have never seen him so completely incoherent and despondent . . . on the verge of complete mental collapse. He seems to have lost at least 40 pounds since he has been incarcerated." Ruby drew Silverman aside and whispered that "there is going to be the greatest purge against the Jews of America in all history. They have already started. It is a plot. Even Tonahill and Burleson are in on it. . . . You are next on the list." Ruby believed that the killings were going on in Dallas even as they were speaking. Silverman was unable to calm him.

As if to further demonstrate Ruby's psychological deterioration, two days later, on April 26, in the early hours of the morning, Ruby asked his guard to get him a glass of water and, very briefly alone, had "run and struck his head against the wall," as Decker told Dr. Louis Jolyon West, a professor of psychiatry at the University of Oklahoma School of Medicine, who had come to Dallas to examine Ruby at the defense's request. (West had conducted radical mind-control psychological experiments, some using LSD, codenamed MK-Ultra, for the CIA. His involvement with Ruby would, of course, provide more fodder for conspiracy theories.)

When West examined Ruby, he found him to be "pale, tremulous, agitated and depressed" and proclaimed him "obviously psychotic." He further reported that, the previous night, Ruby had become convinced that "all the Jews in America were being slaughtered" and that he was the cause of it. Kennedy's assassination, Ruby believed, was now being blamed on him, and that he was the cause of the murders of "twenty-five million innocent [Jewish] people." He was positive that his brother Sam had been "tortured, horribly mutilated, castrated and burned in the street outside the jail."

Ruby claimed he could still hear Sam's screams when West was there. "When Dr. West attempted to convince him that no such events had taken place, Ruby had become furious." West diagnosed Ruby as having "sunk into a paranoid state, manifested by delusions, visual and auditory hallucinations, and suicidal impulses." He did not believe that Ruby was malingering, notably because Jack had rejected any suggestion that he was now "mentally ill," whereas West felt that people who were faking insanity generally welcome any such diagnosis.

West, who was there to try to figure out Ruby's state of mind when he killed Oswald, abandoned that quest in view of what he saw as Ruby's psychotic state. He urged that Ruby be hospitalized immediately, as he was "actively suicidal."

West had specifically met with Ruby in part to help him prepare for a Monday, April 27, court hearing to determine if he required additional psychiatric tests in a hospital. According to Silverman, Ruby had called the rabbi at 7:30 that morning "to make sure that I was not assassinated." The rabbi continued that, while visiting Ruby before the hearing, "I discovered that he was completely incoherent." Ruby said to him, "I have heard the scream of Jews being tortured all last night. They are boiling Jews in vats of oil. They have killed my brother Earl and are after my family. You will never get out of this prison alive. . . . All the Jews are dead. . . . This is the end."

Nonetheless, the hearing did take place, and Ruby did attend, Silverman sitting with him and trying to calm him. "Every few minutes," Silverman noted, "he would turn to me and tell me that I was to be assassinated next and that all his family were murdered."

———————————

After the wall incident, Ruby had been taken to a hospital, where he was found to not have seriously hurt himself. But Sheriff Decker also reported that Ruby had recently been caught fashioning a noose for himself out of the lining of his prison clothes. Other sources indicate that Ruby in fact made an actual attempt to hang himself and another time tried to electrocute himself by standing in a puddle in his cell and sticking his finger in a light socket. All three of the suicide attempts failed. Where was the twenty-four-hour watch?

On Wednesday, April 29, there was a hearing to determine if Ruby was entitled to another trial. Tonahill and Burleson had compiled a list of 205 errors made during the trial, assigning blame for many of them to Judge Brown. Silverman came to visit Ruby shortly before the hearing, at which Ruby was to appear. The rabbi recalled that "he was in an even more emotional state" than he had been on his previous visit. He constantly asked, "Can't you hear the screams downstairs? They are torturing the Jews." He said, "They have my brother Earl and have killed him. You will never get out of the court today alive. I am responsible for this great tragedy."

According to Silverman, Ruby went on like this for quite a while. "He would whisper rapidly and then suddenly stop to hear the screams of Jews being tortured. A few times his mind went completely blank and there were minutes of silence. Suddenly he stood up and kissed me on the cheek. 'I am kissing you goodbye because I will never see you again. They will kill you as soon as you leave my cell.'"

Ruby then produced a pencil and wrote out some illegible names for Silverman on a piece of paper, asking that he contact those people immediately. "It is a kangaroo court," he told the rabbi. "It is all a farce and a plot." Silverman opined, "There is no possibility of Jack's 'putting on an act.' He was far too emotional, irrational, incoherent and obviously mentally deranged to be 'playing games.'"

Silverman sat next to Ruby during the hearing, and every few minutes, he would turn to the rabbi and say things like, "This is the end. They will kill you today. This is the greatest tragedy in history." And later, in his cell, he asked Silverman, "Will God forgive me for all that I have done? I am worse than Hitler." Apparently believing all he was saying to be true, Ruby "grumbled to guards that his family and lawyers were trying to make him out a crazy man."

The hearing itself was "as contentious as the trial had been. Within an hour Tonahill and Bowie were shouting, accusing each other of having 'no guts.'" During the six weeks since the verdict, Ruby had greatly deteriorated. "He appeared in court looking nervous, gaunt and haggard and throughout the hearing muttered to himself." During a recess, he said to Eva "Goodbye, I'm not coming back." Nonetheless, Wade remained convinced, unlike Silverman and West, that Ruby *was* putting on an act in order to convince Brown to declare him insane. Brown, indeed, rejected the defense motion for a new trial.

Silverman saw Ruby again on Wednesday, May 6. Though he found him calmer than he'd been the last time, "he was still despondent and incoherent." Ruby still insisted that massacres and pogroms were going on. He "begged me to see Governor Connally or 'the authorities' in Washington." And he kept asking the rabbi, "You don't think I'm crazy, do you?"

"He mentions Oswald now by name," Silverman noted, "and claims that the American public is accusing him of assassinating not Oswald but Kennedy. He is guilt-stricken about his family. Each time I attempted to take leave of him he begged me to remain a little longer."

Those words are the last in Hillel Silverman's notes about his visits with Jack Ruby. In June, not long after this meeting with his congregant, Silverman left Dallas for good. "I was getting restless," he wrote. "I wanted to move on. I was haunted by this tragic episode, emotionally drained, and I needed to change my venue . . . it was time to go." Silverman would move to Los Angeles to helm a congregation there.

But while Hillel Silverman may have been gone, Earl Warren was finally coming to town.

24 | UNLEASHED

JACK RUBY'S FIRST WARREN COMMISSION TESTIMONY was given on June 7, 1964, in a small converted kitchen in the Dallas County Jail.

Sources differ as to why the Ruby family had decided to accede to Jack's demands to speak to the commission. Unsurprisingly, his various lawyers couldn't agree on whether letting him do so was a good idea or not. Despite that, the interview was scheduled. Ruby himself was, of course, obsessed with speaking with Earl Warren, especially if that testimony would include being hooked up to a lie detector.

Ruby's inner logic—or illogic—seemed to go something like this: If he could speak to Warren, then perhaps Warren could get him a meeting with Lyndon Johnson, who—although Jack thought the guy might have actually been behind Kennedy's murder—might for some reason be willing to listen to Ruby's pleas and call off the extermination of America's Jews, if only as a favor to Johnson's longtime Jewish friend Judge Abe Fortas.

Warren had not wanted to come to Dallas in the first place—it was the heart of "Impeach Earl Warren" country. But he realized it was historically important for him to take Ruby's testimony personally, and so he went. But if he or anyone thought that Ruby's interview would be a polite, orderly affair like so many of the question-and-answer sessions conducted by the commission's lawyers—well, they would be sorely mistaken.

Though their desire to have Ruby testify was now being honored, Hubert and Griffin were not invited to be present at the killer's testimony. Hubert, fed up with what he saw as the commission having ignored much of the work he'd done, had resigned. Griffin had sabotaged himself during a confrontational interview with Patrick Dean—the police sergeant whose testimony was a major element of Wade's case—whose credibility Griffin vocally doubted. Arlen Specter was sent in their place.

So those in the small room (Warren wanted it small so as to keep curiosity seekers out) for Ruby's testimony included commission members Warren and Gerald Ford, commission lawyers J. Lee Rankin and Joseph Ball, assistant DA Jim Bowie, secret service agent Elmer Moore, Sheriff Decker, Joe Tonahill (representing Ruby), and a stenographer. For reasons of space, Specter was told to wait in the sheriff's office, where he watched a televised baseball game between the San Francisco Giants (Warren's hometown team) and the Philadelphia Phillies (the team from where Specter lived).

Ruby was so eager to talk that, even before he was sworn in, he demanded of Warren that he be given a polygraph. "Without a lie detector on my testimony, how do you know if I am telling the truth? I would like to be able to get a lie detector test, or truth serum, of what motivated me to do what I did."

Warren replied, "If you and your counsel want a kind of test, I would arrange it for you. I will be glad to do that, if you want it."

"I do want it," Ruby told the judge.

"We will be glad to."

With the assurance that he would have a follow-up session with a lie detector, Ruby spoke for three hours. As Abrams and Fisher note, "This was Ruby's opportunity to tell his own story in public . . . but Ruby did not make it easy, often failing to respond directly to questions, other times ignoring them or seemingly plucking answers out of thin air. One thought often was interrupted by leaping to a completely different thought." At certain points, "his testimony seemed so disjointed that it was impossible for Warren to follow."

Ruby would go on to tell a sort of greatest-hits version of his story, seeming to say both that his actions were premeditated and that they weren't, that he killed Oswald to spare Jackie Kennedy having to come to testify at Oswald's trial, that he had thought of killing Oswald early on Sunday morning, but also that his shooting the guy was spontaneous. It was standard Jack Ruby word salad, although at times seeming somewhat less off-the-rails than his conversations with Silverman and others.

However, as the session progressed, fewer and fewer coherent statements would make their way out of Ruby's mouth. For instance, he announced that

I am being victimized as part of a plot in the world's worst tragedy and crime. . . . At this moment, Lee Harvey Oswald isn't guilty of committing the crime of assassinating President Kennedy. Jack Ruby is. How can I fight that, Chief Justice Warren?

Ruby stated that, because of what he'd done, the John Birch Society and General Walker had gained significant power:

Unfortunately for me . . . me giving the people the opportunity to get in power, because of the act I committed, has put a lot of people in jeopardy with their lives. Don't register with you, does it? . . . I won't be living long now. I know that. My family's lives will be gone. . . . No one requested me to do anything. I never spoke to anyone about attempting to do anything. No subversive organization gave me any idea. No underworld person made any effort to contact me.

Ruby then blamed the Preludin dieting medication he was taking in the period leading to his murder of Oswald for affecting his thinking, explaining it was "a stimulus to give me an emotional feeling that suddenly I felt . . . that I wanted to show my love for our faith, being of the Jewish faith . . . suddenly the . . . emotional feeling came within me that someone owed this debt to our beloved president to save [Jackie] the ordeal of coming back . . . I had the gun in my right hip pocket, and impulsively . . . I saw him and that is all I can say. I didn't care what happened to me. . . . The next thing, I was on the floor."

Gerald Ford would recall that Ruby's testimony went reasonably well for about forty-five minutes, until Ruby and Tonahill started arguing for reasons that were unclear. The court reporter stopped recording the session. Things became tense.

And then, as Specter recalls, "[Secret service agent] Elmer Moore . . . barged into the sheriff's office [where Specter was watching the ballgame]. 'They want you upstairs,' Moore told me. 'Ruby wants a Jew in the room.'"

Specter arrived in the small room. "Looking straight at me, [Ruby] mouthed the words, 'Are you a Yid?'" Ruby asked him three more times. Specter refused to answer. "I knew from my experience as an appellate lawyer what it would look like in print if I responded."

It's unclear what exactly Specter was concerned about. Perhaps he thought the commission might appear to be giving Ruby some kind of special treatment because of their mutual religious or cultural identity.

At that point, the stenographer ran out of paper and had to reload her machine. As Specter recalls, it was then that "Ruby jumped up, grabbed the chief justice, who was on his left, and pulled him into a corner. Ruby ordered me into the corner also."

Commission lawyer Joe Ball tried to join the group, but Ruby asked him, "Are you Jewish?" When Ball responded that he was not, Ruby snapped, "Well, go away." Ball did just that.

Specter continues:

> Ruby turned back to Warren and me. "Chief," he said, "you've got to get me to Washington. They're cutting off the arms and legs of Jewish children in Albuquerque and El Paso."
>
> I was astonished, and I attributed Ruby's remarks to his being out of touch with reality on the matter he had brought up.
>
> "I—I can't do that, Mr. Ruby," Warren stammered.
>
> "Get to Fortas. He'll get the job done," Ruby said. . . . "Get to Fortas. He'll get it worked out."

The side meeting broke up, and the stenographer went back to work. But Ruby saw Tonahill pass a note to Ford and demanded to see it. Specter observed that "Jack Ruby was indisputably in command." The note was handed over but Ruby couldn't read it without his glasses. Incredibly, Warren loaned Ruby his spectacles.

The note read, "You see? I told you he was crazy." It did not seem to faze Ruby.

Ruby asked again to be taken to Washington. "Do I sound dramatic? Off the beam?" he asked.

"No," replied Warren, "you are speaking very, very rationally."

"I want to tell the truth, and I can't tell it here."

Ruby said to Warren that, because of what he, Ruby, had done, "the Jewish people are being exterminated at this moment. . . . I am being used as a scapegoat. I am as good as guilty as the accused assassin of President Kennedy.

How can you remedy that, Mr. Warren?" Ruby claimed that if he could get to Washington, "maybe my people won't be tortured and mutilated."

Warren responded, "You may be sure that the president and his whole commission will do anything that is necessary to see that your people are not tortured."

Ruby told him, "All I want to do is tell the truth, and the only way you can know it is by polygraph." Warren again assured him: "That we will do for you."

Warren immediately regretted making that promise, but Specter later counseled him that, after promising Ruby that he would get him a polygraph test, there was no way to back out without it looking as if the commission was deliberately passing up an opportunity to get at the truth, maybe even covering something up.

Still, during this three-hour testimony, Ruby spoke of many things. He claimed that while he had known some underworld figures in Chicago. "I have never been a bookmaker, I have never stolen for a living. I am not a gangster." He also denied having been carrying a gun when he saw Oswald at the police station on Friday night November 22. "I lied about it. . . . I didn't have a gun," he said. That undercut one of Belli's arguments for the spontaneous nature of Ruby's shooting Oswald on Sunday: that, although armed, he didn't take the shot on Friday because the idea hadn't yet popped into his brain.

Ruby also warned of the power of the Birch Society, adding, "The Jewish people are being exterminated at this moment. Consequently, a whole new form of government is going to take over our country and I know I won't live to see you another time. . . . If you don't take me back to Washington tonight to give me a chance to prove to the president I am not guilty, then you will see the most tragic thing that will ever happen. . . . I am being used as a scapegoat, and there is no greater weapon you can use to create some falsehood about someone of the Jewish faith.

"I have been used for a purpose, and there will be a certain tragic occurrence happening if you don't take my testimony and somehow vindicate me so my people don't suffer for what I have done. . . . All I want is to take a polygraph and tell the truth. . . . You are the only one who can save me."

And he emphasized, "There was no conspiracy."

Specter later reflected that "it turned out that Jack Ruby had been in charge from the time the deposition began, or even before it began." He recalled that Ford had similarly observed that Ruby "flaunted his power and presence."

It's remarkable that Both Specter and Ford seemed to feel that Ruby took control of the session, that somehow, through sheer force of will, he intimidated them into doing as he wished. Was Ruby able to summon such personal power—despite his plainly obvious weaker position—that he was able, in their view, to take over the room?

It seems strange that with Sheriff Decker in the room—presumably armed—along with a secret service agent and the physically formidable Ford, with just the sheer number of people there, Ruby would have been able to treat this room full of confident and accomplished men as if they were busboys at the Carousel. This portrayal of him is certainly at odds with those of Silverman and others who visited him in his cell. By the same token, this was still Jack Ruby, a *shtarker* who beat up Nazis, brutalized Carousel customers, fought off street toughs—and who cold-bloodedly murdered Lee Harvey Oswald. Somewhere inside him, whether hidden by guile or madness, the take-charge, intimidating thug apparently still lived and could still make his presence known.

Specter notes that "the commission then arranged with the FBI to give Ruby a lie-detector test. . . . Then Ruby's lawyers—who changed periodically—and relatives weighed in. They sent mixed signals. Some warned that Ruby's mental state would make the test meaningless. But Joe Tonahill, still Ruby's primary lawyer, whether Ruby believed that or not, told me he wanted the test." The test date was set for July 18.

Some believe Ruby felt that he needed to testify in Washington because he was afraid he might himself be assassinated in prison in Texas. But why would he be safer in Washington?

Perhaps he felt that, like mobster Joe Valachi—who the year before had testified to Congress about previously unknown inner workings of the mob, and had received federal protection—he would be better guarded in the nation's capital.

Others feel that Ruby's main concern was his family's well-being. This narrative goes that Ruby had been coerced into killing Oswald, perhaps selected as one of multiple hitmen tasked with taking Oswald out, and he had been the "lucky" one who got to do it. He did all he could to avoid being the guy to pull the trigger but was strongarmed into doing it or else face the dire consequences that would be visited on his family. In this scenario, now that he had obeyed orders, Ruby would want it publicly known that he was, in his testimony, denying that there was any conspiracy, that he was sticking to the story that he acted alone. And he wanted to tell the story again, his word validated by the magical lie detector. Then there could be no doubt. His family would be safe, even if he wouldn't be. (The flaw in the logic here, of course, is that if Ruby was lying about operating on his own, wouldn't the polygraph pick that up, thereby invalidating his story?)

Alternatively, perhaps Ruby actually did believe that, once in Washington, hooked up to a polygraph, he could somehow get to tell Lyndon Johnson something earth-shattering that would protect Jack's family—even if, as Ruby regularly implied, Johnson was, himself, part of a conspiracy.

Of course, questions arise: Even if Oswald hadn't spilled the beans in his two days in captivity, why would anyone think that, after seven months, Jack Ruby hadn't already told everything he knew? And why had no one already tried to kill him, an easy target sitting day after day in an antiquated prison and accessible to many?

In the weeks between Ruby's two testimonies before the Warren Commission, Dallas lawyer Clayton Fowler was hired, albeit briefly, as Ruby's chief counsel, brought on in the midst of a defense motion to have Jack declared legally insane. The hope was that if he was declared to be *currently* insane, then at least the death penalty might be averted.

On June 16 Fowler was able to postpone any hearing on Ruby's sanity, feeling that more time was needed to establish just how far gone Jack truly was. "We immediately commenced a series of propaganda . . . stories that would, at a later date, at least soften up the public in their feeling for Jack's mental condition," said Fowler.

As part of this campaign—but perhaps in a more extreme manner than Fowler had imagined—Sol Dann wrote a thirty-five-page document that explained *his* theory of the case. Dann argued that "Ruby had killed Oswald as a reaction to antisemitism, and it was this very same antisemitism that accounted for the jury's verdict." Dann's document—in all capital letters—detailed how, in a manner similar to the way Jack had been fighting antisemitism with his fists and with his refusal to allow ethnic jokes in his clubs,

> Ruby took the law into his own hands . . . just as he took the treatment of Anti-Semitism and Anti-Kennedyism into his own hands. . . . The jury, not unlike Ruby, felt the need to "right a wrong" and respond (K.K.K. style) with a verdict of death for Ruby. . . . But what demented Anti-Semitism in the jury's personal lives made them vulnerable to such needs and pleas . . . led them to "act on impulse" and make their hasty death verdict? . . .
>
> What irony that Ruby, who concerned himself with fighting Anti-Semitism . . . may be executed because of this hate and prejudice. . . . The greatest monument that the people of Dallas could erect to the memory of President John F. Kennedy would be by Judge Brown ordering a new trial.

But before any determination of Jack Ruby's sanity, there would be his second Warren Commission testimony, the long-requested, long-awaited lie-detector session.

25 | WIRED

IT WOULDN'T HAVE BEEN SURPRISING to see a burlesque dancer at the Carousel Club come onstage and perform, dressed in a skimpy, flag-themed outfit, as the superhero Wonder Woman, roping willing audience members—or even host Jack Ruby himself—in her golden lasso of truth. The crowd at the club would have gotten a good laugh out of it.

As far as anyone knows, no such dancer ever appeared there. Nonetheless, the device Ruby so wanted to be hooked up to—the lie detector—owed its existence to research done by Dr. William Moulton Marston, the cocreator of Wonder Woman. Marston was also known for putting on public events where he hooked scantily clad young women up to his truth-divining device to see if they were lying.

Likely unaware of the history or legacy of the polygraph (Judge Brown, described by multiple sources as sometimes reading comic books during trials, would more plausibly have been aware of it), Jack Ruby finally got his day to testify while connected to a lie detector. That day was Saturday, July 18, 1964.

Defense attorney Clayton Fowler, who had launched the let's-prove Jack-Ruby-is-crazy propaganda campaign, was present at the session, as was Joe Tonahill. The test was to be administered at the Dallas County Jail, though, not in Washington as Ruby had requested, by two FBI agents, one of whom was Bell P. Herndon, one of the top polygraph practitioners in the country. Earl Ruby, Sol Dann, and Fowler had repeatedly advised Ruby to not take the test, but Jack was adamant that he wanted to go through with it.

Nonetheless, while the appointment had been made for the wired follow-up to take place on that day, there seem to have been some crossed signals regarding the presence of the FBI polygraph men. Sheriff Decker had called Fowler to let him know, but since it was Saturday, Fowler decided that it was too late to find a judge over the weekend who might stop the test.

Both Fowler and Specter tried to give Ruby one last chance to back out of taking the test. Specter even reminded Ruby that his answers could be used to undermine his appeal. Ruby still wanted to go ahead with it. "I want to answer anything and everything," he told Specter.

During a break, Fowler called Eva so she would know what was going on. Eva called Dann, who called Fowler to tell him he was fired for not finding a way to stop the test, Jack's strong desire to take it notwithstanding. As had happened with dueling lawyers before in this macabre reality show, Fowler then informed Dann that *he* was fired.

Specter recalls the scene:

> [Ruby] had prepared his own list of questions he wanted to be asked. A lie-detector test is supposed to last forty-five minutes. . . . Ruby's polygraph exam lasted from twelve noon until twelve midnight. Everybody had questions he wanted Ruby to answer. And we started with Ruby's own sizable list.

Ruby's testimony, responding to questions that allowed (per polygraph requirements) only yes or no answers, pretty much stuck to the story he'd told the commission the previous month. Herndon told Specter that he thought Ruby "had passed the test with flying colors and was clearly not involved in the assassination." But, Specter continued, "J. Edgar Hoover filed a report that Ruby was out of touch with reality and that the polygraph was worthless."

Nonetheless, Specter believed that Herndon was correct, though the Warren Commission report as issued would disagree, disregarding the test results on the grounds that Ruby's disturbed mental condition rendered them valueless.

Herndon commented, "I think he held up remarkably well. . . . He certainly did not show undue stress . . . and handled the questions better than I thought he would. It did seem like he was getting, in a sense, his day in court, which . . . trial procedure and presumed defense tactics [had] not allowed him in the first trial."

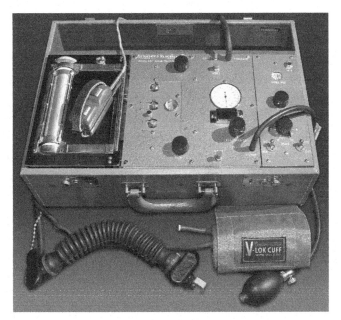

The Keeler model 6317 polygraph machine used on Jack Ruby in his second testimony before the Warren Commission, which took place on July 18, 1964. *Federal Bureau of Investigation, courtesy of Wikimedia Commons*

Dr. William Beavers, a psychiatrist at the polygraph session representing the Ruby family, commented about the test results that "any delusional state did not interfere with awareness of the past . . . with the appearance of an apparently reasonable appreciation of reality in reference to his whereabouts. . . . In short, he seemed to behave like a man with a well-fixed delusional system in which whole areas of his thinking and his behavior [are] not strongly interfered [with] by the delusion." Talk about damning with faint praise.

By the same token, Herndon did add, "There was no area of deception present with regard to his response to the relevant questions." In other words, though he may have been delusional, Ruby did not appear to be lying.

Nonetheless, "when next Jack moved through newsmen at a public hearing, he shouted that 'the plot' was suppressing results of his polygraph session, so the excuse for killing the Jews would not be removed. . . . After the test, he was broken."

For numerous reasons, Dann was displeased with Fowler, and apparently, he *did* have the power to fire him, or at least, had the Ruby family's ear in the matter. In mid-October 1964, Eva Grant filed a request in Dallas District Court that every attorney with the exception of Burleson be removed from Jack's case. As a parting shot, Fowler attested that "perhaps the defendant, Jack Ruby, might be unstable insofar as they [the Ruby family] are unable to employ competent counsel for any period of time." He suggested that Judge Brown should "appoint competent counsel" to help Burleson with his duties going forward.

For his part, Burleson filed a motion with Brown that Charles Bellows (another lawyer the Rubys had brought in) and Dann be added to the list of official Ruby lawyers. This led to a heated argument between Dann and Tonahill in which "the huge Texan [Tonahill] had felt so provoked that he used most unpleasant language—language that Dann contended was strongly anti-Semitic."

Tonahill's version of the argument was that "Sol Dann and his financial exploiters of Jack Ruby wouldn't tolerate us because they could not exploit Jack Ruby. . . . Dann wanted to degrade Jack Ruby's public image and jeopardize his appeal through a commercialization program. . . . Dann . . . is well aware that if Jack Ruby is executed . . . that Jack Ruby will be the first Jew in Texas history ever executed. . . . Such a fact will be utilized by Sol Dann for commercialization exploitation." Tonahill refers in his motion to "the moving grasping hand of Sol Dann and his fellow Ghouls." Perhaps Dann's accusation was not without merit.

In retaliation, in a July 25 letter to Tonahill and Fowler, Dann (in all capitals) demanded that they "fully explain to Dallas press, public and me why you threatened me last Wednesday night with bodily harm and safety of my life. . . . Also, what prompted you to call me . . . anti-Semitic vile epithets similar to those resorted to by prosecution and their witnesses . . . to inflame hate and prejudice . . . against Jack Ruby."

Dann claimed Tonahill had said, "Texas is an unhealthy climate for a Jew. . . . You . . . better get out of Texas if you want to stay healthy." Dann added that "the assault [upon Dann] was interrupted only because of the appearance of representatives of the press and television . . . but for said interruption, Joe Tonahill would have carried out his threats to physically attack your petitioner."

Regardless of whether Dann's accusations were accurate, they were enough to make Fowler so uncomfortable that he did, indeed, withdraw from the case. Melvin Belli, himself—no lawyer left the case for long if at all—wrote to Tonahill, urging *him* to leave the case. In his letter, Belli said of Dann that "as a Jewish lawyer, he is injecting the Jewish issue and he will irreparably hurt the case.... I only speak my piece because of my loyalty and friendship to Jack Ruby ... and with you."

Belli and Carroll's book, *Dallas Justice*, was released that fall. In it, Belli lambasted pretty much everyone involved with the Ruby case, including the Ruby family and the "Oligarchy of Dallas" that "could figuratively press a button and, as if it had signaled transistors in their brains, direct the thinking of this great city's people." The verdict was everyone's fault but his: "We won it. The Dallas jury was wrong."

––––––––––

Around that same time, in late September 1964, ten months after the murders of Kennedy and Oswald, the Warren Commission report was issued. The report, containing interviews with 552 witnesses, was 888 pages long, with an additional 26 lengthy volumes of transcribed interviews and evidence of various types.

The report concluded that Oswald was the lone gunman and that there was no conspiracy involving Jack Ruby or anybody else at play. It would excite controversy and conspiracy theories from the moment of publication, and even those who gave it credence believed the commission inadvertently damaged its own credibility, if only by the report being released so soon (in part due to pressure from Johnson, who wanted it completed well before the November elections, an understandable—if not especially noble—political goal) and, ironically, by discussing possible conspiracies at all. As Carroll puts it,

> At the Trib, we nodded in agreement.... It added up. Three shots fired, all from the rear, all fired by Oswald, two striking the President, the first probably not fatal going on to hit the governor, one other missing, one tearing into the President's head ... painstaking investigation has proven every element of it to be true.... This should have been highlighted, underlined, stressed. It was the key to the report, the explanation that cleared up the conspiracy nonsense and the claims about multiple gunmen.... What "really" happened was accurately reported by the Warren Commission but in such tentative, legalistic wording, with so many hedgings and digressions, with so much lawyerly obfuscation, that it not only failed to clear up the confusion; to some extent, the commission stoked it.

And Carroll observes, regarding the controversial single-bullet theory,

> Specter wrote that he went "out of my way to include material that contradicted the conclusion." That no doubt reflected admirable professional restraint, but it made for a confusing description of the most important finding, a point that should have been made clear and straightforward.

Despite Carroll's critique, though, it's unlikely that, had the report been written more clearly, it would have forestalled the plethora of conspiracy theories that blossomed in the wake of its release and ever since.

On May 24, 1964, Arlen Specter (left) of the Warren Commission demonstrates the assumed projectile path that was at the heart of his single-bullet (a.k.a. "magic bullet") theory. The Jewish Specter was later called in to be part of Ruby's first Warren Commission testimony when Ruby insisted there be at least one other Jew in the room besides himself. He would also be present for Ruby's long-requested polygraph test. (Other figures in the photo are unidentified.) *Exhibit 903 in* Hearings Before the President's Commission on the Assassination of President Kennedy *(Washington, DC: US Government Printing Office, 1964), 18:96, courtesy of Wikimedia Commons*

In November 1964, Lyndon Johnson coasted to a landslide victory over Republican Barry Goldwater, who many thought of as extremist almost in the Edwin Walker mode. John F. Kennedy's goal of retaining Democratic control of the White House had been attained. And, like four years earlier, Texas went Democratic. All mention of the various Johnson-related scandals were shunted aside, out of the public spotlight. At his January 20, 1965, inaugural, Johnson said, "I will repeat today what I said on that sorrowful day in November last year: I will lead and I will do the best I can."

Though he hadn't taken the stand in his own defense during his trial, Jack Ruby had more than made up for it in his testimony before the Warren Commission. And, of course, he had never stopped his impromptu news conferences, regardless of whether what he said contradicted anything he'd said earlier.

For instance, on March 8, 1965, during a break in one of the many hearings held regarding him, Ruby held an impromptu news conference. Despite his disavowal of being involved with, or having knowledge of, any conspiracies, Ruby decided it was time to say to reporters,

> Everything pertaining to what's happening has never come to the surface. The world will never know the true facts of what occurred, my motives. The people that had so much to gain, and had such an ulterior motive for putting me in the position I'm in will never let the true facts come above board to the world.

When a reporter asked, "Are these people in high positions, Jack?" he simply replied, without elaboration:

Yes.

Ruby loved to write notes and letters that were as portentous, and ultimately as contradictory and confusing, as his nonstop spoken verbiage. The notes would be smuggled out by visitors and guards, perhaps from a genuine desire to help him, perhaps also to sell them on the memorabilia market. Ruby lawyer Elmer Gertz speaks of a note Ruby gave him which read, in part,

> This is all so hopeless. . . . These hearings are just to stall for time . . . they are killing our people here now in this very building. . . . They are torturing people right here.

There was also a 1965 letter to a former fellow inmate, Thomas E. Miller, somehow smuggled out and ultimately found on an auction website, in which Ruby seems to be laying the blame for everything on Lyndon Johnson:

> Oh the way I fucked up this world[.] [W]ho would ever dream that the mother fucker [Johnson] was a Nazi, and found me as the perfect setup for a frame[?] It was perfect for them. Remember they had the president killed, and now with me in the picture, they'll make it look as though Castro or the Russians had it done. Anyone in their right mind would know that the Russians or Castro would never do something like that. . . . It would only create worse hostilities. After it was done they would only put another man in office to take Kennedy's place. Remember the only one who had all to gain was Johnson himself. Figure that out. Remember all points.

Miller eventually sold the note, which was, of course, fodder for conspiracy theorists. Did Ruby truly believe what he was saying? And even if he did, does that mean it was in any way true?

Conversely, in March of the same year, at a hearing, Ruby mocked any thought of a conspiracy, saying with irony that he must have been involved in "the most perfect conspiracy in the history of the world, that a man was going to accept a call and come from his apartment down to the Western Union [in order to somehow then kill Oswald]. . . . I didn't conspire . . . to do all those things. . . . All these circumstances were against me."

As satisfying as it would have been to sift some consistent, logical statement of motives from Ruby's many proclamations, that would be an impossible task. Dr. Walter Bromberg addressed Ruby's constantly shifting narratives:

> Ruby talked readily, compulsively. He didn't talk to his audience, he just talked as he moved—physiologically, so to speak—bobbing his head forward like a boxer, rolling up phrase after phrase, which became entangled with malapropisms, flashes of aggression, and self-aggrandizement . . . just beyond the firm ground of reality. . . . He spoke of himself as a phenomenon, without conscious appreciation of any inappropriateness. A messianic tendency peeped through the tangle of immature braggadocio.

Bromberg's observations—which could apply to Ruby's written statements, as well—provide a clue to how Ruby could be almost catatonic in his cell while speaking to a visitor, and yet seem to take charge at impromptu press conferences or as he had at his testimonies before the Warren Commission. Bringing his experience and temperament as a street brawler, salesman, and nightclub bouncer into play, Ruby could confront people far more intelligent and accomplished—and with legal authority over him—and seemingly maneuver them into, at least on a short-term basis, doing his bidding.

Assistant DA Bill Alexander thought all the squabbling among Ruby's lawyers and family was deliberate and performative so that a case could be made that Ruby did not have competent representation. Joe Tonahill (still there) responded by calling Alexander a "tarantula-eyed one hundred percent liar."

He then accused Dann and the others of wanting to eject him from the case so they could bring in "commie lawyers," who he felt would discredit Jack. Ultimately, Tonahill accused the prosecution's Wade and the defense's Dann of colluding to get rid of him to make sure Ruby was convicted and executed. Dann's rebuttal was not much more rational, though, as it focused on the alleged right-wing plot by Jew-haters to connect Ruby to Oswald and both of them to a Communist plot to kill the president.

Wills and Demaris sum up the situation: "To go from lawyer to lawyer in the Ruby defense is a dizzying experience. . . . At the core of the affair, Jack himself, was hallucinating up conspiracies on a worldwide scale."

Ruby was, at a certain point, judged competent enough to pick his own lawyers, whereupon he dumped Tonahill. But another ruling declared he was no longer competent, so Tonahill got to stay. Ruby did manage to announce to the world, "Me, Jack Ruby, Jack Rubenstein, am the greatest scapegoat in the history of the world." Then Ruby was again judged competent enough to fire Tonahill, and he did. Unsurprisingly, Tonahill still didn't go away.

Finally, Judge Brown, who was scheduled to preside over Ruby's official sanity hearing, voluntarily resigned from the case, largely over controversy regarding his book deal. In addition, he had written, "It is my opinion they will never find Ruby insane," thereby bringing his objectivity into question.

By November 1965 it seemed that the prosecution was becoming concerned about the possible success of an appeal for Ruby. Wade suddenly made "a public, unsolicited offer to Ruby's lawyers: he would request that the State Board of Pardons and Paroles reduce Ruby's death sentence to life—on the condition that the defense join him in that plea." In theory, Ruby could be out on parole in ten years or less. Burleson turned the offer down—indicating that he had the authority to do so.

On November 8, 1965, Melvin Belli's lunch companion, *New York Journal American* columnist Dorothy Kilgallen, was found dead of an overdose of alcohol and barbiturates. Rumors that the death was a murder (as opposed to an unintentional suicide) and that she was killed because she knew too much about the assassination were never substantiated—but, of course, never fully refuted. It's likely that her comments about her exclusive interview with Ruby in which he told her the real story were overblown. But as her notes relating to it are said to have vanished mysteriously, it's unlikely we'll ever know.

Ruby's sanity hearing was finally scheduled for June 1966. Because his lawyers couldn't agree that it was necessary, they decided to have it canceled. When the court ruled it had to proceed, the defense simply chose not to participate. Without opposition, the prosecution easily proved Ruby was competent. Four of their six witnesses were prison guards who testified that Ruby seemed sane to them, and prison doctor John Callahan said the same thing.

The sixth witness—testifying on behalf of the *state*—was Jack Ruby himself. Ruby declared, "Never at any time have I tried to make anyone believe I was of unsound mind." He was judged to be sane.

———————————

Speaking of "commie lawyers," the most significant progressive attorney in Ruby's appeal was William Kunstler, best known today for his defense, several years later, of the Chicago Eight.

Kunstler had actually started out intending to represent *Oswald*. Indeed, on Sunday, November 24, 1963, Kunstler was heading for the airport to catch a plane from New York to Dallas. "I wanted to be Oswald's defense attorney," he recalls, "because I believed he would get short shrift in Texas; his rights were certain to be violated. And I was not at all convinced that Oswald was, in fact, the president's murderer."

When Kunstler heard that Ruby had murdered Oswald, he changed his mind and canceled the trip, apparently not especially concerned, at that point, about Jack Ruby's fate. Kunstler believed that Wade was furious at Ruby for cheating him out of the opportunity to prosecute Oswald and so threw the book at Ruby. Interestingly, Kunstler reflects, "I can identify with Wade's desire for glory a bit, though: it really would have been something to be the attorney who defended Oswald."

But two years later, in the fall of 1965, Kunstler was with his client Martin Luther King Jr. in La Guardia Airport when Earl Ruby rushed up to them and pleaded with King, "Can we have Bill?"

King replied, "Sure."

Kunstler felt that, although his plate was filled with civil rights cases, he had to take on Ruby's, since "it was an important death-penalty case. Besides, Martin had said, 'Do it.'"

Lawyer William Kunstler (seen here in 1970), who would gain his greatest fame for representing the Chicago Eight, was instrumental in challenging Ruby's death sentence. *Courtesy of Los Angeles Times Photographic Collection, https://digital.library.ucla.edu/catalog/ark:/21198/zz0002vt1g*

Arriving in Dallas a week later, Kunstler was greeted by hundreds of hostile demonstrators who called him a Communist and told him to go back to New York. Undeterred, Kunstler met with the then-current team of Ruby's lawyers: Sol Dann, Phil Burleson, ACLU lawyer (as was Kunstler) Sam Houston Clinton, and Elmer Gertz. Although they didn't always get along with each other, they welcomed the New Yorker.

As Gertz explains,

> There was nothing lovable . . . about [Ruby]. It was hard to defend his mad act. We, his defense team, only had the redemption of American justice as our cause. Of course, we wanted to win Jack's case, but we had an even greater desire to challenge the mockery of justice that had occurred.

The lawyers were all working essentially for free, the Ruby family having run out of money. Tonahill, claiming that Ruby still wasn't competent, legally, to fire him, continued hanging around too. Kunstler and the others were able to convince a county judge that Ruby *was* competent to choose his own lawyers, and so, finally, Tonahill was ejected from the case.

With Brown and Tonahill gone (well, Tonahill was actually sticking around as "a friend of the court," there to offer advice, should anybody choose to ask him), the Kunstler team could proceed.

In the summer of 1966, the lawyers presented their case before the Texas Court of Criminal Appeals, the highest court in the state. The largest crowd in the history of that institution packed the three-hundred-seat courtroom. The lawyers' main argument was that Ruby's "conviction should be overturned because he had only gotten the semblance of a fair trial."

Sam Houston Clinton told the panel, "First there was a trial by inflamed public opinion. . . . Then there was a trial by newspaper and television. Then there was a trial by ritual—with 11 of the 12 jurors [having seen the murder on TV] going through the ritual of saying they could set aside their opinions," There was also, he asserted, a "trial by ordeal," with the jury forced to endure the closing arguments until past one o'clock in the morning.

Elmer Gertz brought up Judge Brown's conduct, including a passage from the judge's unpublished book where Brown wrote that Ruby did not get a fair trial but that he wasn't going to lose any sleep over it. Gertz also pointed out that "the atmosphere in the halls and around the courthouse resembled a circus" and that "the press undoubtedly had an effect on the jury."

The lawyer also cited numerous unsubstantiated and prejudicial claims about Ruby that were published in the media, including that he was a mobster, connected to hoodlums and organized crime; that he was a Communist; that he had done business with Castro; and that he had previously known Oswald.

The defense made sixteen different claims in total. Kunstler himself focused on several issues, including Patrick Dean's testimony. "The record is replete with Dean lying," he said, pointing out inconsistencies in Dean's statements. He declared that the prosecution, with Dean, "invented a fabrication . . . that [Ruby] intended to kill Oswald after he saw him Friday night."

Bill Alexander rebutted those charges, essentially saying that Ruby having killed Oswald on TV where lots of people saw it did nothing to lessen his guilt.

And besides—films of the murder were run during the trial. The jurors would have seen them then in any case.

Having heard both sides, the court adjourned for the summer, as was its custom, promising to deliver a ruling when it reconvened in the fall.

———————

While the court was on its break, Burleson and the other Ruby lawyers tried several other motions, including, partnered with the Texas Civil Liberties Union, petitioning the US Supreme Court, claiming that Ruby "had not had the remotest semblance of a fair trial." The Supreme Court, too, was in recess for the summer. It wasn't clear whether, on its return, it would agree to take the case up.

But on October 5, 1966, the Texas Court of Criminal Appeals unanimously overturned Jack Ruby's murder conviction and death sentence.

Judge William A. Morrison wrote the opinion, in which he said that the conversation Dean claimed to have had with Ruby could not have been seen as being made spontaneously immediately after the shooting, that Ruby's statement to Dean "constituted an oral confession of premeditation made while in police custody and therefore was not admissible . . . and calls for a reversal of this conviction. The judgement is reversed, and the case is remanded with directions that the venue be changed to some other county other than Dallas." (Wichita Falls, ninety miles from Dallas, would eventually be chosen.)

Morrison added, in a rebuke cloaked in legalese: "Judge Joe B. Brown, who tried this case, has recused himself from any further connection with the case and, we have concluded, properly so." Morrison also stated that there was "such strong feeling in the Dallas County climate that it was not humanly possible to give Ruby a fair and impartial trial."

In a concurring opinion, the court's Judge McDonald added,

> Dallas was being blamed . . . for President Kennedy's assassination and for allowing the shooting of Oswald by Ruby. . . . [It is] fair to assume that the citizenry of Dallas consciously and subconsciously felt Dallas was on trial and the Dallas image was uppermost in their minds to such an extent that Ruby could not be tried there fairly. . . .

The press had a field day with stories stating directly, indirectly, by hints and innuendoes that a Communist conspiracy existed between Oswald and Ruby. Ruby was referred to as a "tough guy," a "Chicago mobster," a strip-joint owner. Anti-Semitism against Ruby was sparked by pretrial publicity that Ruby's name had been changed from Rubenstein to Ruby.

The judges, in effect, vindicated Belli's objections to Dallas as a venue and his challenges to Brown's admission of Dean's statements.

Jack Ruby was now innocent in the eyes of the law.

Kunstler recalls, "It was a great victory, because [Ruby] had certainly never schemed to kill . . . Oswald. Jack's was the act of a madman, perhaps, but not one who planned." Kunstler referred to Ruby as a "meshuggana" and believed that he did, indeed, suffer from psychomotor epilepsy.

Kunstler also noted that when Ruby told him he had killed Oswald "for the Jews," he believed him. The lawyer found it credible that, because Oswald had belonged to Fair Play for Cuba, an organization "with a number of Jewish members," this had led Ruby to thinking that "the Kennedy assassination would be linked to Jews." Kunstler adds that

> during our last visit, he handed me a note in which he reiterated his desire to protect American Jews from a pogrom that could occur because of anger over the assassination. He also told me, "I wanted to save Mrs. Kennedy from being put through the ordeal of a trial."

Ruby had also given Kunstler a letter intended for Earl. The long, rambling composition had included the statements that

> if only you had believed me all along . . . you would have saved Israel, but now they are doomed, because they think the U.S. are for them, but they are wrong because Johnson wants to see them slaughtered and tortured. . . . The Arabs are going to overrun Israel. They are going to get help from both Russia and the U.S. It's now too late to

do anything, and we are all doomed. . . . Forgive me for all this terrible tragedy I've caused. . . . But you still may be able to save Israel . . . tell the Russians how Egypt has been using them all along . . . then they will understand what kind of person Johnson is, and they may be able to save Israel.

The note goes on with the hard-to-parse ideas that

Russia will be in a position to tell Johnson that there [sic] first move if any trouble starts is not to bomb the U.S., but to wipe out Germany, that one thing Johnson don't want to happen, because he is counting on them to be the master race, also all the other former Axis partners South America, Egypt, Italy, and Japan. . . . You may have lost your family [to conspirators], but . . . you can save millions of people who are doomed to be slaughtered. This country has been overthrown.

Interestingly, Kunstler—contrary to the other lawyers and Jack's family—believed that with statements such as these, Jack, believing himself to be sane, was (in Jack's own eyes) *pretending* to be crazy—which wouldn't have affected whether he'd gotten a fair trial (or whether he actually was insane). Nonetheless, he and the other lawyers did seem to pull together for their client, which Kunstler was quite pleased about. In a letter to the group, Kunstler wrote:

Much of our seeming success . . . was due in large measure to the friendship and spirit of cooperation that had developed among us. . . . The Ruby lawyers have become an institution second only to the Smith Brothers, the Dolly Sisters, and the King Family. Long may we wave.

The civil rights lawyer later looked back at the assassinations and opined:

Some conspiracy theorists claim that Jack had close ties to the FBI, but I think he was much too unstable for that. Jack Ruby, one of the most confusing and confused people I ever met, could not have had a responsible part in a conspiracy. His murder of Oswald was clearly an act of individual insanity. . . .

I certainly believe that CIA goons plot and carry out assassinations, but I just don't see Jack as part of those schemes. . . . It seemed incredible to me . . . that if enormously powerful networks like the military-industrial complex and the CIA were behind the Kennedy murder, they would trust even the smallest link in the plot to the likes of Jack Ruby. He . . . was not someone who could be trusted with a responsibility that important. . . .

Besides, after he was sentenced to death, he was the type of man who certainly would have traded any conspiracy information for his life.

Returning to Dallas, Burleson gave Ruby the news, which he received "with the calm of disbelief, hardly grasping its significance." Burleson noted Ruby's near nonchalance, adding, "I'm kind of in shock myself."

Tonahill, in Austin, was jubilant. He announced he was going to see Ruby and personally give him a copy of the decision. Ruby, who had long wanted Tonahill off the case, refused to see him.

Eva Grant said, "My heart feels a little lighter tonight." Eileen Kaminsky, her and Jack's sister, said that she was "pleasantly surprised. He's a wonderful person who wouldn't hurt anybody."

Marguerite Oswald claimed to be glad her son's killer's conviction was reversed because, at a new trial, "the truth will now come to light." Her daughter-in-law, Marina, was also glad Ruby wouldn't be put to death. "I think he's been punished enough already," she said. "He's a human being, too."

Oswald's brother, Robert, who actually had moved to Wichita Falls back in 1964, did not plan to attend the new trial. He believed that his brother was, indeed, guilty of killing the president and that Ruby had received a fair trial. Robert Oswald said, "It doesn't bother me personally to have the trial here in Wichita Falls, but for my family it is unfortunate. It would serve no purpose for me to go. . . . I'll follow the trial's progress through the newspapers."

Noted *New York Herald Tribune* reporter Jimmy Breslin interviewed Judge Brown, who claimed, "Why, Belli and Jack Ruby asked me to keep the trial in Dallas." The judge also said he was glad to be out of the case. "You can get old handling this case," he noted. "I'm glad it ain't mine."

When Breslin told Belli what Brown had said, Belli was amused and enraged. "Judge Brown made his first mistake the day his mother told him to go to law school and he went there instead of staying home," cracked the lawyer. "I asked for the trial to stay in Dallas? We spent two weeks making motions. I knew the decision would get thrown out because Brown wouldn't move the trial."

In any case, thanks to Kunstler, Burleson, and the others, Jack Ruby was now legally innocent, with a new trial scheduled for Wichita Falls in February 1967.

That trial would never take place.

26 | FINAL TESTIMONY

ANY CELEBRATION BY JACK RUBY and his family of the overturned conviction was short-lived. In December 1966, before his new trial could even begin, Ruby was discovered to have multiple life-threatening medical problems. Jack was suffering from pneumonia, circulatory disease, and cancer.

Sheriff Decker had been hospitalized with emphysema and hadn't seen Ruby for a while. He went to visit his star prisoner to introduce him to the sheriff from Wichita Falls, to whom he would soon give Ruby over for the new trial.

Decker realized that something was very wrong physically with Ruby and had Dr. J. M. Pickard, the country health officer, visit him. At first, the doctor's diagnosis was pneumonia, but no alarms were sounded other than labeling the condition as "serious." It seems like there had been a general passing of the buck regarding Ruby's health between Decker and his staff and the various doctors and guards who observed him.

Somehow, everyone who saw Ruby regularly "had not noticed the swiftness of his decline; his growing nausea, vomiting, 'tight chest' seemed to have no explanation—nerves, perhaps, and a cold." The guards didn't—or wouldn't—see the shape he was in. Even friends and relatives who saw him regularly—except for Eva ("For three weeks he's been deathly sick," she reported)—didn't notice how badly he was doing. Maybe they didn't want to. He was treated for his complaints with Pepto-Bismol.

In any case, Ruby's condition was suddenly taken seriously by authorities and he was rushed to Parkland. Fluid had accumulated in his right lung. Some of the fluid was removed, with some set aside for testing.

It turned out that, according to his guards, Ruby had been vomiting frequently and couldn't keep food down starting right after his verdict was overturned. He had also had a coughing spell and had been complaining of chest pains for a while. Perhaps Ruby's symptoms were seen by his guards and others as simply psychosomatic responses to the emotional toll of being condemned to death, then reprieved, and then having to adjust to the idea that he'd have to go through another trial. Or perhaps they hoped he'd just die.

In addition to the pneumonia, cancer was then discovered in Ruby's lungs, liver, and brain, and ultimately in his lymph system, indicating that it had spread everywhere. It was inoperable and progressing rapidly. Eva hinted that she thought the prosecution somehow had induced the cancer.

It looked certain that Ruby wouldn't leave the hospital alive. But the hospital and the police didn't want him to die prematurely. "There are a lot of people in Dallas—and the world, for that matter—who would like to see Ruby dead," said a Parkland spokesperson. Sheriff Decker instituted maximum security precautions.

Possibly giving a glimpse into the dying Jack Ruby's state of mind, his niece, Joyce Ruby Berman, possesses a letter written in Parkland by Ruby to her father, Earl.

Typed by either Ruby or someone he was dictating it to (or possibly writing on his behalf), full of words and phrases crossed out with *x*'s, the letter seems to genuinely be from Jack, but with an awareness that it might have an audience beyond family. Interestingly, the letter is signed in script, with a pen, with Jack signing his first *and* last names, oddly formal for a letter to a sibling. The letter reads:

> Dear Brother Earl,
> I don't know how to begin to thank you for all you've done for me these last three years. What would I have done if you hadn't been out there doing your very best for me? I don't think just thanking you will ever compensate you for your devotion, your time and money, but I feel I must tell you in some way how I feel.

Earl, I want you to know I never knew Oswald, I was never involved in any conspiracy and I did not plan to shoot him. After it happened I didn't know what I had done. Oh, Earl, how I wish this had never happened. I never realized this could cause so much grief to everyone. How I wish I had these last 3 years to live over again—my life would have been so different. I would have been with all my family whom I love so much. You've all been so wonderful being so loyal to me. I'll never forget it as long as I live.

Earl, I know you've been coming down here to confer with the lawyers all the time, and I was able to see you for short periods, but now that I am in Parkland, I want to talk to you face to face without that glass between us and I want to see you. This is the same hospital where our Beloved President Kennedy died. He was a wonderful man.

Earl, thanks again from the bottom of my heart.

(signed) Jack Ruby

Gone from Ruby's mind, at least in this letter, are any thoughts of overarching plots and schemes, of danger to his family or to the Jewish people or to the United States. After this letter, he would make at least one more series of statements regarding how he wanted to be remembered.

Fading, Ruby asked for another lie-detector test. If the end was near, he wanted to make sure, once again, that the world would know his version of his story was the way it really happened. That request would not be granted, largely because it was assumed that Ruby's various ailments and any treatments he had been receiving for them would have made a polygraph test completely unreliable.

But there would be a last, on-the-record—literally and figuratively—declaration and statement by Jack Ruby, this one undertaken for financial as well as historic, legalistic, and, perhaps, conscience-clearing reasons.

The Ruby family was long out of funds, having depleted their resources for Jack's defense. So when Elmer Gertz and Earl Ruby were in Dallas to meet about the upcoming retrial, Burleson informed them that he had been contacted by journalist and photographer Lawrence Schiller. Schiller had been in the room when Ruby shot Oswald and had been involved with the Billy Woodfield-ghostwritten Ruby articles. He wanted to get Jack's participation in a long-playing Capitol Records album he had been assigned to create about the JFK assassination. Schiller had previously been involved with LP documentaries on topics including the death of Lenny Bruce, the use of LSD, and homosexuality.

Schiller had already interviewed others for the JFK record and was willing to pay for Ruby's participation. The day Schiller met with Earl and Gertz in Chicago, Ruby was diagnosed with terminal cancer, adding a ticking clock's pressure to getting Jack's words recorded.

Not willing to risk the red tape—and possible refusal—of getting official permission from the police and hospital to interview Jack, Schiller arranged for Earl and Gertz to visit Jack in the hospital and record his words with a small tape recorder hidden in an attaché case. They designed a set of questions that, while not putting words in Jack's mouth, would make it reasonably easy for him to reaffirm the story he had been telling, with the chance for him to make any changes or adjustments he thought necessary. If this was indeed to be his last testament, then it would be his final chance to affirm, deny, or modify what he'd been saying all along. Of course, there's no telling what anyone would say under such circumstances, especially someone who had said as many contradictory things as Jack Ruby. But this would be at least an effort to get his last recollections and reflections recorded for posterity.

On December 16, 1966, after securing a new power-of-attorney document for Earl (power of attorney had been held by Eva) by sneaking it into Jack's room for his signature so that Earl would have the authority to finalize the deal with Schiller and Capitol on Jack's behalf, the recording was made. Whether Eva was aware of this shift is unclear. In any case, while she and Eileen kept the guard in Jack's room distracted with small talk, it was up to Earl and Gertz to make the recording. Just to make sure the guard didn't tumble to what was going on, the two now filled Jack in on what they were doing in Yiddish. Gertz recalled that "although Jack appeared to be much more rational than when we had seen him in the Dallas County Jail, he still whispered, mostly to Earl, of his earlier obsessions. But now to the slaughtering of Jews induced by his act was added [that] there was something conspiratorial about his illness. It had been induced, somehow, by the prosecution."

The tape—which would eventually be cut down from the recorded fifteen minutes to four for the released record album—does indeed have Jack reiterate what he'd been saying all along: that shooting Oswald was spontaneous and unplanned. Ruby repeated, "All I did is walk down there, down to the bottom of the ramp, and that's when the incident happened."

He was asked when he finally realized that "something had happened."

He responded, "Well, it happened in such a blur that, before I knew it, I was down on the ground. The officers had me on the ground."

Asked when he realized he had "done something," he responded, "Well, really it happened so fast and everything else, I can't recall what happened from the time I came to the bottom of the ramp until the police officers had me on the ground."

On the tape, Ruby denied ever having met Oswald before. He denied that anyone had given him inside information on when and where Oswald was being moved. Strangely, he wasn't asked directly if he had been a part of any conspiracy, although that seems to have been the entire point—finances aside—of making the recording: making it clear that Jack had not been involved with anyone else in the killing of Oswald.

Perhaps that's why Earl and Gertz granted an interview, before the record's existence was publicly revealed, to Bernard Gavzer of the Associated Press. In it, Gertz told Gavzer,

> Jack saw himself as a kind of instrument. He did not have the delusion that God told him to do it, or that he was an instrument of any people, but that it happened without his conscious will. Jack . . . is aware of . . . all the books and articles which are constructing incredible stories of a conspiracy in which he is claimed to have had a part. He says, "How can they think I am hiding anything or protecting anyone else? There is nothing to hide; there was no one else." . . . Jack still thinks millions of people believe there was a sinister plot to kill Oswald and he is preoccupied with wanting to prove there was not.

Gertz also told Gavzer that Ruby had asked his sister Eileen to bring him pastrami, corned beef, kosher dill pickles, rye bread, lox, cream cheese, green onions, and bagels. "It was a badge of his Jewishness, West Side Chicago style," Gertz told the reporter. "Of course, Jack couldn't hold that food down, but to deny it to him would be like denying a condemned man his last meal."

The Rubys were pleased with Gavzer's article, which appeared on front pages nationwide, feeling that, along with the recording, it would give their brother a last chance to make his case before he passed away.

As it became clear to the public that Ruby's days were numbered, Hillel Silverman, by then established as the spiritual leader of Sinai Temple in Los Angeles, was contacted by Dallas TV station KRLD. He recalled that the station "called me and asked if I would come and speak to him before he passed away. And I really didn't want to go, because I was afraid they'd want to know what his last words were. 'Did he confess?' 'Was it a conspiracy?' By the time I got on the plane, he died, so I didn't go."

Jack Leon Ruby died on January 3, 1967, in Parkland Hospital—where John F. Kennedy and Lee Harvey Oswald had died—innocent in the eyes of the law, as Oswald had been. But his strange saga was far from over.

27 | GOING HOME

BECAUSE SO MUCH OF WHAT HAD OCCURRED involving the murders of Kennedy and Oswald was even then thought of as some kind of sleight of hand—"greatest magic trick ever under the sun," as Bob Dylan would chime in decades later—the Ruby family and lawyers were determined that there would be as much transparency as possible regarding the aftermath of Jack's death, so that anyone who wanted to could see the findings with their own eyes. That transparency would include an autopsy.

Although Eva was opposed to an autopsy on religious grounds, Earl and Gertz decided that the only way to avoid the controversies such as had surrounded Kennedy's and Oswald's deaths (and continue to surround them) was to do one and make the results widely available. Their wishes prevailed, and the procedure was done. Gertz recalls, "Experts from Dallas and Washington and elsewhere, governmental and private, eventually participated in the autopsy, which was detailed and lengthy."

The examination revealed that the malignancy had reached every vital organ, including Ruby's brain. "There was," observes Gertz, "the lingering thought that perhaps the origin of the cancer was deep down in the cells and had existed and been felt at the very moment that Oswald had been shot." There was, though, no way to know for sure.

In a meeting with Dallas Country medical examiner Dr. Earl F. Rose, lawyer Alan Adelson—hired by the Ruby family to try to take care of the numerous loose ends Jack had left unresolved—was told that Ruby had ultimately died of a blood clot that traveled from his leg and lodged in his lungs. Rose also explained to Adelson and Eva Grant that "there is no way known to me or to medical science that one can be injected with cancer."

Rose also made it clear that Ruby's ailments should have been detected and treated more than a year before they officially were and that the family might have a case against Ruby's doctors for medical malpractice. This was a route they ultimately elected not to take, fearing that, with Jack condemned to death anyway, neglect of his health would not be given much weight. They also feared that such actions would distract from their goal of retrieving Jack's property, not simply for any perceived value but also to keep it from being displayed in an exploitive manner. (Lee Harvey Oswald's ornate original tombstone, for instance, was, over the years, stolen, hidden, recovered, and last seen in 2017 in the hands of a Dallas bar owner. A newer, simpler one now sits atop his grave.) In this, they would only achieve partial success, and even that would take decades. Controversy over multiple versions of Ruby's will would entangle the fates of his possessions—most importantly, that of the gun with which he'd shot Oswald—for years to come.

———————

Hugh Aynesworth's reporter's instincts kicked into gear the day Ruby died. Aynesworth got the go-ahead from *Newsweek* magazine on his request to cover the story. He had never actually liked Jack Ruby, but a story is a story.

Arriving at Parkland, Aynesworth was grabbed by Earl, Eva, and Eileen, who demanded he come with them. They drove him to Dallas's Weiland-Merritt Funeral Home, where the body had been taken. The funeral director asked them where they would like Jack sent. The family agreed they wanted him to be buried out of the old Original Weinstein & Sons Funeral Home in Chicago.

At some point, Earl and an executive at Weiland-Merritt started negotiating over the costs of preparing and shipping Jack's body to Chicago for burial. "The price of the casket nearly choked poor Earl," Aynesworth recalled. The reporter then took Earl aside and suggested that maybe all they needed to get Jack to Chicago was a simple pine box. Money aside, Aynesworth had heard that some states required a locally made casket to bury someone in.

Upon Earl's demanding that setup, the funeral parlor executive suddenly remembered he had such a box and sold them the simpler item. The coffin was then shipped to the Chicago chapel. In Chicago, the family would replace the wooden box with one made of bronze.

Aynesworth was also assigned by *Newsweek* to make the trip to Chicago for the funeral. He and Phil Burleson ended up sharing a motel room near the Weinsteins' funeral home. (No connection is known between these Weinsteins and the Dallas strip club owners.) Having been invited by the family, Burleson and Aynesworth came to visit them at Eileen's house, just outside Chicago, the night before the funeral. That evening, one of the pallbearers fell ill and had to cancel on the funeral. Someone suggested replacing him with a boyhood friend of Jack's, but it turned out the fellow had been dead for five years. Earl then asked Aynesworth if he could fill in. Aynesworth was torn:

> The Rubys were a decent family, compassionate and loving. They did not deserve the pain that Jack caused them. What Earl asked was a simple favor that I'd be happy to do under any other circumstances. However, it seemed hypocritical if I, who genuinely disliked Jack Ruby, helped carry him to his grave.

The reporter declined the request, and an ex-schoolmate of Jack's, Joe Kellman, was found to take his place, despite Kellman having told the Warren Commission that he had only met Ruby five or six times over their lifetimes and that he didn't even know Ruby had moved to Dallas until news broke of Ruby having killed Oswald. Ultimately, Ruby's pallbearers included Kellman, Eileen's husband, and four of Ruby's lawyers: Michael Levin (a boyhood friend of the family who was also the chairman of the Jack Ruby Appeal Committee), Burleson, Kunstler, and Gertz. Inside the coffin, Ruby's body was "attired in a black suit, a black tie and a white shirt, and the traditional Jewish shawl and skullcap."

The funeral took place on Monday, January 9, 1967. The Original Weinstein & Sons Funeral Home did indeed handle the proceedings. All seven of Jack Ruby's siblings attended.

Adelson drove to the funeral with Burleson and Aynesworth, the sole reporter welcomed by the Ruby family. Fourteen policemen guarded the chapel in case of any disturbances, but there were none. The funeral was officiated over by Rabbi David Graubart, "a friend of the Ruby family." Hillel Silverman was not invited to participate in the ceremony, though he seemed to have been willing—albeit grudgingly—to visit Jack in his last hours alive.

The ceremony took all of ten minutes. Graubart's eulogy included these words:

> The eyes of the world are upon us now.
>
> Jack Ruby linked himself with one of the most tragic moments in American history. He acted as a patriot, but as a misguided patriot and avenger.
>
> Jack Ruby thought he could acquire his spiritual world in one moment, to use the idiom of the ancient rabbis. Jack Ruby unfortunately destroyed his world in one moment.
>
> Shall we condemn him? No, I speak as a religionist who believes that man is beloved of God because he is created in His image.
>
> The ancient rabbis of old taught us not to judge our fellow man until we come into their place. Jack Ruby was a man who knew affliction, sorrow, and suffering. We dare not condone this act, yet we dare not sit in judgment.

During the ceremony, the casket had been closed. When the funeral ended, Earl Ruby called Adelson over as the crowd was filing out and informed him that the news media wanted to open the casket to get a last look at Jack. Aynesworth had pointed out to Adelson that "with all the conspiracy talk already around, I worried that someday someone would say that the man in Jack Ruby's grave was not Jack Ruby." Adelson agreed that they would have to open the casket. "Who was to know if Jack was really in the casket? I had heard rumors that Kennedy was not really dead, but was hidden away in South America." The casket was opened for a few reporters, who saw that it was, indeed, Jack Leon Ruby who was inside it.

Adelson reported the day as being cold: "It must have been ten degrees . . . although the sun was shining brightly." According to John Justin Smith in the *Chicago Daily News*, "Three squad cars led the procession [of some twenty autos] to the Westlawn Cemetery. . . . Jack Ruby would have liked that. He was given to hanging around policemen and police stations."

Smith continued, "About 50 persons gathered at the grave for the burial service, and some 35 of the uninvited looked on from the other side of a wire fence about 50 feet away from the Ruby burial plot."

Earl Ruby had actually given permission to TV news to televise the burial, which was to take place at Westlawn, where Ruby's deceased family members were interred. The TV personnel started setting up their equipment as if they were covering a sporting event, which shocked Earl. He hadn't closely read the permission form he'd signed and had assumed the coverage would be simple and unobtrusive. The family was able to have the press, with the exception of Aynesworth, removed, although some still filmed it from outside the nearby cemetery fence.

The *New York Times* noted, "Ruby's three brothers and four sisters sat on folding chairs alongside the grave during the brief ceremony. . . . The sisters' heads were bowed and all were silent as Ruby's three brothers recited the Kaddish, a Jewish mourners prayer. The sisters rose for the prayer but, following Jewish tradition, did not join in it." The rabbi and Jack's three brothers each then shoveled some dirt into the grave.

Jack's flag-draped veteran's coffin was buried next to his parents' graves. The flag that draped the coffin was folded and given to Eva, who said she would give it to Earl, "who had done so much for us." The family then proceeded to Eileen Kaminsky's house, just outside Chicago, where they would sit shivah for their brother for the following week.

Somehow appropriately for a life so enshrouded in ambiguity, Jack Ruby's headstone bears a different birthdate, April 25, 1911, than any of the several he gave during his lifetime.

Death, however, is not the end of Jack Ruby's story.

The headstone on Jack Ruby's grave, in Westlawn Cemetery on the northwest edge of Chicago. The stone displays a different birthdate than any of the several Ruby gave over the course of his life. *Courtesy of Grandeland/Wikimedia Commons, https:// commons.wikimedia.org/wiki/File:JackRuby.JPG*

28 | AFTERLIFE

JACK RUBY IS DEAD AND BURIED, but his deeds and his presence have lingered for six decades. Down through the years, the country has had to deal with the repercussions of Ruby shooting Oswald, and his family has had to live with their own personal repercussions of that event.

Here are just a few examples. In the aftermath of Ruby's death, Earl Ruby was contacted by country music superstars Hank Snow and Tennessee Ernie Ford, who'd played at Jack's clubs. According to Earl, Ford "called me up and said he'd like to have . . . one of Jack's letters to me. . . . I said forget it." It's unknown what Snow wanted, but Earl implied it was something equally inappropriate. Even celebrities macabrely wanted Jack Ruby souvenirs.

Less amusingly, Ruby's estate was contested, although, as Earl described it, the estate consisted of "a watch, a ring, a suit, and a handgun." Ruby had handwritten a will in the 1950s that named lawyer Jules Mayer as executor. Though Jack and his family wanted to create a new will, even as late as the day he died, they were unable to effect the change that would have put his siblings in charge of his estate.

However, for better or worse, the Warren Commission, in order to make it more palatable for anyone with relevant physical evidence to give it to them, made most of it returnable after the report was issued, and hence fair game for sale to memorabilia collectors. For this reason, many items related to the Kennedy and Oswald murders are in the hands of private collectors and small museums.

So it took until 1991 for Earl to wrest control of his brother's estate from Mayer and gain possession of the infamous Colt Cobra revolver Jack had used to shoot Oswald. Earl then sold it for $220,000 to prominent collector Anthony Pugliese III.

In 2008 Pugliese attempted to auction the weapon off, but was unable to get his $1 million minimum bid. The highest auction price at that point was actually twenty thousand *less* than Pugliese had paid. He seems to still be in possession of the gun.

And, as we have seen, Ruby family members suffered the repercussions of simply being related to Jack Ruby. As recently as 2013, in an interview with journalist Steve North, Sam Ruby's son Fred was, at his request, referred to as "Craig Ruby." (Since then, he has allowed use of his actual first name.) He said the family encountered "bomb threats and huge legal bills" and that, because of his surname, he was "an easy target for bullies" at his Dallas junior high school.

And in a surreal footnote, a 2018 rave review on the Yelp website of Detroit's Earl Ruby Cleaners and Tailors—which Earl called Cobo Cleaners and sold long ago, but which new ownership now named after him (one would hope to take advantage of his good reputation, not his connection to history)—notes unironically that "the employees are always extremely friendly and polite despite the fortified wall of bulletproof glass that separates us."

It's sixty years since John F. Kennedy and Lee Harvey Oswald were murdered and fifty-six years since Jack Ruby died. You can say a lot of things about the era. It was the beginning of the "the Sixties," the start—or at least acceleration—of the age of conspiracy obsession. It was the first televised trauma where America—and the world—shared, first in real time, then repeated endlessly, the shock to the system of those killings.

Somehow, it seems that the assassinations that took place after the Kennedy and Oswald murders should fit, along with those two, a theme, a pattern, a story. A conspiracy. The murders of Malcolm X, Martin Luther King Jr., Robert F. Kennedy (and the defanging-by-scandal of his brother Edward), and John Lennon, the attempts on the lives of Ronald Reagan and George Wallace, somehow must all be part of some bigger picture.

And somehow, Jack Ruby must fit into this bigger picture. But what was that picture?

JFK assassination conspiracy theorists started disseminating their ideas from the get-go—Mark Lane's *Rush to Judgment*, for instance, was among the first books to do so. Polls generally indicate that a large percentage of American don't buy the theory of Ruby and Oswald as lone killers. Even so, many skeptics have a hard time buying into a *specific* theory, even if they believe that there was *some* kind of conspiracy to kill Kennedy and that Jack Ruby may well have been involved with it. Even Lyndon Johnson, after he was out of office, publicly voiced the belief that some kind of conspiracy was likely at play. (He did not, however, implicate himself in such an operation.)

The Select Committee on Assassinations of the US House of Representatives was convened in 1976 in response to growing public sentiment that, intentionally or not, the investigations of the murders of John F. Kennedy and Martin Luther King Jr. ignored important evidence that would have indicated conspiracies behind them. The committee reinvestigated these killings and indeed concluded that conspiracies were involved, though it pointedly avoided specifying exactly who was conspiring with whom to do what. (In the late '70s, apparently, Robert F. Kennedy's 1968 assassination was not yet widely considered to be the handiwork of a cabal.)

Mark Lane, seen here in 1967. His book *Rush to Judgment* was among the first to challenge the findings of the Warren Commission. *University of Michigan yearbook* Michiganensian, *1968, courtesy of Wikimedia Commons*

Regarding Jack Ruby, the committee's conclusions included the following:

> Ruby's shooting of Oswald was not a spontaneous act, in that it involved at least some premeditation.
>
> Similarly, the Committee believed that it was less likely that Ruby entered the police basement without assistance, even though the assistance may have been provided with no knowledge of Ruby's intentions. The assistance may have been in the form of information about plans for Oswald's transfer or aid in entering the building or both.
>
> The scientific evidence available to the committee indicated that it is probable that more than one person was involved in the President's murder. That fact compels acceptance. And it demands re-examination of all that was thought to be true in the past. . . .
>
> Nevertheless, the committee frankly acknowledged that it was unable firmly to identify the other gunman or the nature and extent of the conspiracy.

Some years later, however, the most significant "scientific evidence" that the committee used to support that finding—data gleaned from close examination of sound recordings of the Kennedy killing—was invalidated.

Documents relating to Kennedy's and Oswald's killings that had previously been deemed too sensitive for public view are regularly released by the National Archives. The most recent such data drops happened in December 2022 and June 2023. Relating to Jack Ruby, some of Earl Ruby's tax returns have been released, indicating that his dry-cleaning business did, indeed, seem to be profitable. Unsurprisingly, there are those who believe that the government will forever hold back any documents that would reveal the "actual truth."

Earl Ruby had an interesting take on the murders of Kennedy and Oswald and his brother's role in history. In 1991 he reflected to senior reporter Steve North on the TV newsmagazine *Now It Can Be Told* that

I don't think it'll ever be over. It's just like in the assassination of Lincoln. Every so many years, other thoughts and theories are presented to the public. And I'm sure that's what's gonna go on with Jack.

———————

Of course, Jack Ruby's death did not end the many life stories with which his own was entwined. Here are the fates of some of the notable figures in Ruby's saga:

- On January 17, 1967, two weeks after Ruby passed, his lifelong friend Barney Ross died of cancer. Shortly before that, Ross had requested of an old friend, "When I check out, make sure you give my business to Hershey." Hershey was one of Chicago's Weinstein brothers, and Ross's funeral was indeed held, as was Jack Ruby's, in the Original Weinstein & Sons Funeral Home.
- The University Club of Chicago owner (and Ruby rival), Dallas mob boss Benny Bickers, died on February 14, 1967. Hillel Silverman's friend Mickey Mantle—a co-owner of the club—was a pallbearer at the funeral.
- Judge Joe B. Brown died on February 20, 1968. His book about the Ruby trial was finished years later by his son, also a judge. Also, jury foreman Max Causey's son released a book of his father's notes taken during and after the trial.
- On October 11, 1968, Melvin Belli appeared in the "And the Children Shall Lead" episode of the original *Star Trek* series, playing Gorgan, the human embodiment of an evil entity. Belli's 1964 book about the Ruby trial, *Dallas Justice: The Real Story of Jack Ruby and His Trial*, explained why he didn't really fail. (Indeed, the reversal of the verdict would indicate that at least some of his strategy was correct.) Belli would go on to represent many celebrity clients over the years (and have a prominent role in the Maysles brothers' Rolling Stones documentary, *Gimme Shelter)*, though he would always be best remembered for his failed defense of Jack Ruby.
- William Kunstler would continue his mission of fighting for the underdog, including with the 1969–1970 Chicago Eight trial. Interestingly, in a 2010 documentary about him made by his daughters, *William Kunstler: Disturbing the Universe*, a copy of Kaplan and Waltz's *The*

Trial of Jack Ruby: A Classic Study of Courtroom Strategies is seen on his desk in footage shot decades after the trial. Was Jack Ruby still on his mind after all those years?

- DA Henry Wade would be the defendant in 1973's landmark *Roe v. Wade* decision (announced on the day Lyndon Johnson died), which was overturned by the Supreme Court in 2022.
- Candy Barr would make some halfhearted attempts at a show business comeback. She would be pardoned for her marijuana arrest by Governor Connally in 1969, narrowly miss being put away on another pot bust, and write a book of poetry, *A Gentle Mind . . . Confused.* She quietly (well, aside from a short affair with Hugh Hefner) lived out the last years of her life in her hometown, Edna, Texas, where she died in 2005 at age seventy.
- Hillel Silverman would play himself in a 1978 made-for-TV movie, *Ruby and Oswald,* directed by comic book legend Stan Lee's cousin Mel Stuart (also director, most famously, of *Willy Wonka & the Chocolate Factory,* but also of a 1964 documentary about the Kennedy and Oswald murders, *Four Days in November*). Hillel's son, Jonathan, would become a well-known actor, most memorably in 1989's *Weekend at Bernie's.*
- Rabbi Silverman would pass away on April 10, 2023 at age ninety-nine. To literally the end of his life, he held to his belief that Jack Ruby was a troubled, unhinged, tragic soul who did what he did for any number of possible reasons—but did it all on his own, not as part of any conspiracy.

  In his obituary for Silverman, journalist Steve North—who was friendly with the rabbi as well as with Ruby's siblings—wrote:

  "During his final hospitalization, a family member at his bedside asked about the rabbi's former congregant one last time: Did Ruby have anything to do with a conspiracy?

  "The family shared a video of that moment with me, in which Silverman adjusts his oxygen mask, shakes his head and firmly says: 'No!'"
- Many people connected to, or believed to be connected to, the assassinations would die young, including "Little Lynn" Carlin, who was shot to death in 1966. Some think that any number of these deaths were arranged to silence people who knew too much. It can also be argued that many people in both Ruby's and Oswald's orbits were marginal characters, people whose lives often intersected with violence and erratic behavior. Most notorious of these "suspicious" deaths, perhaps,

was that of Dorothy Kilgallen, who some believe had information that would have revealed the assassinations' secrets.

———————

Ruby's Carousel Club, after a brief period as a police department gym, was razed in 1972. The Weinsteins' strip clubs are gone, too, as is much of the downtown Dallas that Jack Ruby knew.

Dallas's civic fathers and mothers chose to preserve Dealey Plaza—including the Grassy Knoll—much as they were on November 22, 1963. The Texas Theatre, where Oswald was captured, still remains as it was that day. Even Campisi's Egyptian Restaurant is still decorated as if it were still 1963. (An autographed photo on one of the restaurant's walls of Al Pacino as Michael Corleone is inscribed, To Joe Campisi, from One Godfather to Another.)

But no such historic status, official or unofficial, was reserved for the grungy blocks where the Carousel Club was based. A huge government and business plaza, made up of enormous, boxlike edifices, now stands on the venue's site, a tombstone of sorts for a place and an era and the man who came to symbolize them: Jack Ruby.

———————

It's customary, in the final pages of biographies, to reflect on what the subject's legacy might be. This rumination usually falls along the lines of saying that though the person may have had flaws—even large, significant flaws—overall he or she did some really important things. The notable exceptions are when the subject is someone like Hitler or Al Capone. It's impossible to frame figures like that in a positive light. But you can at least say of them that they may have been evil, but you can't deny that they affected history.

It would be hard to put Jack Ruby in the territory of Hitler, Stalin, Capone, and Pol Pot. But because of what he did in that basement garage in November 1963, he's also more than just a regular person, even a regular criminal. Jack Ruby changed history, and his actions reverberate to the present day. But does that mean he has a legacy?

He certainly impacted history, helped change the way we view the very notions of justice and even our concept of agreed-upon truth. Whether he was a lone nut or part of a conspiracy, the repercussions of his actions will be with us forever. Whatever forces may have propelled him into the limelight, he was ultimately alone, the decision to pull the trigger his and his only.

And yet, we don't really know what to do with him. You couldn't exactly call what he did a victory for the little guy, could you? At best, he represents the worst of vigilante justice.

And at worst? Well, people will be speculating about that forever.

And so, we have done with Jack Leon Ruby what we so often do with violent, history-changing figures: we make them into icons, into, dare I say, celebrities. Perhaps, for someone like Jack Ruby, who so desperately wanted to be famous, becoming an irony-larded icon—a funhouse-mirror version of a celebrity—is the most appropriate status to wind up with.

After all, mentions of and allusions to Jack Ruby abound in our culture. Starting with the period immediately after his death, directly or indirectly, Jack Ruby's name, image, and persona regularly turn up.

Ruby has become an almost camp figure, fodder for artists and entertainers as well as for conspiracy theorists, a character simultaneously sinister and sympathetic. The image of the chubby everyman, exacting some form of revenge on behalf of a nation that may or may not have asked for that favor, has become, for some, an ironic icon. Just look at some of the uses to which his name and image have become attached:

- Early in 1967, shortly after Ruby's death, the popular *Esquire* magazine devoted an issue to the JFK assassination, featuring a photo of Ruby's murder of Oswald as part of the cover. In addition to a portion of an early version of Wills and Demaris's *Jack Ruby* biography, the issue included a three-page comic about Ruby's fateful forty-eight hours, adapted from the Warren Commission report, edited by John Berendt (who would write the book *Midnight in the Garden of Good and Evil*) and drawn by Marvel Universe genius cocreator Jack Kirby.
- The late Lawrence Lindo, a prominent Jamaican reggae music producer, took on the professional name of Jack Ruby. His son, Jack Ruby Jr., is a well-known reggae DJ.
- Ruby was a character in Oliver Stone's *JFK*, and of course in the Danny Aiello–starring movie *Ruby*. *JFK* was justly criticized for playing fast and loose with history, validating a generally debunked conspiracy the-

ory, immortalizing speculation about Ruby as ironclad fact. *Ruby* was pretty much completely a fantasy, portraying Jack Ruby as a criminal and conspiratorial mastermind.

- Don DeLillo's landmark 1988 novel *Libra* portrayed a sympathetic, albeit fictionalized, version of Ruby, which lingers in the memories of many.

- Around the fiftieth anniversaries of the Kennedy and Oswald murders, Stephen King wrote the 2011 bestseller *11/22/63*, which played on an alternate-reality version of that weekend. The book was made into a popular 2016 TV series. Even with his role changed in this storyline, Jack Ruby plays a part.

- The Ruby Revue (featuring the Conspiracy Club), a neo-burlesque troupe centered in Dallas, performs regularly. Carousel Club alumna Tammi True, who died in 2019 at age eighty-one, performed with the group until nearly the end of her life.

- Recently, five thousand bullets were fired from Ruby's Colt Cobra pistol. Each bullet was then put up for sale as a collectible item, complete with a spent cartridge case. Each has a plaque that reads, AN ORIGINAL BULLET SHOT FROM THE "MOST FAMOUS GUN IN THE WORLD." In 2017 bullet #435 was auctioned for $1,287.00.

The spent cartridge from one of five thousand souvenir bullets fired through Jack Ruby's Colt Cobra .38. *Courtesy of Steve North*

- A set of Ruby's fingerprints from the day he was booked for killing Oswald, signed by Jack at the time, was auctioned off in 2021 for $18,308.
- Dealey Plaza, the Texas Theatre, and the Texas School Book Depository have become popular tourist attractions. Dallas city hall and police headquarters, where Ruby shot Oswald, is today part of the University of North Texas at Dallas College of Law, but the school has recently put up exhibits inside the building relating to the infamous event that took place there.
- Bob Dylan, the prolific Nobel Prize–winning singer-songwriter and visual artist, has shown a marked interest in the JFK assassination, and in Jack Ruby in particular:

  ○ A month after the killings of Kennedy and Oswald, Dylan excited controversy when he said that "I saw some of myself" in Lee Harvey Oswald.
  ○ In his 2020 seventeen-minute rumination on the JFK assassination, "Murder Most Foul," released during the frightening early days of the coronavirus pandemic, Dylan advises those looking for the truth about the murders to "ask Oswald and Ruby—they oughta know."
  ○ In November 2022, Dylan's book *The Philosophy of Modern Song* featured three photos of Ruby (including that of his shooting of Oswald). Dylan discussed him in the context of examining the 1956 song "Ruby, Are You Mad?" (The Ruby of the song is not, and has no connection to, Jack.)
  ○ Dylan has produced two Ruby-themed visual works. One riffs on the image of Ruby shooting Oswald, the other on a photo of Ruby hanging out with Carousel dancers.

- In the summer of 2020, the second season of Netflix's popular *The Umbrella Academy* series was set in November 1963 Dallas and prominently featured a historically accurate (dachshunds and all) Jack Ruby.
- In general, the name Jack Ruby has become a touchstone for discussions of mysterious deaths. For instance, when reviled political influencer Jeffrey Epstein turned up dead in 2019, a Florida columnist noted that his supposed suicide "may be the most curious jailhouse death since Jack Ruby shot Lee Harvey Oswald."

The idea of Jack Ruby embodying and symbolizing a regular guy who forced his way into history is a powerful one. Maybe that's his legacy, a perverse twist on the idea that "one person can make a difference."

Clockwise from upper left: TV and print journalist Steve North with Jack Ruby's siblings Sam Ruby, Earl Ruby, and Eva Grant in 1989 at a Los Angeles deli. Jack's siblings seemed to never lose faith in their brother's essential goodness of heart. *Courtesy of Steve North*

Perhaps the last reflections on Jack Ruby should come from Earl Ruby, forever loyal to his brother's memory. In 2003, three years before his death, Earl told a reporter for the *Toledo Blade* that "Jack never meant to kill Oswald. He just wanted to make him suffer."

Years earlier, Earl had observed that, contrary to the recollections of other family members, "We never had any problems. Nobody ever threatened us or anything like that.

"He owed me $16,000. When the FBI asked why I gave him the money, I said I loved Jack. I didn't care if I got it back. . . . He was my brother, that's why. I wanted to help him get on his feet. And I thought, 'One of these days he's gonna hit it. And do well.' That's the way we were. We were brothers.

"He believed in America. He really did. He liked the Presidents. Roosevelt. Eisenhower. Truman. But especially Kennedy, and his whole family. He loved 'em all. That's the way he was.

"I don't know if you would say I'm 'proud' of what he did. But I'm not ashamed of him, that he did it. I'm really not ashamed."

ACKNOWLEDGMENTS

IT WAS MORE THAN TEN YEARS AGO that I decided to tell the far-more-incredible-than-I-had-realized story of Jack Ruby. A good decade's worth of research and thinking—and talking endlessly to my ever-patient friends and family—about Ruby's strange saga has gone into the making of this book.

Many people have been helpful and encouraging along the way—so many that I'm sure I'll overlook some. But as best I can, here's a list of people without whom this book would not have been possible. To anyone I neglect to mention, my deepest apologies.

First, though, there are a couple of people to whom I have to give special thanks, whose contributions made a significant difference to the direction and content of *Jack Ruby*.

One is Rabbi Hillel Silverman (who passed away in April 2023, at age ninety-nine), who was extraordinarily generous with his knowledge, memories, and insights relating to his congregant Jack Ruby.

The other is broadcast and print journalist Steve North, who had and has personal and professional connections with a number of the key players in the story, and whose own deep knowledge and insights have been invaluable.

In addition to them, there are numerous people and institutions who helped bring this book into being. My deepest thanks and appreciation go to:

Michael Benson, John Berendt, Joyce Ruby Berman, Mitch Blank, Sidney Blumenthal, Matt Bucher, Brian Chuck, Ron Deutsch, Edward Jay Epstein, Jules Feiffer, Blanche Fingeroth, Ethan Fingeroth, Jacob Fingeroth, Jim Fingeroth, Pat Fingeroth, Devon Freeny, Andrew J. Friedenthal, Rick Geary, Mike Gold, Marc Gordon, Don Graham, Glenn Hauman, Richard Hyfler, Robert Hyfler, Chris Jansen, Eve Jedda, Richard Kahn, David Kasakove, Peter Kuper, Chris Latshaw, the freewheelin' Evander Lomke, Deb Matlovsky, Kevin Moran, Dean Motter, Robert Nedelkoff, Jerome Pohlen, the Pop Culture Roundtable biographers group, Carl Rollyson's *A Life in Biography* podcast, Fred Ruby, John Ruskay, Gus Russo, Geoff Schumacher at the Mob Museum, the staff of the Sixth Floor Museum at Dealey Plaza (including: Stephen Fagin, Krishna Shenoy, and Mark Davies), J. David Spurlock, Varda Steinhardt, Steven Tice, Larry Tye, David Uslan, Michael Uslan, Joseph Webb, Gary Weinstein, Steven Weinstein, Robert Welch, Mark Zaid, Alexandra Zapruder, and Howard Zimmerman.

NOTES

Preface: "You Killed My President, You Rat!"

"You killed my president": Jack Ruby, testimony, June 7, 1964, in Hearings Before the President's Commission on the Assassination of President Kennedy (Washington, DC: US Government Printing Office, 1964), 5:200. This document is cited subsequently as Warren Commission Hearings.

"Jack Ruby, that bastard child": Kinky Friedman, "Jack Was an Ace," *Texas Monthly*, September 2003, https://www.texasmonthly.com/articles/jack-was-an-ace/.

1. Killing the Killer

"shootout town": Wills and Demaris, *Jack Ruby*, 10.

"You killed my president": Jack Ruby, testimony, 200.

"You all know me": Wills and Demaris, *Jack Ruby*, 59.

2. Death of a Dream

"heading into nut country" and *"if somebody wants"*: O'Donnell and Powers, *"Johnny, We Hardly Knew Ye,"* chap. 1.

"You can't say Dallas": "Kennedy Assassination—1963 Year in Review," United Press International, 1963, https://www.upi.com/Archives/Audio/Events-of-1963/Kennedy -Assassination/.

"better leave this Willie fella": Willie Nelson with David Ritz, "Willie Nelson's Dallas Diaries," *D Magazine*, January 20, 2023, https://www.dmagazine.com/publications/d -magazine/2023/january/willie-nelsons-dallas-diaries/.

"two Dallas policemen were": Earl Ruby, unpublished interview by Gus Russo, 2003, private collection.

"Are you so money hungry?": Posner, *Case Closed*, 370.

3. Worlds Apart

In 1871, Jack Ruby's father: "A Biography of Jack Ruby," appendix 16 in *Report of the President's Commission*, 779.

"His sons Jack and Earl" to *"He was a carpenter":* Berkow, *Maxwell Street*, 320.

"boy's truancy, incorrigibility at home": Clinical evaluation, Institute for Juvenile Research, exhibit 1291 in Warren Commission Hearings, 22:429.

"disruption and confusion": Belli with Carroll, *Dallas Justice*, 267.

"undescended testicles": Hartogs and Freeman, *Two Assassins*, 78.

"he has some sex knowledge": Clinical evaluation, Institute for Juvenile Research, 431.

"In our last conversation": Clinical evaluation, 431.

"felt an obligation": Hyman Rubenstein, testimony, June 5, 1964, in Warren Commission Hearings, 15:10.

described him as "a hustler": Rubenstein, 10.

"Jacob learned to fight when": Benson, *Gangsters vs. Nazis*, 103–104.

"the Jungian shadow of Ross": Century, *Barney Ross*, 19.

"Sparky and Beryl were": Sussman, *Max Baer and Barney Ross*, chap. 3.

"flew into an uncontrollable rage" and *"Throughout his life, Jack Ruby":* Century, *Barney Ross*, 20.

"Gangsters make excellent protagonists": Kraus, *Kosher Capones*, 136.

"appears to have suffered from": Hartogs and Freeman, *Two Assassins*, 222.

4. A World Gone Mad

"Marx, the jig is up!": Groucho Marx, *Groucho and Me* (orig. publ. 1959; Boston: Da Capo, 2009), chap. 15, digital ed.

"several Chicago friends": "Biography of Jack Ruby," 786.

"One friend, who stated" and *"advice and support":* "Biography of Jack Ruby," 787.

"was always guiding me": Eva Grant, testimony, May 28, 1964, in Warren Commission Hearings, 14:442.

"a young man who dressed": Virginia Belasco, interview by FBI, December 2, 1963, exhibit 1248 in Warren Commission Hearings, 22:358.

"acted as hired muscle": Kraus, *Kosher Capones*, 208n13.

"You guys get caught": Benson, *Gangsters vs. Nazis*, 107.

"Your brother is terrific": Rubenstein, testimony, 20.

"an irregular household": "Biography of Jack Ruby," 783.

"According to the Michael Reese Hospital" and *"By order of the county court":* "Biography of Jack Ruby," 783.

5. War at Home, War Abroad

"being called . . . names, referring" and *"Somebody called me"*: Earl Ruby, testimony, June
    3, 1964, in Warren Commission Hearings, 14:411.

"said words like Sheeny": Grant, testimony, May 28, 1964, 484.

"extremely sensitive to insulting": Berkow, *Maxwell Street*, 322.

"conniver with much nerve" and *"when Bob Hope"*: Stephen Andrew Belancik, interview
    by FBI, June 19, 1964, exhibit 1294 in Warren Commission Hearings, 22:441.

"I'm frank enough to admit": Century, *Barney Ross*, 103.

"He'd gone through money": Century, 110.

"mad that I got involved": Grant, testimony, May 28, 1964, 453.

"shortly after his [Guthrie's] election": Steve Guthrie, interview by FBI, December 6, 1963,
    exhibit 1251 in Warren Commission Hearings, 22:360.

"before she opened the Singapore": "Biography of Jack Ruby," 792.

"hooked up with a con-artist": Kantor, *Ruby Cover-Up*, 209.

"For all I know" to *"his sinister associates hung out"*: Kantor, 210–211.

"My uncle was very involved": Fred Ruby, interview by the author, September 8, 2022.

6. The Old Frontier

it turned out, he was: Knight News Wire, "Jack Ruby Revealed as FBI Informant," *Detroit
    Free Press*, July 31, 1975.

"wasn't surprised": Abe Weinstein, interview, 1994, Sixth Floor Museum at Dealey Plaza,
    Dallas, TX.

"My club [the Colony Club]": Josh Alan Friedman, "Jack Ruby: Dallas' Original J.R.,"
    LCD 20 (1997): http://www.wfmu.org/LCD/20/ruby.html.

"a 7-foot bouncer named": Rachel Stone, "This Son of Abe's Colony Club Warmed Up
    TV Audiences, Managed a Magic Club, Now Charms High-Rollers," *Oak Cliff
    Advocate*, September 27, 2021, https://oakcliff.advocatemag.com/2021/09/larry
    _weinstein-colony-club/.

"He had a wonderful heart": Wills and Demaris, *Jack Ruby*, 14.

"was not a burlesque house": Schwarz and Rustam, *Candy Barr*, 105–106.

"I loved it at Abe's": Schwarz and Rustam, 111.

"made girls available": Schwarz and Rustam, 132.

"Eva Ruby's nightspot": Schwarz and Rustam, 48–49.

"always eager to help": Schwarz and Rustam, 149.

"July 26, 1953": "Biography of Jack Ruby," 800.

Jack was "devoted": Alice Reaves Nichols, testimony, April 14, 1964, in Warren Com-
    mission Hearings, 14:120.

referred to as "Virginia Fitzgerald": "Biography of Jack Ruby," 787.

"a gradual thing": Nichols, testimony, 115.

"a very fine person": Eva Grant, testimony, July 25, 1964, in Warren Commission Hearings, 15:330.

"several times each week": Elaine Rogers, interview by FBI, November 27, 1963, exhibit 1459 in Warren Commission Hearings, 22:880.

"merely to cover up": Marilyn Moone, interview by FBI, November 26, 1963, exhibit 1460 in Warren Commission Hearings, 22:881.

"seemed to have been drinking": Edward McBee, interview by FBI, December 19, 1963, exhibit 1635 in Warren Commission Hearings, 23:110.

"took off all his clothes": Patricia Kohs, interview by FBI, December 15, 1963, exhibit 1499 in Warren Commission Hearings, 22:917.

"one of Hank Williams' last friends": Kinky Friedman, interview, *Quote Unquote*, June 1994, transcribed in Stephen Stratford, "Nigel Cox on Kinky Friedman," *Quote Unquote* (blog), December 2, 2016, http://quoteunquotenz.blogspot.com/2016/12 /nigel-cox-on-kinky-friedman.html.

"go to hell": "Biography of Jack Ruby," 796.

a *"mental breakdown"*: "Biography of Jack Ruby," 794.

"Well, it looks like it is the end": Earl Ruby, testimony, 417.

7. The Personal and the Political

"I would have said": Earl Ruby, testimony, 423.

"depressed . . . and was thinking": Earl Ruby, 372.

"hostility or belligerence" to *"'Maybe we can find'"*: Earl Ruby, 426.

"informed Irving Alkana": "Biography of Jack Ruby," 794.

"bosomy women were working": Nelson with Ritz, "Willie Nelson's Dallas Diaries."

"In 1954, Ruby's Vegas associate": "Biography of Jack Ruby," 794–795.

"SAM RUBY: We sued": Sam Ruby, testimony, May 29, 1964, in Warren Commission Hearings, 14:496–497.

"has become well known": "Jack Ruby Signed Agency Contract," online auction ending November 11, 2020, RR Auction, https://www.rrauction.com/auctions/lot -detail/34363190595321-jack-ruby-signed-agency-contract.

"Curry planned to have" to *"interest her in selling"*: Eileen Curry, interview by FBI, June 9, 1964, exhibit 1762 in Warren Commission Hearings, 23:370.

"set up a numbers game" to *"impressed him as being"*: Jack Hardee Jr., interview by FBI, December 24, 1963, exhibit 1763 in Warren Commission Hearings, 23:372–373.

"chanced to be" to *"hoodlums and safe-crackers"*: FBI agent Ralph J. Miles, report, n.d., exhibit 1764 in Warren Commission Hearings, 23:374.

"For years, the neighbors": Silverman, *Time of My Life*, 55.

"was a member of my congregation": Silverman, 59.

"He [Ruby] was looked upon" to *"She was a sicko"*: Hillel Silverman, interview by the author, August 2013.

"The top people in Dallas": Schwarz and Rustam, *Candy Barr*, 133.

"a group of politicians": Schwarz and Rustam, 134.

"The downtown club district": Schwarz and Rustam, 136.

8. Converging Forces

"had run crime syndicate": Kantor, *Ruby Cover-Up*, 22.

"relative luxury": Kantor, 256.

"like cats and dogs": George Senator, April 21, 1964, in Warren Commission Hearings, 14:212.

"popped Eva on the nose": Hyman Rubenstein, testimony, 26.

"like a disagreeable man": Grant, testimony, May 28, 1964, 462.

"On about 15 occasions" to *"frequently felt contrite"*: "Biography of Jack Ruby," 804–805.

Comedian Gabe Kaplan: "Gabe Caplan," July 12, 2021, in *Gilbert Gottfried's Amazing Colossal Podcast*, https://podcasts.apple.com/ie/podcast/gabe-kaplan/id883308059?i =1000528580168.

"three and one half mile": Bret Stout, "Amazing Untold History of Fort Worth," Bretstout1.com, n.d., http://bretstout1.com/amazing-untold-history-of-fort-worth .htm.

"the club was burned out" to *"would pop in"*: Robertson, *Testimony*, chap. 8.

"Forget about it": Jewel Brown, interview by David Mac, Blues Junction Productions, n.d, http://bluesjunctionproductions.com/monthly_artist_spotlight_jewel_brown.

a *"mental case"* and a *"phony"*: Joseph Glaser, interview by FBI, December 3, 1963, exhibit 1765 in Warren Commission Hearings, 23: 374.

9. The New Frontier

"I want to show": Jack Ruby, testimony, 200.

"He would feed people": Earl Ruby, unpublished interview.

"Ruby's financial records were chaotic": "Biography of Jack Ruby," 798

"I would say that" to *"I was really angry"*: Breck Wall, interview by Bob Porter, Oral History Collection, Sixth Floor Museum at Dealey Plaza, December 28, 1993, video, 47:41, https://emuseum.jfk.org/objects/4677/breck-wall-oral-history.

"Ruby apparently believed": "Biography of Jack Ruby," 797.

"came up with this thing": Steven Weinstein, interview by the author, September 27, 2022.

"Jack likes to live": Senator, testimony, 177.

"It is a word" and *"When I read"*: Senator, testimony, 312–313.

"She is very nervous": Wills and Demaris, *Jack Ruby*, 246.

"He fired me at least": Wills and Demaris, 24, 25.

"Connie was a student": Jim Williamson, "A Dark Day: Area Residents Share Special Ties to Kennedy Assassination," *Texarkana Gazette*, November 22, 2013, https://www.texarkanagazette.com/news/2013/nov/22/dark-day-areresidents-share-special-ties-kenn/.

"Dear Jack" to *"Juanita took [Ruby's] advice"*: Schwarz and Rustam, *Candy Barr*, 255–257.

"yanked me up the night": Schwarz and Rustam, 263.

"I saw some of myself": Joe Taysom, "Remembering Bob Dylan's 1964 Sympathetic Speech About John F. Kennedy Murderer Lee Harvey Oswald," *Far Out Magazine*, May 7, 2020, https://faroutmagazine.co.uk/bob-dylan-lee-harvey-oswald-john-f-kennedy-sympathy-letter/.

a stocky, "Jewish-looking" man: Huey Reeves, testimony, March 27, 1964, in Warren Commission Hearings, 13:253–254.

"too young": Hillel Silverman, interview by FBI, November 27, 1963, exhibit 1485 in Warren Commission Hearings, 22:907.

"the extreme right-wing": Adelson, *Ruby-Oswald Affair*, 50.

"[Jack] ran the spotlight": Tammi True [pseud.], interview by Ginger Valentine, *21st Century Burlesque*, August 27, 2013, https://21stcenturyburlesque.com/tammi-true-interview-ginger-valentine/.

10. Gathering Storm

"a symbol of the communist conspiracy": Minutaglio and Davis, *Dallas 1963*, 241–242.

did from November 20 to 24, 1963: M. A. Moyer and Betty Windsor, "Timeline of Jack Ruby's Activities," Dr. Kenneth A. Rahn Sr. personal website, 1998, https://www.kenrahn.com/JFK/Issues_and_evidence/Jack_Ruby/Timeline_of_Ruby.html.

"underworld characters": Mrs. Harris D. Bryant, interview by FBI, January 6, 1964, exhibit 2396 in Warren Commission Hearings, 25:375.

may have been with him: Gloria Fillmon/Rettig, interview by FBI, December 19, 1963, exhibit 2379 in Warren Commission Hearings, 25:356.

"You probably don't know me": W. F. Dyson to J. E. Curry, November 25, 1963, exhibit 2002 in Warren Commission Hearings, 24:160.

"Lee Oswald. He's with the CIA": Oliver with Buchanan, *Nightmare in Dallas*, 94.

"Ruby called our apartment": Gary Cartwright, "Who Was Jack Ruby? How a Small-Time Strip Joint Operator Ushered in America's Age of Violence," *Texas Monthly*, November 1975, https://www.texasmonthly.com/news-politics/who-was-jack-ruby/.

11. Murder Most Foul

"Ruby called asking if": Williamson, "A Dark Day."

"headed for our second-floor": Aynesworth with Michaud, *JFK: Breaking the News*, 104–105.

"If this Weissman is a Jew": Minutaglio and Davis, *Dallas 1963*, 317.

"It is clear by now": Minutaglio and Davis, 309.

"In Dallas, Texas, three shots": "Walter Cronkite on the Assassination of John F. Kennedy" NPR, November 22, 2013, https://www.npr.org/transcripts/246628793.

"someone ran into the room": Aynesworth with Michaud, *JFK: Breaking the News*, 105.

"Everyone gathered to watch": Aynesworth with Michaud, 106.

"I don't know why": Jack Ruby, testimony, 185.

"Jack called and he was crying": Meghan Keneally, "Jack Ruby 'Wanted to Leave Dallas as Soon as Kennedy Was Shot but His Sister Told Him to Stay' Not Knowing He Was Going to Kill Oswald." *Daily Mail*, November 20, 2013, https://www.dailymail.co.uk/news/article-2510815/Jack-Ruby-wanted-leave-Dallas-soon-Kennedy-shot-sister-told-stay-knowing-going-kill-Oswald.html.

12. Frenzy

"We were together": Hillel Silverman, interview by Stephen Fagin, Oral History Collection, Sixth Floor Museum at Dealey Plaza, June 28, 2006, MP3 audio, 38:58, https://emuseum.jfk.org/objects/26203/rabbi-hillel-silverman-oral-history.

"Seth Kantor I remember": Silverman, interview by Fagin.

"I knew him": Andrew Armstrong Jr., testimony, April 14, 1964, in Warren Commission Hearings, 13:353.

"nervous": Curtis LaVerne Crafard, testimony, April 8, 1964, in Warren Commission Hearings, 13:452.

"half-sobbing": Billy Joe Willis, interview by FBI, November 26, 1963, exhibit 2414 in Warren Commission Hearings, 25:505.

"upset," and "crying": Kay Helen Olsen, August 6, 1964, in Warren Commission Hearings, 14:645.

"happy, jovial": Victor Robertson, interview by FBI, June 9, 1964, exhibit in Warren Commission Hearings, 21:312.

"I wanted to get drunk": Dr. Walter Bromberg, medical history report to attorney Melvin Belli, January 11, 1963, 17, via Portal to Texas History, https://texashistory.unt.edu/ark:/67531/metapth190058/m1/17/.

"three bottles of celery tonic": Kantor, *Ruby Cover-Up*, 93.

"That lousy commie" to *"[He] went into the bathroom"*: Kantor, 93.

"broken, a broken man" and *"Ruby looked so bad"*: Kantor, 94.

"Shortly after 7 p.m.": Kantor, 96–97.

"the pocket-sized revolver": Kantor, 94.

"it turned out to be": Silverman, interview by Fagin.

"Jack Ruby went up": Steven Weinstein, interview.

"put on display in": Kantor, *Ruby Cover-Up*, 100.

"There was no premeditation": Hillel Silverman, notes on Jack Ruby visits, "Unanswered Questions, Premeditation," private collection.

"If Ruby had considered": Kantor, *Ruby Cover-Up*, 101.

"Ruby was no longer": Kantor, 102.

"'Hi, Henry,' he said": Aynesworth with Michaud, *JFK: Breaking the News*, 107.

"if he was in England": Jack Ruby, testimony, 191.

"sullen, quiet, looking": Danny Patrick McCurdy, testimony, June 26, 1964, in Warren Commission Hearings, Volume 15:534.

"happy about being able": Jack Ruby trial transcript, 791, via *JFK Assassination: Jack Ruby Murder Trial*, BACM Research/PaperlessArchives.com, accessed April 24, 2023, https://downloads.paperlessarchives.com/p/jdrm9m/.

"a little weasel of a guy": Ruby trial transcript, 783

turned tearful and agitated: Ruby trial transcript, 776

"Ruby was giving": Kantor, *Ruby Cover-Up*, 106.

in a *"very jovial mood"*: Kenneth E. Griffith, interview by FBI, August 20, 1964, exhibit 2297 in Warren Commission Hearings, 25:232.

"patently upset and emotionally disturbed": George Senator, interview by FBI, November 24, 1963, exhibit 5401 in Warren Commission Hearings, 21:430.

"thought the John Birch Society": Aynesworth with Michaud, *JFK: Breaking the News*, 108.

"Recalling that the News ad": Aynesworth with Michaud, 109.

"Ruby looked through a slot": Kantor, *Ruby Cover-Up*, 110–111.

13. Mania

"Our president was a victim": A printed copy of Rabbi David Seligson's eulogy for JFK is in the author's collection.

"put his head through": Frederic Rheinstein, testimony, July 22, 1964, in Warren Commission Hearings, 15:356.

"*walking around, talking*": Aynesworth with Michaud, *JFK: Breaking the News*, 109.
"*a hangout for many*" : Traces of Texas, "Moment in Time," Facebook, August 21, 2017, https://www.facebook.com/TracesofTexas/posts/this-nifty-moment-in-time-photo -of-downtown-dallas-in-the-1940s-was-sent-in-by-t/1622000624498727/.
"*I believe I told Ruby*" to "*[The photo] upset him*": Frank Bellocchio, testimony, June 27, 1964, in Warren Commission Hearings, 15:470–471.
"*You know I'll be there*": Garnett Claud Hallmark, interview by FBI, December 11, 1963, exhibit in Warren Commission Hearings, 20:68–69.
"*He told me he had tried*": Aynesworth with Michaud, *JFK: Breaking the News*, 109.
"*we couldn't do enough*": Robert L. Norton, testimony, June 27, 1964, in Warren Commission Hearings, 15:552.

14. Assault on History

"*Has he been brought down*": Ira N. Walker Jr., testimony, April 15, 1964, in Warren Commission Hearings, 13:292–293.
he was "*going out*": Elnora Pitts, testimony, March 31, 1964, in Warren Commission Hearings, 13:232.
"*a strange look on his face*": Kantor, *Ruby Cover-Up*, 129.
"*If something happened*": Jack Ruby, polygraph testimony, July 18, 1964, in Warren Commission Hearings, 14:532.
"*[Ruby] had on his snap-brim*": Kantor, *Ruby Cover-Up*, 134.
"*Have they brought him*": Ira N. Walker Jr., testimony, April 15, 1964, in Warren Commission Hearings, 13:294.
"*[Chief Curry] denied that he was put*": Aynesworth with Michaud, *JFK: Breaking the News*, 115.
"*If Graves had [also] been*": James R. Leavelle to Gary Dunaier, May 24, 2017, private collection.

15. Hero of the People

"*Jews do have guts*": Aynesworth with Michaud, *JFK: Breaking the News*, 176.
"*for Mrs. Kennedy's sake*": Wills and Demaris, *Jack Ruby*, 71.
"*Well, we'll send them*": Kantor, *Ruby Cover-Up*, 231.
"*was about as handicapped*": Kantor, 222.
"*I'm sitting in the office*": Berkow, *Maxwell Street*, 331–334.
"*Earl, I think we're*": "Earl Ruby's Life Defined by His Impulsive Brother," *Toledo Blade*, September 28, 2003. https://www.toledoblade.com/JackLessenberry/2003/09/28 /Earl-Ruby-s-life-defined-by-his-impulsive-brother/stories/200309280005.

"Tom Howard had tried": Kaplan and Waltz, *Trial of Jack Ruby*, 20.

"Five lawyers showed up": Wills and Demaris, *Jack Ruby*, 84.

"the most famous criminal lawyer": Aynesworth with Michaud, *JFK: Breaking the News*, 170.

"Rose arrived at Ruby's apartment": Dave Reitzes, "Dead in the Wake of the Kennedy Assassination: The Men Who Gathered in Ruby's Apartment," Kennedy Assassination Home Page, n.d., https://www.jfk-assassination.net/death11.htm.

"WE LOVE YOUR GUTS": Wills and Demaris, *Jack Ruby*, 86–87.

"I was at a sleepover": Joyce Ruby Berman, interview by the author, October 6, 2022.

"somebody came to speak": Berman, interview.

"There was a Civic Light Opera": Fred Ruby, interview.

16. Search for Justice

"thought that a successful": Kaplan and Waltz, *Trial of Jack Ruby*, 32.

"The FBI . . . made sure": Belli with Carroll, *Dallas Justice*, 48–49.

"somebody had to kill him": Wills and Demaris, *Jack Ruby*, 72.

"I was having lunch" to *He was sobbing"*: Tony Zoppi, interview by Wes Wise and Bob Porter, Oral History Collection, Sixth Floor Museum at Dealey Plaza, June 1, 1992, video, 1:07:32, https://emuseum.jfk.org/objects/4559/tony-zoppi-oral-history.

"In dramatic contrast": Kaplan and Waltz, *Trial of Jack Ruby*, 11.

"I said, 'Jack, if you're'": Wills and Demaris, *Jack Ruby*, 60.

"I want you to know": Silverman, notes.

"I have a feeling": Silverman, interview by Fagin.

"I brought with me" to *"Jack Ruby said to me"*: Silverman, notes, "Religious Outlook."

"the man who shot" to *"a tank, and there"*: Wall, interview.

"I was right to kill Oswald": Wills and Demaris, *Jack Ruby*, 72.

"We had a type of": Wall, interview.

"Jack talked as if": Wills and Demaris, *Jack Ruby*, 72.

"He never expected to spend": Wills and Demaris, 73.

"had been taking his turn": Abrams and Fisher, *Kennedy's Avenger*, 44.

"dry writ": Wills and Demaris, *Jack Ruby*, 73.

"Judge Joe B. Brown had": Kaplan and Waltz, *Trial of Jack Ruby*, 17, 20.

17. Into the Maze

"satisfy itself that the truth": "Special Section: The Warren Commission Report," *Time*, October 2, 1964, https://time.com/3422341/the-warren-commission-report/.

"the strippers have been": Abrams and Fisher, *Kennedy's Avenger*, 48.

"*a square room*": Belli with Carroll, *Dallas Justice*, 46–47.

"*The Ruby family had*": Kaplan and Waltz, *Trial of Jack Ruby*, 32.

"*a distraught little man*" to "*On and on he chattered*": Belli with Carroll, *Dallas Justice*, 44.

"*I try to be clinical*": Wills and Demaris, *Jack Ruby*, 118.

"*We already have one*": Belli with Carroll, *Dallas Justice*, 45.

"*[Ruby's] main jail activities*" and "*Ruby read very little*": Belli with Carroll, 49.

"*I told him everything*" to "*Ruby turned out to be*": Belli with Carroll, 47.

"*While Ruby was silent*": Abrams and Fisher, *Kennedy's Avenger*, 68–70.

"*By then, [due to] my own*": Belli with Carroll, *Dallas Justice*, 63.

"*is extremely sensitive to*": Gertz, *Moment of Madness*, 20.

"*San Antonio, being largely*": Gertz, 21.

"'*I feel wonderful*'": Gertz, 13.

"*It had apparently been*": Gertz, 15.

"*After the first bail hearing*": Belli with Carroll, *Dallas Justice*, 54.

Belli was requesting bail: Belli with Carroll, 89–90.

"*[Ruby said:] I am more sympathetic*": Silverman, notes, "Bond Hearing."

"*I did not intend to be*" to "*I reported to Jack*": Silverman, notes, "Henry Wade."

"*He continually recites this*": Silverman, notes, "Religious Outlook."

"*psychomotor epilepsy*" to "*where consciousness is impaired*": Kaplan and Waltz, *Trial of Jack Ruby*, 58.

"*The whole of the second*" to "*that a Jewish boy like that*": Kaplan and Waltz, 58–59.

"*before any final diagnosis*" to "*Ruby displayed a variety*": Kaplan and Waltz, 60.

"*Ruby became agitated*": Kaplan and Waltz, 61.

"*The prosecution, now forewarned*": Kaplan and Waltz, 62.

"*because of a conspiracy*": Abrams and Fisher, *Kennedy's Avenger*, 51.

"*Jack was tremendously upset*": Silverman, notes.

"*I will stay*": Silverman, notes, "Lawyers."

"*I am . . . giving Earl all*": Silverman, notes.

18. The Power of the Press

"*I have never talked*" and "*the negotiations in connection*": Kaplan and Waltz, *Trial of Jack Ruby*, 67.

"*Members of the Ruby family*": Kaplan and Waltz, 68.

"*notes, drafts and edited versions*" to "*The final initialed and approved*": "Jack Ruby's 'My Story'—Notes Drafts," Alexander Historical Auctions, November 6, 2008, https://www.alexautographs.com/auction-lot/jack-rubys-my-story-notes-drafts_TUPQ49XIYO/.

"*millions of salt*" to "*I am not a white slaver*": Jack Ruby, *My Story*, part 1, *Press-Telegram* (Long Beach, CA), January 28, 1964.

"*I was up early*" to "*I said, 'My God'*": Jack Ruby, *My Story*, part 3, *Press-Telegram* (Long Beach, CA), January 30, 1964.

"*Well, I've been hit*": Jack Ruby, *My Story*, part 4, *Press-Telegram* (Long Beach, CA), January 31, 1964.

"*In both cases, one of*" to "*lucrative contract for*": Kaplan and Waltz, *Trial of Jack Ruby*, 67.

"*The only real asset*": Kaplan and Waltz, 68.

"*I will not take a nickel*": Silverman, notes, "Lawyers."

"*He complained that*" and "*Jack denied writing this*": Silverman, notes, "Psychiatric Tests."

"*With only a grade school*": Kantor, *Ruby Cover-Up*, 235–236.

carrying a water pistol: Abrams and Fisher, *Kennedy's Avenger*, 70.

"*It was a bizarre spectacle*": Abrams and Fisher, 80.

"*great reservations*": "Dallas's Leaders Doubt Ruby Can Get Fair Trial," *New York Times*, February 12, 1964, https://www.nytimes.com/1964/02/12/archives/dallass-leaders -doubt-ruby-can-get-fair-trial.html.

"*Never in my life*": Abrams and Fisher, *Kennedy's Avenger*, 78.

"*hog-calling contest*": Belli with Carroll, *Dallas Justice*, 86.

"*As it later became known*": Abrams and Fisher, *Kennedy's Avenger*, 84–85.

"*Jack Ruby couldn't get*": Abrams and Fisher, 72.

"*This is unbelievable*": Abrams and Fisher, 74.

"*the true test of whether*": Abrams and Fisher, 84.

"*to seat the entire press*": Kaplan and Waltz, *Trial of Jack Ruby*, 84.

"*The entire Ruby family*" and "*he was greeted by such*": Kaplan and Waltz, 85.

"*Jack is most nervous*": Silverman, notes.

"*the newspapermen make him*" to "*Ruby, for the first time*": Silverman, notes, "Change of Venue Hearing."

19. A Jury of His Peers

"*I brought him a Sabbath*": Silverman, notes, "Religious Outlook."

"*The only thing [Belli] wanted*": Kaplan and Waltz, *Trial of Jack Ruby*, 95.

"*of the 162 questioned*": Belli with Carroll, *Dallas Justice*, 135.

"*In my thirty-five years*": Causey, *Jack Ruby Trial Revisited*, 19.

"*If I made one mistake*": Belli with Carroll, *Dallas Justice*, 131.

"*regarded picking a jury as*": Kaplan and Waltz, *Trial of Jack Ruby*, 106.

"*Rose made me sit up*": Belli with Carroll, *Dallas Justice*, 139.

"*Can we get any more*": Abrams and Fisher, *Kennedy's Avenger*, 95.

"*terribly distraught and disturbed*" to "*It seems to me that*": Silverman, notes, "The Trial."

"was deeply involved": Abrams and Fisher, *Kennedy's Avenger*, 101.

"are also on trial": Abrams and Fisher, 98.

"You don't have to worry": Kaplan and Waltz, *Trial of Jack Ruby*, 111.

"the intelligence level": Kaplan and Waltz, 114.

"Belli picked a perfect jury": Wills and Demaris, *Jack Ruby*, 120.

"wanted to draw Stubblefield": Silverman, notes, "The Trial."

"fully prepared to cope": Kaplan and Waltz, *Trial of Jack Ruby*, 114.

20. Jailbreak

"this 'state of the art' model": Abrams and Fisher, *Kennedy's Avenger*, 87.

"From beginning to end": Gertz, *Moment of Madness*, 43.

"Reliable sources report": Gertz, 19.

"JUDGE BROWN: Mr. Ruby": Kaplan and Waltz, *Trial of Jack Ruby*, 118–119.

"a pale pudgy guy": Carroll, *Accidental Assassin*, 62.

"While the legal gladiators": Carroll, 63.

"The Joe B. Brown show": Carroll, 72.

"a pretty volatile": Brown, *Dallas and the Jack Ruby Trial*, 89.

"I hope the son of a bitch" to *"Oswald is shot!"*: Kaplan and Waltz, *Trial of Jack Ruby*, 135.

"I intended to shoot": D. R. Archer, testimony, Ruby trial transcript, 254.

"I hope I killed": Dr. Robbert Stubblefield, testimony, Ruby trial transcript, 1265.

"You rat": Thomas Don McMillon, testimony, Ruby trial transcript, 300.

"You all know me": Kaplan and Waltz, *Trial of Jack Ruby*, 146.

"The day had been a complete": Kaplan and Waltz, 161.

"the jury selection seems": Wills and Demaris, *Jack Ruby*, 128–129.

"Ruby was most distraught" to *"He wanted to continue"*: Silverman, notes, "The Trial," 5–6.

"You didn't think I": Glen D. King, testimony, Ruby trial transcript, 486.

"that he saw no reason": Gertz, *Moment of Madness*, 49.

"[Ruby] said . . . something to the effect" to *"'Jews,' Belli yelled"*: Abrams and Fisher, *Kennedy's Avenger*, 174–175.

"some ten to twelve": Abrams and Fisher, 180.

"Just as the defense": Carroll, *Accidental Assassin*, 72.

"escaped from the Dallas County Jail" to *"had grabbed Edna Biggs"*: Jack Langguth, "7 Flee Dallas Jail, Passing the Door of Ruby Courtroom," *New York Times*, March 7, 1964, https://www.nytimes.com/1964/03/07/archives/7-flee-dallas-jail-passing-the-door-of-ruby-courtroom.html.

"Dallas, which looked tragic": Carroll, *Accidental Assassin*, 73–74.

21. Heartbreak

"These are my children": William G. Serur, Ruby trial testimony, March 4, 1964, exhibit 2411 in Warren Commission Hearings, 25:484.

"They [the seats] were all eat[en] out": Serur, Ruby trial testimony, 485.

he was "unpredictable": William E. Howard, testimony, Ruby trial transcript, 486.

"As always," Silverman wrote to "only to make sure that": Silverman, notes.

"far more animated": Abrams and Fisher, Kennedy's Avenger, 204.

"go into a tantrum and scream": Ruby trial transcript, 678.

"he wouldn't step on a fly": Transcript, 693.

"he understood his own trouble": Transcript, 692.

he stopped at the defense table: Abrams and Fisher, Kennedy's Avenger, 204.

Ruby "was in grief": Ruby trial transcript, 716.

"he had a moody look": Transcript, 724–725.

"[Jack] knocked him [the driver]": Kaplan and Waltz, Trial of Jack Ruby, 184.

"At the outset": Carroll, Accidental Assassin, 70.

"the first to convincingly record": Prasad Vannemreddy, MD, MCh, James L. Stone, MD, and Konstantin V. Slavin, MD, "Frederic Gibbs and His Contributions to Epilepsy Surgery and Electroencephalography," Neurosurgery 70, no. 3 (March 2012): https://journals.lww.com/neurosurgery/Abstract/2012/03000/Frederic_Gibbs_and _His_Contributions_to_Epilepsy.31.aspx.

"The brunt of our defense": Belli with Kaiser, My Life, 264.

"organic brain damage": Ruby trial transcript, 872.

"psychomotor variant": Martin L. Towler, testimony, Ruby trial transcript, 995.

"behaving as an automaton" and doesn't "know what": Towler, 1001.

"six hundred feet": Belli with Kaiser, My Life, 268.

"was not capable of" to "a mental cripple": Gertz, Moment of Madness, 56.

"a very short-lived": Carroll, Accidental Assassin, 71.

a book he was reading: Abrams and Fisher, Kennedy's Avenger, 279.

"would have no significance": Ruby trial transcript, 1246.

"The barber had just placed": Belli with Kaiser, My Life, 265.

E. H. "Billy" Combest: Ruby trial transcript, 1382–1383.

"had not even bothered" to "He was disturbed that": Silverman, notes, "The Trial," 8.

"Ruby was mentally ill": Gertz, Moment of Madness, 60.

"seemed to be in sort of": Kaplan and Waltz, Trial of Jack Ruby, 275.

"very unstable, very emotional": Ruby trial transcript, 1454.

"at the time of the shooting": Transcript, 1458.

"I have found that on many": Transcript, 1454–1455.

"It is also my opinion": Kaplan and Waltz, Trial of Jack Ruby, 276.

"In a sense, this": Kaplan and Waltz, 291.

"was very despondent": Alice Nichols, testimony, Ruby trial transcript, 1633.

"WADE: And I believe": Nichols, 1635.

"the day John F. Kennedy": Kantor, *Ruby Cover-Up*, 245.

"and this additional stress": Kaplan and Waltz, *Trial of Jack Ruby*, 291–292.

"some . . . said he resembled": Belli with Carroll, *Dallas Justice*, 214

"Jack Ruby," Gibbs testified: Ruby trial transcript, 1641.

"Dr. Gibbs's answer": Causey, *Jack Ruby Trial Revisited*, 83.

"was not as despondent" to *"What will you do"*: Silverman, notes, "The Trial," 8.

22. Pleading for a Life

"a directed verdict of guilty": Belli with Kaiser, *My Life*, 273

"This final session": Abrams and Fisher, *Kennedy's Avenger*, 323.

"The jury, if it finds": "Ruby Jury Gets Case After a Long Delay," *New York Times*, March 14, 1964, https://www.nytimes.com/1964/03/14/archives/ruby-jury-gets -case-after-a-long-delay.html.

"American justice is on trial" and *"You denied him the very thing"*: Summation, Ruby trial transcript, 24–25.

"wanted to become famous": Summation, 26.

"He is nothing but a thrill killer": Summation, 37.

"the Lord knows": Summation, 26.

"that you do something": Summation, 67.

"Have you watched": Summation, 100.

"bounced around the courtroom": Abrams and Fisher, *Kennedy's Avenger*, 336.

"the oldest defense": Summation, Ruby trial transcript, 106.

"the martyr, the hero": Summation, 118–119.

"I felt like Alice": Belli with Kaiser, *My Life*, 274.

"The cry goes out": Summation, Ruby trial transcript, 135–136.

"This poor sick fellow": Summation, 135–136.

"Acquit him, not guilty": Summation, 153–154.

"Would it have been": Kaplan and Waltz, *Trial of Jack Ruby*, 333.

"of the right to see": Summation, Ruby trial transcript, 161–162.

"Any word of a conspiracy": Abrams and Fisher, *Kennedy's Avenger*, 342.

"Ladies and gentlemen": Summation, Ruby trial transcript, 162.

"turn this man loose": Summation, 160–161.

"I ask you": Summation, 165.

"Dallas is sure crowding": Kaplan and Waltz, *Trial of Jack Ruby*, 339.

"The single factor mentioned": Kaplan and Waltz, 339.

"Is this your verdict?": "Ruby Sentenced to Death Speedily by Dallas Jury; Oswald Killer to
Appeal; Defense Angered," *New York Times,* March 15, 1964, https://www.nytimes
.com/1964/03/15/archives/ruby-sentenced-to-death-speedily-by-dallas-jury-oswald
-killer-to.html.

"It's bad": Belli with Carroll, *Dallas Justice,* 256.

"We the jury find": "Ruby Sentenced," *New York Times,* https://www.nytimes.com
/1964/03/15/archives/ruby-sentenced-to-death-speedily-by-dallas-jury-oswald-killer
-to.html.

23. Condemned

"May I thank the jury": Belli with Carroll, *Dallas Justice,* 257.

"I can't shake hands": Belli with Kaiser, *My Life,* 276–277.

"shocked even me": Brown, *Dallas and the Jack Ruby Trial,* 133.

"The town's a little bit shaken": Abrams and Fisher, *Kennedy's Avenger,* 351.

"Perhaps twelve other jurors": Causey, *Jack Ruby Trial Revisited,* 95.

"calm but distant": Abrams and Fisher, *Kennedy's Avenger,* 351.

"I was completely shocked" to *"I want to take a lie detector"*: Silverman, notes, "The Trial."

"We believe that the possibility": Shenon, *Cruel and Shocking Act,* 286.

"The evidence seemed overwhelming": Burt Griffin, testimony, September 28, 1978, in
*Hearings Before the Select Committee on Assassinations of the US House of Repre-
sentatives* (Washington, DC: US Government Printing Office), 5:474–475.

"After Oswald shot at": Burt Griffin, interview by Jesse Bethea, Columbus Underground,
November 23, 2018.

"I believed that Ruby": Belin, *November 22, 1963,* 432.

"Ruby was innocent": Belin, 433.

"He was really too stupid": Silverman, interview by the author.

"agreed that there could be": Belin, *November 22, 1963,* 433.

"agreed immediately to appear": Silverman, notes, "Post-Trial."

"You have my sympathy": Silverman, "Post-Trial."

"looked terribly depressed" to *"If anything should happen"*: Silverman, "Post-Trial."

"lest he mutilate himself" to *"there is going to be"*: Silverman, "Post-Trial."

"run and struck his head": Kaplan and Waltz, *Trial of Jack Ruby,* 344.

"pale, tremulous, agitated" to *"actively suicidal"*: Kaplan and Waltz, *Trial of Jack Ruby,* 345.

"to make sure that I" to *"Every few minutes"*: Silverman, notes, "Post-Trial."

"he was in an even more" to *"This is the end"*: Silverman, "Post-Trial."

"grumbled to guards": Wills and Demaris, *Jack Ruby,* 147.

"as contentious as the trial" to *"Goodbye, I'm not"*: Abrams and Fisher, *Kennedy's Avenger,*
355–356.

"he was still despondent" to *"He mentions Oswald now"*: Silverman, notes, "Post-Trial."
"I was getting restless": Silverman, *Time of My Life*, 62.

24. Unleashed

"Without a lie detector" to *"We will be glad"*: Jack Ruby, testimony, 181–182.
"This was Ruby's opportunity": Abrams and Fisher, *Kennedy's Avenger*, 357.
"his testimony seemed so": Shenon, *Cruel and Shocking Act*, 370.
"I am being victimized" to *"a stimulus to give me"*: Jack Ruby, testimony, 198–200.
"[Secret service agent] Elmer Moore" to *"Are you Jewish"*: Specter and Robbins, *Passion for Truth*, 113.
"Ruby turned back to": Specter and Robbins, 114.
"Jack Ruby was indisputably" to *"That we will do for you"*: Specter and Robbins, 114; Jack Ruby, testimony, 210–213.
"I have never been" to *"There was no conspiracy"*: Ruby, 204–205, 210–212.
"it turned out that": Specter and Robbins, *Passion for Truth*, 114.
"the commission then arranged": Specter and Robbins, 116.
"We immediately commenced" and *"Ruby had killed Oswald"*: Kaplan and Waltz, *Trial of Jack Ruby*, 347.
"Ruby took the law": Kaplan and Waltz, 349.

25. Wired

"I want to answer": Shenon, *Cruel and Shocking Act*, 422.
"[Ruby] had prepared his own" and *"had passed the test"*: Specter and Robbins, *Passion for Truth*, 116-117.
"I think he held up": Wills and Demaris, *Jack Ruby*, 200.
"any delusional state" to *"when next Jack moved"*: Wills and Demaris, 201.
"perhaps the defendant" to *"the huge Texan"*: Kaplan and Waltz, *Trial of Jack Ruby*, 351.
"Sol Dann and his": Wills and Demaris, *Jack Ruby*, 172–173.
"fully explain to Dallas press" and *"Texas is an unhealthy"*: Gertz, *Moment of Madness*, 136–137.
"the assault [upon Dann]": Wills and Demaris, *Jack Ruby*, 173.
"as a Jewish lawyer": Gertz, *Moment of Madness*, 140.
"Oligarchy of Dallas": Belli with Carroll, *Dallas Justice*, 2–3.
"We won it": Belli with Carroll, 259.
"At the Trib" to *"Specter wrote that"*: Carroll, *Accidental Assassin*, 81–82.
"I will repeat today": Lyndon Baines Johnson, inaugural address, January 20, 1965, via the Avalon Project, Yale Law School, https://avalon.law.yale.edu/20th_century/johnson.asp.

"Everything pertaining to" to *"Yes"*: "Jack 'Ruby' Rubenstein Press Conference," Internet Archive, uploaded March 28, 2021, https://archive.org/details/jack-ruby-interview.

"This is all so": Gertz, *Moment of Madness*, 469–470.

"Oh the way I": RR Auction, "Jack Ruby Handwritten Letter from Jail Identifying LBJ as the Kennedy Assassination Mastermind," October 23, 2013, https://www.rrauction.com/auctions/lot-detail/33049970417260.

"the most perfect conspiracy": Gertz, *Moment of Madness*, 185.

"Ruby talked readily": Gertz, 470–471.

"tarantula-eyed one": Kaplan and Waltz, *Trial of Jack Ruby*, 359.

"To go from lawyer": Wills and Demaris, *Jack Ruby*, 180.

"Me, Jack Ruby": Kaplan and Waltz, *Trial of Jack Ruby*, 360.

"It is my opinion": Kaplan and Waltz, 362.

"a public, unsolicited": Abrams and Fisher, *Kennedy's Avenger*, 373–374.

"Never at any time": Abrams and Fisher, 375.

"I wanted to be Oswald's" to *"it was an important"*: Kunstler with Isenberg, *My Life as a Radical Lawyer*, 154–155.

"There was nothing lovable": Adelson, *Ruby-Oswald Affair*, 67.

"conviction should be": Abrams and Fisher, *Kennedy's Avenger*, 377.

"First there was a trial" to *"the atmosphere in the halls"*: Abrams and Fisher, 378.

"The record is replete": Abrams and Fisher, 379.

"invented a fabrication": Gertz, *Moment of Madness*, 422

"had not had the remotest": Abrams and Fisher, *Kennedy's Avenger*, 380.

"constituted an oral confession" to *"such strong feeling"*: Abrams and Fisher, 381.

"Dallas was being blamed": Rubenstein v. State, 407 S.W.2d 793 (1966), https://law.justia.com/cases/texas/court-of-criminal-appeals/1966/37900-3.html.

"It was a great victory": Kunstler with Isenberg, *My Life*, 157.

"during our last visit": Kunstler with Isenberg, 158.

"if only you had believed" to *"Russia will be in"*: Gertz, *Moment of Madness*, 473–474.

"Much of our seeming success": Gertz, 423–424.

"Some conspiracy theorists": Kunstler with Isenberg, *My Life*, 179–180.

"with the calm of": Gertz, *Moment of Madness*, 443.

"My heart feels a little" to *"the truth will now"*: Gertz, 444.

"I think he's been": Gertz, 445.

"It doesn't bother me": Gertz, 468.

"Why, Belli and Jack Ruby" to *"Judge Brown made his"*: Gertz, 445–446.

26. Final Testimony

"had not noticed": Wills and Demaris, *Jack Ruby*, 202.
"For three weeks": Gertz, *Moment of Madness*, 476.
"There are a lot of people": Gertz, 477.
"Dear Brother Earl": Jack Ruby to Earl Ruby, private collection of Joyce Ruby Berman.
"although Jack appeared to be": Gertz, *Moment of Madness*, 484.
"All I did is walk" to *"Well, really it happened"*: Gertz, 485–486.
"Jack saw himself" to *"Of course, Jack couldn't"*: Gertz, *Moment of Madness*, 496–497.
"called me and asked": Silverman, interview by the author.

27. Going Home

"greatest magic trick ever": "Murder Most Foul," Bob Dylan official website, accessed April 18, 2023, https://www.bobdylan.com/songs/murder-most-foul/.
"Experts from Dallas": Gertz, *Moment of Madness*, 502–503.
"there is no way": Adelson, *Ruby-Oswald Affair*, 37.
"The price of the casket": Aynesworth with Michaud, *JFK: Breaking the News*, 192.
"The Rubys were a": Aynesworth with Michaud, 192–193.
"attired in a black suit": Associated Press, "Jack Ruby Rests in Funeral Home," *Daily Illini*, January 6, 1967, https://idnc.library.illinois.edu/?a=d&d=DIL19670106.2.5.
"a friend of the Ruby": "Jack Ruby to Be Buried Friday in Chicago Beside His Parents," *Jewish Telegraphic Agency Daily News Bulletin*, January 5, 1967, https://www.jta.org/archive/jack-ruby-to-be-buried-friday-in-chicago-beside-his-parents.
"The eyes of the world": Gertz, *Moment of Madness*, 505
"with all the conspiracy": Aynesworth with Michaud, *JFK: Breaking the News*, 193.
"Who was to know": Adelson, *Ruby-Oswald Affair*, 6.
"It must have been": Adelson, 7.
"Three squad cars led": Berkow, *Maxwell Street*, 329.
"Ruby's three brothers": "Ruby Buried in Chicago Cemetery Alongside Graves of His Parents," *New York Times*, January 7, 1967, https://www.nytimes.com/1967/01/07/archives/ruby-buried-in-chicago-cemetery-a-longside-graves-of-his-parents.html.
"who had done so": "Ruby Buried in Chicago," *New York Times*.

28. Afterlife

"called me up and": Adelson, *Ruby-Oswald Affair*, 319.
"a watch, a ring": Adelson, 323.

"bomb threats and huge legal bills": Steve North, "My History with the Family of Lee Harvey Oswald's Jewish Killer," ReformJudaism.org, November 19, 2013, https://reformjudaism.org/blog/my-history-family-lee-harvey-oswalds-jewish-killer.

"the employees are always": David F., comment on "Earl Ruby Cleaners and Tailors," Yelp, October 22, 2018, https://www.yelp.com/biz/earl-ruby-cleaners-and-tailors-detroit.

"Ruby's shooting of Oswald": "Findings," in *Final Report of the Select Committee on Assassinations* (Washington, DC: Government Printing Office, 1979), https://www.archives.gov/research/jfk/select-committee-report/part-1c.html.

"I don't think it'll ever": Earl Ruby, interview by Steve North, in *Now It Can Be Told*, aired November 22, 1991, via Steve North personal archive.

"When I check out": Berkow, *Maxwell Street*, 346.

Candy Barr: Myrna Oliver, obituary for Candy Barr, *Los Angeles Times*, January 3, 2006, https://www.latimes.com/archives/la-xpm-2006-jan-03-me-barr3-story.html.

"During his final hospitalization": Steve North, obituary for Hillel Silverman, Jewish Telegraphic Agency, April 12, 2023, https://www.jta.org/2023/04/12/obituaries/hillel-silverman-longtime-rabbi-whose-congregant-killed-jfks-assassin-is-dead-at-99.

"I saw some of myself": Taysom, "Sympathetic Speech," https://faroutmagazine.co.uk/bob-dylan-lee-harvey-oswald-john-f-kennedy-sympathy-letter/.

"ask Oswald and Ruby": "Murder Most Foul," Bob Dylan official website, https://www.bobdylan.com/songs/murder-most-foul/.

"may be the most curious": Gil Smart, "Epstein and Florida Sex Trafficking Cases Show Justice Slipping Through Our Fingers," TCPalm.com, August 12, 2019, https://www.tcpalm.com/story/opinion/columnists/gil-smart/2019/08/12/epstein-and-florida-sex-spa-cases-wheres-justice/1984942001/.

"Jack never meant" to *"I don't know if"*: Berkow, *Maxwell Street*, 332–333.

BIBLIOGRAPHY

Abrams, Dan, and David Fisher. *Kennedy's Avenger: Assassination, Conspiracy, and the Forgotten Trial of Jack Ruby.* Toronto: Hanover Square, 2021.

Adelson, Alan. *The Ruby-Oswald Affair: Reflections by Alan Adelson.* Seattle: Romar, 1988.

Aynesworth, Hugh, with Stephen G. Michaud. *JFK: Breaking the News.* Richardson, TX: International Focus, 2003.

Belin, David W. *November 22, 1963: You Are the Jury.* New York: Quadrangle, 1973.

Belli, Melvin M., with Maurice C. Carroll. *Dallas Justice: The Real Story of Jack Ruby and his Trial.* New York: David McKay, 1964.

Belli, Melvin M., with Robert Blair Kaiser. *My Life on Trial: An Autobiography.* New York: William Morrow, 1976.

Benson, Michael. *Encyclopedia of the JFK Assassination.* New York: Checkmark, 2002.

———. *Gangsters vs. Nazis: How Jewish Mobsters Battled Nazis in Wartime America.* New York: Citadel, 2022.

———. *Who's Who in the JFK Assassination: An A-to-Z Encyclopedia.* New York: Citadel, 1993.

Berkow, Ira. *Maxwell Street: Survival in a Bazaar.* Garden City, NY: Doubleday, 1977.

Biderman, Rose G. *They Came to Stay: The Story of the Jews of Dallas 1870–1997.* Austin: Eakin, 2002.

Brown, Judge Joe B., Sr. *Dallas and the Jack Ruby Trial: Memoir of Judge Joe B. Brown, Sr.* Edited by Diane Holloway, Ph.D. San Jose, CA: Authors Choice, 2001.

Caro, Robert A. *The Years of Lyndon Johnson.* Vol. 4, *The Passage of Power.* New York: Vintage, 2013.

Carroll, Maurice. *Accidental Assassin: Jack Ruby and 4 Minutes in Dallas.* Xlibris, 2013.

Causey, Max. *The Jack Ruby Trial Revisited: The Diary of Jury Foreman Max Causey.* Edited by John Mark Dempsey. Denton, TX: University of North Texas Press, 2000.

Century, Douglas. *Barney Ross: The Life of a Jewish Fighter.* New York: Nextbook/Schocken, 2006.

DeLillo, Don. *Libra.* New York: Viking, 1988.

Epstein, Edward Jay. *The Assassination Chronicles: Inquest, Counterplot, and Legend.* New York: Carroll & Graf, 1992.

———. *The JFK Assassination Diary: My Search for Answers to the Mystery of the Century.* EJE, 2013.

Flippo, Chet. *Your Cheatin' Heart: A Biography of Hank Williams.* New York: St. Martin's Press, 1981.

Gertz, Elmer. *Moment of Madness: The People vs. Jack Ruby.* Chicago: Follett, 1968.

Graff, Harvey J. *The Dallas Myth: The Making and Unmaking of an American City.* Minneapolis: University of Minnesota Press, 2008.

Hartogs, Dr. Renatus, and Lucy Freeman. *The Two Assassins.* New York: Thomas Y. Crowell, 1965.

Hill, Patricia Evridge. *Dallas: The Making of a Modern City.* Austin: University of Texas Press, 1996.

Hunter, Diana, and Alice Anderson. *Jack Ruby's Girls.* Atlanta: Hallux, 1970.

Kantor, Seth. *The Ruby Cover-Up.* New York: Zebra/Kensington, 1978.

Kaplan, John, and Jon R. Waltz. *The Trial of Jack Ruby: A Classic Study of Courtroom Strategies.* New York, Macmillan, 1965.

Kraus, Joe. *The Kosher Capones: A History of Chicago's Jewish Gangsters.* Ithaca, NY: Northern Illinois University Press, 2019.

Kunstler, William M., with Sheila Isenberg. *My Life as a Radical Lawyer.* New York: Birch Lane, 1994.

Lane, Mark. *Rush to Judgment.* New York: Holt, Rinehart and Winston, 1966.

Mailer, Norman. *Oswald's Tale: An American Mystery.* New York: Random House, 1995.

Minutaglio, Bill, and Steven L. Davis. *Dallas 1963.* New York: Twelve/Hachette, 2013.

O'Donnell, Kenneth P., and David F. Powers. *"Johnny, We Hardly Knew Ye": Memories of John Fitzgerald Kennedy.* New York: Open Road, 2013. Digital ed.

Oliver, Beverly, with Coke Buchanan. *Nightmare in Dallas.* Nevada, TX: Extreme Services, 2003.

O'Neill, Tom, with Dan Piepenbring. *Chaos: The Truth Behind the Manson Murders.* London, Windmill Books, 2019.

Phillips, Michael. *White Metropolis: Race, Ethnicity, and Religion in Dallas, 1841–2001.* Austin: University of Texas Press, 2006.

Posner, Gerald. *Case Closed: Lee Harvey Oswald and the Assassination of JFK.* New York: Anchor Books, 2003.

Report of the President's Commission on the Assassination of President Kennedy. Washington, DC: US Government Printing Office, 1964. https://www.archives.gov/research/jfk/warren-commission-report.

Robertson, Robbie. *Testimony.* New York: Crown Archetype, 2016. Digital ed.

Ross, Barney, and Martin Abramson. *No Man Stands Alone: The True Story of Barney Ross.* New York: J. B. Lippincott, 1957.

Russo, Gus. *Live By the Sword: The Secret War Against Castro and the Death of JFK.* Baltimore: Bancroft, 1998.

Russo, Gus, and Harry Moses, eds. *Where Were You? America Remembers the JFK Assassination.* Guilford, CT: Lyons, 2013.

Scheim, David E. *Contract on America: The Mafia Murder of President John F. Kennedy.* New York: Shapolsky, 1988.

Schwarz, Ted, and Mardi Rustam. *Candy Barr: The Small-Town Texas Runaway Who Became a Darling of the Mob and the Queen of Las Vegas Burlesque.* Lanham, MD: Taylor Trade, 2008.

Shaw, Mark. *Melvin Belli: King of the Courtroom.* Fort Lee, NJ, Barricade, 2007.

Shenon, Philip. *A Cruel and Shocking Act: The Secret History of the Kennedy Assassination.* New York: Picador, 2013.

Silverman, Hillel E. *The Time of My Life: Sixty Fulfilling Years as a Congregational Rabbi.* Jersey City, NJ: KTAV, 2009.

Specter, Arlen, with Charles Robbins. *Passion for Truth: From Finding JFK's Single Bullet to Questioning Anita Hill and Impeaching Clinton.* New York: William Morrow, 2000.

Sussman, Jeffrey. *Max Baer and Barney Ross: Jewish Heroes of Boxing.* New York: Rowman & Littlefield, 2016. Digital ed.

Tereba, Tere. *Mickey Cohen: The Life and Crimes of L.A.'s Notorious Mobster.* Toronto: ECW, 2012.

Wills, Gary, and Ovid Demaris. *Jack Ruby.* New York: Da Capo, 1994.

Zapruder, Alexandra. *Twenty-Six Seconds: A Personal History of the Zapruder Film.* New York: Twelve/Hachette, 2016.

Zemeckis, Leslie. *Behind the Burly Q: The Story of Burlesque in America.* New York: Skyhorse, 2013.

INDEX

Page numbers in *italics* denote images.